Preston Lee's

3-in-1 BOOK SERIES!

Beginner ENGLISH + Conversation ENGLISH + Read & Write ENGLISH
Lesson 1 - 40   Lesson 1 - 40

For Turkish Speakers

Preston Lee Books
prestonleebooks@gmail.com

No unauthorized photocopying

All rights reserved. No part of this publication may be reproduced, stored in a retrieval system, or transmitted, in any form or by any means, without the prior permission in writing of Preston Lee Books.

This book is sold subject to the condition that it shall not, by the way of trade or otherwise, be lent, resold, hired out, or otherwise circulated without the publisher's prior consent in any form of binding or cover than that in which it is published and without a similar condition including this condition being imposed on the subsequent purchaser.

Copyright © 2019 Matthew Preston, Kevin Lee
All rights reserved.

ISBN: 9781651215272
Imprint: Independently published

Preston Lee's Beginner ENGLISH

Page 4

Preston Lee's Conversation ENGLISH
Lesson 1 - 40

Page 209

Preston Lee's Read & Write ENGLISH
Lesson 1 - 40

Page 375

Preston Lee's
Beginner ENGLISH

For Turkish Speakers

CONTENTS

Lesson 1: My family Ailem — Page 8
Lesson 2: My pencil case Kalem kutum — Page 12
Lesson 3: In the classroom Sınıfta — Page 16
Lesson 4: The weather Hava durumu — Page 20

Test 1 — Lesson 1 - 4 — Page 24

Lesson 5: Places Yerler — Page 26
Lesson 6: Sports Spor — Page 30
Lesson 7: At the zoo Hayvanat bahçesinde — Page 34
Lesson 8: Colors Renkler — Page 38

Test 2 — Lesson 5 - 8 — Page 42

Lesson 9: Activities Aktiviteler — Page 44
Lesson 10: Food & Drinks Yiyecek ve içecekler — Page 48
Lesson 11: At the fruit market Manavda — Page 52
Lesson 12: Shapes Şekiller — Page 56

Test 3 — Lesson 9 - 12 — Page 60

Lesson 13: At the supermarket Süpermarket   Page 62
Lesson 14: At the ice cream shop Dondurma dükkanında Page 66
Lesson 15: In the refrigerator Buzdolabında   Page 70
Lesson 16: Jobs Meslekler   Page 74

| Test 4 | Lesson 13 - 16 | Page 78 |

Lesson 17: Names İsimler   Page 80
Lesson 18: More places Daha çok yer   Page 84
Lesson 19: Meats Etler   Page 88
Lesson 20: Vegetables Sebzeler   Page 92

| Test 5 | Lesson 17 - 20 | Page 96 |

Lesson 21: At school Okulda   Page 98
Lesson 22: School subjects Okul dersleri   Page 102
Lesson 23: Chores Ev işleri   Page 106
Lesson 24: At the toy store Oyuncak mağazasında   Page 110

| Test 6 | Lesson 21 - 24 | Page 114 |

Lesson 25: In the kitchen Mutfakta   Page 116
Lesson 26: In the toolbox Alet çantası   Page 120
Lesson 27: Transportation Ulaşım   Page 124
Lesson 28: Clothes Giysiler   Page 128

| Test 7 | Lesson 25 - 28 | Page 132 |

Lesson 29: **More clothes** Daha fazla giysi — Page 134
Lesson 30: **In the living room** Oturma odasında — Page 138
Lesson 31: **In the bathroom** Banyoda — Page 142
Lesson 32: **In the bedroom** Yatak odasında — Page 146

| Test 8 | Lesson 29 - 32 | Page 150 |

Lesson 33: **Around the house** Evin etrafında — Page 152
Lesson 34: **Hobbies** Hobiler — Page 156
Lesson 35: **Countries** Ülkeler — Page 160
Lesson 36: **Landscapes** Manzaralar — Page 164

| Test 9 | Lesson 33 - 36 | Page 168 |

Lesson 37: **Everyday life** Günlük yaşam — Page 170
Lesson 38: **Languages** Diller — Page 174
Lesson 39: **Pets** Evcil hayvanlar — Page 178
Lesson 40: **Fast food** Hazır yemek — Page 182

| Test 10 | Lesson 37 - 40 | Page 186 |

Lesson 41: **At the cinema** Sinemada — Page 188
Lesson 42: **Music** Müzik — Page 192
Lesson 43: **Feelings** Duygular — Page 196
Lesson 44: **The calendar** Takvim — Page 200

| Test 11 | Lesson 41 - 44 | Page 204 |

| Answers | Test 1 - 11 | Page 206 |

Lesson 1: My family

Ailem

| Section A | Words |

1. **mother**
   Anne
2. **grandmother**
   Büyükanne
3. **sister**
   Kız kardeş
4. **baby sister**
   Bebek kız kardeş
5. **aunt**
   Yenge

6. **father**
   Baba
7. **grandfather**
   Büyükbaba
8. **brother**
   Erkek kardeş
9. **baby brother**
   Bebek erkek kardeş
10. **uncle**
    Amca

| Section B | Make a sentence |

Who is she?

She is my mother.

Who is he?

He is my father.

Note: isn't = is not

Section C — Make a question

Is <u>she</u> your <u>mother</u>?
Yes, she is. / No, she isn't.

Is <u>he</u> your <u>father</u>?
Yes, he is. / No, he isn't.

Section D — Learn a verb

see – seeing – saw – seen görmek

He **sees** my father on Fridays.
I will be **seeing** him this afternoon.
My brother **saw** you yesterday.
I haven't **seen** that movie yet.

Section E — Learn an idiom

Like one of the family

Meaning: To be like a person in one's family.

"Our dog is treated *like one of the family*."

| Section F | Write |

Trace and write the words

1. Who is she?

She is my mother.

2. Who _____ he?

He is my father.

3. Who _____ _____?

She _____ my grandmother.

4. Who _____ _____?

He _____ _____ grandfather.

5. Is she your sister?

Yes, she is.

6. Is _____ your brother?

No, he isn't.

7. Is she your mother?

Yes, _____ _____.

8. Is _____ _____ father?

_____, _____ _____.

Section G | Let's have fun

My family!

Find the words!

```
c i o b j t d c z b g g r o v k
o i j m w d o g f a j r k s s q
q d e g q l z t c b z a q c u o
u w n r c e o z s y i n t t t v
n f f a t h e r o b a d y s y r
c d l n b h j m u r x f d v t q
l z a d m g g y e o x a c m n v
e h p (m o t h e r) t z t j y t f
f u e o v q q f d h e h b x s n
n z v t u x l w j e z e k o u v
t a a h s i s t e r o r y a l r
t o u e y v s h b r o t h e r j
j n n r u d o s x j v t y k y o
j b t y t d b a b y s i s t e r
```

~~mother~~   brother
father   baby sister
grandmother   baby brother
grandfather   aunt
sister   uncle

Lesson 2: My pencil case

Kalem kutum

> What is this?
> It is an eraser.

Section A — Words

1. **a pencil**
   Kalem
2. **an eraser**
   Silgi
3. **glue**
   Tutkal
4. **a pencil sharpener**
   Kalemtıraş
5. **whiteout**
   Daksil
6. **a pen**
   Dolma kalem
7. **a ruler**
   Cetvel
8. **tape**
   Bant
9. **a marker**
   Keçeli kalem
10. **a crayon**
    Pastel boya

Section B — Make a sentence

What is this?

It is <u>a pencil</u>.

What are these?

They are <u>pen</u>s.

Section C — Make a question

Is this <u>an eraser</u>?
Yes, it is. / No, it isn't.

Are these <u>ruler</u>s?
Yes, they are. / No, they aren't.

Section D — Learn a verb

buy – buying – bought – bought satın almak

I will **buy** some pencils for you.

My sister was **buying** a new ruler.

My father **bought** an eraser.

My mother hasn't **bought** some glue yet.

Section E — Learn an idiom

Cross your fingers

Meaning: To wish for luck.

"*Cross your fingers* and hope this marker has ink."

| Section F | Write |

Trace and write the words

1. What is this?

It is a pencil.

2. What _____ these?

They are pens.

3. What _____ _____?

It _____ a ruler.

4. What _____ _____?

They _____ markers.

5. Is this an eraser?

Yes, it is.

6. Is _____ a pencil sharpener?

No, it isn't.

7. Is _____ a crayon?

No, _____ isn't.

8. _____ _____ rulers?

Yes, _____ _____.

Section G | Let's have fun

My pencil case!

Unscramble the words!

1. encpil   <u> pencil   </u>

2. enp   _____

3. relru   _____

4. eugl   _____

5. reshrapne cpneli   _____

6. arerse   _____

7. emrakr   _____

8. hwteituo   _____

9. yocarn   _____

10. ptae   _____

Lesson 3: In the classroom

Sınıfta

What are these?
These are old books.

Section A — Words

1. **chair**
   Sandalye
2. **blackboard**
   Karatahta
3. **poster**
   Afiş
4. **globe**
   Küre
5. **clock**
   Saat
6. **desk**
   Sıra
7. **whiteboard**
   Beyaz tahta
8. **bookshelf**
   Kitaplık
9. **computer**
   Bilgisayar
10. **book**
    Kitap

Section B — Make a sentence

What is this?

This is a <u>big</u> <u>chair</u>.

What are these?

These are <u>small</u> <u>desk</u>s.

Learn: big, small, new, old

Section C — Make a question

Is the <u>blackboard</u> <u>big</u>?
Yes, it is. / No, it is <u>small</u>.

Are the <u>desks</u> <u>new</u>?
Yes, they are. / No, they are <u>old</u>.

Section D — Learn a verb

look – looking – looked – looked bakmak

Please **look** at the blackboard.

They are **looking** at the whiteboard.

My father **looked** at your bicycle yesterday.

We have already **looked** at many houses.

Section E — Learn an idiom

Class clown

Meaning: A student who often makes everyone laugh in the classroom.

"Peter is the *class clown*. Even the teacher laughs sometimes."

| Section F | Write |

Trace and write the words

1. What is this?

This is a big chair.

2. What _____ these?

These are small desks.

3. What _____ _____?

This is a _____ _____.

4. What _____ _____?

These are _____ _____.

5. Is the blackboard big?

Yes, it is.

6. Are _____ desks new?

No, they _____ old.

7. Is the _____ small?

No, it is big.

8. Are the _____ _____?

Yes, _____ _____.

Section G Let's have fun

In the classroom!

1. chair
2. desk
3. blackboard
4. whiteboard
5. poster

b l a c k b o a r d

6. bookshelf
7. globe
8. computer
9. clock
10. book

Lesson 4: The weather

Hava durumu

How is the weather on Friday?
It is sunny.

| Section A | Words |

1. **snowy**
   Karlı
2. **sunny**
   Güneşli
3. **rainy**
   Yağmurlu
4. **windy**
   Rüzgarlı
5. **cloudy**
   Bulutlu
6. **hot**
   Sıcak
7. **cold**
   Soğuk
8. **warm**
   Ilık
9. **cool**
   Serin
10. **freezing**
    Çok Soğuk

| Section B | Make a sentence |

How is the weather on <u>Monday</u>?

It is <u>snowy</u>.

It is not <u>hot</u>.

Learn: Sunday, Monday, Tuesday, Wednesday, Thursday, Friday, Saturday

Section C — Make a question

Is the weather <u>cold</u> on <u>Wednesday</u>?
Yes, it is. / No, it isn't. It is <u>hot</u>.

Is the weather <u>sunny</u>?
Yes, it is. / No, it isn't. It is <u>rainy</u>.

Section D — Learn a verb

feel – feeling – felt – felt hissetmek

My sister always **feels** tired after school.

I'm not **feeling** well.

I **felt** something on the back of my neck.

I haven't **felt** this happy for a long time!

Section E — Learn an idiom

It's raining cats and dogs

Meaning: It's raining heavily.

"You can't play outside right now. *It's raining cats and dogs.*"

| Section F | Write |

Trace and write the words

1. How is the weather on Monday?

It is snowy.

2. How is the weather _____ Thursday?

It is cloudy. It _____ not rainy.

3. How is the _____ _____ Friday?

It is _____.

4. How is _____ _____ _____ Tuesday?

It is cold. It is _____ _____.

5. Is the _____ hot?

Yes, it _____.

6. Is _____ _____ windy on Wednesday?

No, it isn't. It is _____.

7. Is the _____ _____ on Saturday?

Yes, _____ _____.

8. Is the weather _____?

No, it _____. It is _____.

22

Section G | Let's have fun

The weather!

snowy   sunny   rainy   windy   cloudy

hot   cold   warm   cool   freezing

Write the words

Sunday	Monday	Tuesday	Wednesday	Thursday	Friday	Saturday
Ra_n_	W_n_y	Cl_u_y	S_n_y	C_ _d	H_ _	W_r_

Circle the correct answer

1. Is the weather cold on Thursday?

   Yes, it is.   No, it's not. It's hot.

2. Is the weather windy on Monday?

   Yes, it is.   No, it's not. It's hot.

3. Is the weather rainy on Wednesday?

   Yes, it is.   No, it's not. It's sunny.

4. Is the weather cold on Friday?

   Yes, it is.   No, it's not. It's hot.

Test 1   Lesson 1 - 4

Write the answer next to the letter "A"

A: ___ **1.** Who ___ she? She is ___ mother.

a. is, my   b. are, her   c. am, his   d. is, me

A: ___ **2.** ___ he your father? Yes, ___ is.

a. Is, she   b. Are, he   c. Is, he   d. Are, she

A: ___ **3.** We ___ a movie now.

a. are seeing   b. seen   c. is seeing   d. saw

A: ___ **4.** "The housekeeper is one ___ the family."

a. off   b. is   c. from   d. of

A: ___ **5.** What are ___? ___ are markers.

a. this, They   b. these, It   c. it, They   d. these, They

A: ___ **6.** Are ___ rulers? No, ___ aren't.

a. it, these   b. them, it   c. these, they   d. this, it

A: ___ **7.** I ___ a pencil yesterday.

a. buy   b. buying   c. bought   d. buys

A: ___ **8.** Tom: "I hope I pass my test." Mary: "___ your fingers."

a. Hold   b. Cross   c. Pull   d. Look at

A: ___ **9.** What ___ these? These are ___ posters.

a. are, those   b. is, small   c. is, old   d. are, big

A: ___ **10.** Is the ___ small? No, it is ___.

a. it, old   b. globe, big   c. chair, desk   d. this, new

A: ___ **11.** He is ___ at the whiteboard.

a. looks   b. looking   c. looked   d. look

A: ___ **12.** "Johnny is the class ___. He's so funny."

a. clown   b. clowned   c. clowning   d. clowns

A: ___ **13.** How is the ___ on Tuesday? It is ___. It is not hot.

a. weather, cold   b. rainy, sunny   c. cool, old   d. hot, rain

A: ___ **14.** Is the weather ___ on Friday? Yes, ___ is.

a. cold, it   b. cold, snowy   c. hot, sunny   d. it, cold

A: ___ **15.** She ___ feel cold.

a. very   b. isn't   c. doesn't   d. do

A: ___ **16.** "Look at the heavy rain. It's raining ___ and ___."

a. lots, water   b. dogs, cats   c. cat, dog   d. cats, dogs

Answers on page 206

Lesson 5: Places

Yerler

> Where is he going?
> He is going to the gym.

Section A — Words

1. **park**
   Park
2. **beach**
   Plaj
3. **night market**
   Akşam pazarı
4. **store**
   Mağaza
5. **supermarket**
   Süpermarket
6. **restaurant**
   Restoran
7. **swimming pool**
   Yüzme havuzu
8. **department store**
   Alışveriş merkezi
9. **cinema**
   Sinema
10. **gym**
    Spor salonu

Section B — Make a sentence

Where is <u>she</u> going?

She is going to the <u>park</u>.

Where is <u>he</u> going?

He is going to the <u>beach</u>.

Section C — Make a question

Is <u>he</u> going to the <u>store</u>?
Yes, he is. / No, he isn't.

Is <u>she</u> going to the <u>supermarket</u>?
Yes, she is. / No, she isn't.

Section D — Learn a verb

walk – walking – walked – walked yürümek

I **walk** at the park on Sundays.

She will be **walking** to the store tomorrow morning.

My grandmother **walked** to the supermarket last week.

I've never **walked** to the night market before.

Section E — Learn an idiom

Have a change of heart

Meaning: To change your mind about something.

"I've *had a change of heart* about this place. Let's go to another restaurant."

| Section F | Write |

Trace and fill in the words

1. Where is she going?

She is going to the park.

2. Where is he going?

He is going to the beach.

3. Where is _____ _____?

She is going to the _____.

4. Where is _____ _____?

He is _____ to the _____.

5. Is he going to the store?

Yes, he is.

6. Is she going to the gym?

No, she isn't.

7. Is he going to the _____?

Yes, _____ is.

8. Is she going to the _____?

No, _____ _____.

Section G Let's have fun

Places!

1. Where is he going? [Department store]

He is going to the department store.

2. Where is she going? [Gym]

_____

3. Where is he going? [Restaurant]

_____

4. Where is she going? [Supermarket]

_____

5. Where is he going? [Cinema]

_____

Lesson 6: Sports

Spor

Section A — Words

1. **basketball**
   Basketbol
2. **soccer**
   Futbol
3. **badminton**
   Badminton
4. **golf**
   Golf
5. **hockey**
   Hokey
6. **cricket**
   Kriket
7. **tennis**
   Tenis
8. **baseball**
   Beyzbol
9. **volleyball**
   Voleybol
10. **football**
    Amerikan futbolu

What are you playing?
I am playing golf.

Section B — Make a sentence

What are <u>you</u> playing?

I am playing <u>basketball</u>.

What are <u>they</u> playing?

They are playing <u>soccer</u>.

Note: aren't = are not / I'm = I am

Section C — Make a question

Are <u>you</u> playing <u>basketball</u>?
Yes, I am. / No, I'm not.

Are <u>they</u> playing <u>soccer</u>?
Yes, they are. / No, they aren't.

Section D — Learn a verb

play – playing – played – played oynamak

I **play** basketball at the park on the weekends.

She will be **playing** tennis in the school competition.

My brother and I **played** badminton last night.

My grandfather has **played** golf for a long time.

Section E — Learn an idiom

A good sport

Meaning: Someone who can accept losing or be made fun of.

"We made fun of Johnny, but he was *a good sport* and laughed with us."

| Section F | Write |

Trace and fill in the words

1. What _____ you playing?

   _____ am _____ basketball.

2. _____ is _____ playing?

   She _____ playing tennis.

3. What are they _____?

   They are playing _____.

4. What _____ they _____?

   _____ are playing _____.

5. _____ you playing volleyball?

   Yes, _____ am.

6. _____ she _____ football?

   No, _____ isn't.

7. Are they playing _____?

   Yes, _____ are.

8. Are we playing _____?

   No, _____ _____.

| Section G | Let's have fun |

Sports!

Connect the sentences

What are you playing? •   • We are playing soccer.

What are they playing? •   • I am playing tennis.

What are you playing? •   • He is playing basketball.

What is he playing? •   • They are playing baseball.

Are you playing golf? •   • No, she isn't.

Is she playing hockey? •   • Yes, they are.

Is he playing football? •   • Yes, I am.

Are they playing volleyball? •   • No, he isn't.

Lesson 7: At the zoo

Hayvanat bahçesinde

How many lions are there?
There are two lions.

Section A — Words

1. **monkey**
   Maymun
2. **lion**
   Aslan
3. **tiger**
   Kaplan
4. **rhino**
   Gergedan
5. **bear**
   Ayı
6. **penguin**
   Penguen
7. **giraffe**
   Zürafa
8. **elephant**
   Fil
9. **kangaroo**
   Kanguru
10. **crocodile**
    Timsah

Section B — Make a sentence

How many <u>monkey</u>s are there?

There is one monkey.

There are <u>three</u> monkeys.

Learn: one, two, three, four, five, six, seven, eight, nine, ten

Note: there's = there is

Section C — Make a question

Is there one <u>rhino</u>?
Yes, there is. / No, there isn't.

Are there <u>five</u> <u>bear</u>s?
Yes, there are. / No, there aren't.

Section D — Learn a verb

like – liking – liked – liked beğenmek

I **like** the kangaroo.

The penguins are **liking** the new fish.

We **liked** the lions best at the zoo yesterday.

The bear hasn't **liked** any of the food we prepared.

Section E — Learn an idiom

Let the cat out of the bag

Meaning: To let someone know a secret.

"He let the cat out of the bag about the surprise party."

| Section F | Write |

Trace and fill in the words

1. How many monkeys are there?

There is one monkey.

2. How many penguins are there?

There _____ five penguins.

3. How many _____ are there?

There _____ one _____.

4. How many _____ are there?

There _____ six _____.

5. Is there one rhino?

Yes, there is.

6. Are there four bears?

No, there aren't.

7. Is there one _____?

Yes, there _____.

8. Are there four _____?

No, _____ _____.

Section G — Let's have fun

At the zoo!

Read and write

ANIMAL	AMOUNT
Monkey	6
Giraffe	
Lion	
Tiger	
Penguin	
Elephant	
Bear	
Kangaroo	
Crocodile	

1. How many monkeys are there?
   There are six monkeys.

2. How many giraffes are there?
   There are four giraffes.

3. How many lions are there?
   There is one lion.

4. How many penguins are there?
   There are seven penguins.

5. How many elephants are there?
   There are two elephants.

6. How many bears are there?
   There is one bear.

7. How many kangaroos are there?
   There are three kangaroos.

8. How many crocodiles are there?
   There is one crocodile.

9. How many tigers are there?
   There are seven tigers.

Lesson 8: Colors

Renkler

| Section A | Words |

1. **red**
   Kırmızı
2. **blue**
   Mavi
3. **orange**
   Turuncu
4. **pink**
   Pembe
5. **black**
   Siyah
6. **yellow**
   Sarı
7. **green**
   Yeşil
8. **purple**
   Mor
9. **brown**
   Kahverengi
10. **white**
    Beyaz

What is your favorite color?
My favorite color is red.

| Section B | Make a sentence |

What color is this?

It is <u>red</u>.

What is your favorite color?

My favorite color is <u>yellow</u>.

Note: it's = it is

Section C — Make a question

Is this <u>pencil</u> <u>purple</u>?
Yes, it is. / No, it's <u>blue</u>.

Is your favorite color <u>green</u>?
Yes, it is. / No, it isn't.

Section D — Learn a verb

draw – drawing – drew – drawn çizmek

My uncle can **draw** a green crocodile.

She is **drawing** a black bear.

The teacher **drew** a pink elephant on the blackboard.

I had first **drawn** a brown monkey, but didn't like it.

Section E — Learn an idiom

Feeling blue

Meaning: Feeling unhappy.

"He's *feeling blue* today because he lost the game."

Section F — Write

Trace and fill in the words

1. What color is this?

   It is green.

2. What _____ your favorite color?

   My favorite color is purple.

3. What color is _____?

   It is _____.

4. What is your favorite _____?

   My _____ color is _____.

5. Is this pencil blue?

   Yes, it is.

6. Is your favorite color pink?

   No, it isn't.

7. Is this eraser _____?

   No, it's _____.

8. Is your favorite color _____?

   Yes, it _____.

Section G | Let's have fun

Colors!

1. What color is this? _____. It is yellow.

2. _____? My favorite color is green.

3. _____? Yes, it is.

4. _____? No, it isn't.

Test 2 Lesson 5 - 8

Write the answer next to the letter "A"

A: ___ **1.** Where ___ she going? She is ___ to the beach.

a. does, going b. is, going c. are, go d. is, go

A: ___ **2.** Is ___ going to the store? Yes, she ___.

a. we, can b. her, is c. she, is d. he, is

A: ___ **3.** Yesterday, they ___ to the cinema.

a. are walk b. walk c. walked d. walking

A: ___ **4.** "I changed my mind about going. I had a change of ___."

a. eyes b. think c. clothes d. heart

A: ___ **5.** What are ___ playing? We ___ playing tennis.

a. you, are b. we, is c. they, can d. she, are

A: ___ **6.** ___ you playing soccer? No, ___ not.

a. Is, she's b. Are, I'm c. Can, can d. Are, he's

A: ___ **7.** They want to ___ baseball.

a. played b. playing c. plays d. play

A: ___ **8.** "We laughed at John, but he was a ___ sport."

a. well b. good c. easy d. difficult

42

A: ___ **9.** How many ___ are there? There ___ two tigers.

a. tiger, are　　b. number, is　　c. tiger, is　　d. tigers, are

A: ___ **10.** Is ___ one kangaroo? No, there ___.

a. there, isn't　　b. number, isn't　　c. this, is　　d. this, aren't

A: ___ **11.** He ___ the penguins.

a. like　　b. liking　　c. likes　　d. was like

A: ___ **12.** "He told everyone my secret and let the cat ___ the bag."

a. out from　　b. into　　c. out of　　d. out

A: ___ **13.** What is your ___ color? My favorite color ___ purple.

a. best, is　　b. best, are　　c. favorite, are　　d. favorite, is

A: ___ **14.** Is this desk ___? Yes, ___ is.

a. red, they　　b. color, pink　　c. green, it　　d. yellow, he

A: ___ **15.** She can ___ a yellow lion.

a. drawing　　b. draw　　c. draws　　d. drew

A: ___ **16.** "I'm pretty unhappy today. I'm feeling ___."

a. red　　b. green　　c. color　　d. blue

Answers on page 206

Lesson 9: Activities

Aktiviteler

Section A — Words

1. **play piano**
   Piyano çalmak
2. **read books**
   Kitap okumak
3. **play video games**
   Video oyunu oynamak
4. **surf the internet**
   İnternette gezinmek
5. **take photos**
   Fotoğraf çekmek
6. **watch TV**
   Televizyon izlemek
7. **sing songs**
   Şarkı söylemek
8. **study English**
   İngilizce çalışmak
9. **play cards**
   Kart oynamak
10. **go shopping**
    Alışverişe gitmek

Section B — Make a sentence

What do you like to do?

I like to play piano.

What don't you like to do?

I don't like to sing songs.

Note: don't = do not

Section C — Make a question

Do you like to <u>play video games</u>?
Yes, I do. / No, I don't.

Don't you like to <u>read books</u>?
Yes, I do. / No, I don't.

Section D — Learn a verb

read – reading – read – read okumak

I can **read** English books.

My sister was **reading** the newspaper this morning.

I **read** a really interesting article last week.

My brother hasn't **read** this book yet.

Section E — Learn an idiom

Shop around

Meaning: To shop at different stores to find the best price.

"You should *shop around* before you buy this piano."

Section F | Write

Trace and fill in the words

1. What do you like to do?

I like to read books.

2. What don't you like to do?

I don't like to _____ cards.

3. What do you _____ to do?

I like to _____ _____.

4. What don't you like to _____?

I don't like to _____ _____.

5. Do you like to take photos?

No, I _____.

6. Don't you like to go shopping?

Yes, I do.

7. Do you like to _____ _____?

Yes, I _____.

8. Don't you like to _____ _____?

No, I _____.

Section G | Let's have fun

Activities!

Unscramble the sentences!

    like to / video games / I / play

1. _____.

    I / like to / read books / don't

2. _____.

    I / study English / like / to

3. _____.

    don't / go shopping / I / like to

4. _____.

    like / take / I / photos / to

5. _____.

    the / don't / I / to / like / internet / surf

6. _____.

Lesson 10: Food & Drinks

Yiyecek ve içecekler

How much tea is there?
There is a lot of tea.

Section A — Words

1. **cake**
   Pasta
2. **cheese**
   Peynir
3. **milk**
   Süt
4. **tea**
   Çay
5. **soda**
   Soda
6. **pizza**
   Pizza
7. **water**
   Su
8. **juice**
   Meyve suyu
9. **coffee**
   Kahve
10. **pie**
    Turta

Section B — Make a sentence

How much <u>cake</u> is there?

There is <u>a little</u> cake.

How much <u>pizza</u> is there?

There is <u>a lot of</u> pizza.

Learn: a little, a lot of

Section C — Make a question

Is there a lot of <u>juice</u>?
Yes, there is. / No, there isn't.

Is there a little <u>water</u>?
Yes, there is. / No, there isn't.

Section D — Learn a verb

want – wanting – wanted – wanted istemek

I **want** a lot of tea.

Wanting to improve your English takes practice.

They **wanted** a cheese cake, but the shop didn't have one.

My father has **wanted** to eat pizza all week.

Section E — Learn an idiom

Put food on the table

Meaning: To make money for the household expenses.

"I need this job to *put food on the table*."

| Section F | Write |

Trace and fill in the words

1. How much juice is there?

There is a little juice.

2. How much coffee is there?

There _____ a lot of coffee.

3. How much _____ is there?

There is a _____ _____.

4. How much _____ is there?

There is a _____ of _____.

5. Is there a lot of cheese?

Yes, there is.

6. Is _____ a little tea?

No, there isn't.

7. Is there a _____ of _____?

Yes, there _____.

8. Is _____ a little _____?

No, _____ _____.

Section G   Let's have fun

Food + Drinks!

Circle the odd word

1. cake   pizza   cheese   (soda)   pie

2. soda   tea   cake   juice   milk

3. pizza   coffee   cheese   pie   cake

4. pie   soda   water   tea   coffee

5. cheese   cake   tea   pie   pizza

6. pizza   milk   coffee   juice   water

7. cake   juice   cheese   pie   pizza

8. water   soda   milk   juice   cheese

Write the word

1.
2.
3.
4.
5.
6.
7.
8.

Lesson 11: At the fruit market

Manavda

What do you want?
I want an apple.

Section A — Words

1. **orange**
   Portakal
2. **pear**
   Armut
3. **watermelon**
   Karpuz
4. **strawberry**
   Çilek
5. **cherry**
   Vişne
6. **lemon**
   Limon
7. **banana**
   Muz
8. **grape**
   Üzüm
9. **pineapple**
   Ananas
10. **apple**
    Elma

Section B — Make a sentence

What do you want?

I want an <u>orange</u>.

What don't you want?

I don't want a <u>lemon</u>.

Note: Say *an* before all words that begin with a, e, i, o, u.

Section C — Make a question

Is there one <u>pear</u>?
Yes, there is. / No, there isn't.

Are there <u>five</u> <u>grape</u>s?
Yes, there are. / No, there aren't.

Section D — Learn a verb

need – needing – needed – needed gerekmek

I **need** two watermelons for the picnic.

People **needing** vitamin C should eat more oranges.

Yesterday, I **needed** to buy some apples.

I haven't **needed** to use the heater this year.

Section E — Learn an idiom

A bad apple

Meaning: The one bad person in a good group.

"He is *a bad apple* on this basketball team."

Section F | Write

Trace and fill in the words

1. What do you want?

I want an apple.

2. What don't you want?

I don't _____ a cherry.

3. What _____ you want?

I want a _____.

4. What _____ you _____?

I don't _____ a _____.

5. Is there one grape?

Yes, there is.

6. Are there seven strawberries?

No, there aren't.

7. Is _____ one _____?

No, _____ isn't.

8. Are _____ three _____?

Yes, _____ _____.

| Section G | Let's have fun |

At the fruit market!

Write the missing word

| orange | lemon | pear | strawberry | banana |
| watermelon | grape | pineapple | cherry | apple |

1. orange

lemon
pear
strawberry
pineapple
watermelon
apple
cherry
banana
grape

2. _____

apple
orange
strawberry
banana
pear
lemon
grape
pineapple
cherry

3. _____

strawberry
apple
orange
watermelon
pineapple
pear
cherry
banana
grape

4. _____

lemon
pear
strawberry
orange
watermelon
apple
cherry
banana
pineapple

5. _____

lemon
grape
strawberry
pineapple
watermelon
apple
cherry
orange
banana

6. _____

pear
orange
watermelon
banana
strawberry
apple
cherry
lemon
grape

7. _____

grape
pear
orange
pineapple
watermelon
apple
banana
cherry
lemon

8. _____

lemon
pear
strawberry
cherry
watermelon
banana
orange
pineapple
grape

Lesson 12: Shapes

Şekiller

What color is this circle?
This is a green circle.

Section A — Words

1. **square**
   Kare
2. **circle**
   Çember
3. **star**
   Yıldız
4. **heart**
   Kalp
5. **octagon**
   Sekizgen
6. **triangle**
   Üçgen
7. **rectangle**
   dikdörtgen
8. **oval**
   Oval
9. **diamond**
   Elmas
10. **pentagon**
    Beşgen

Section B — Make a sentence

What color is this <u>square</u>?

This is a <u>red</u> square.

What color is that <u>triangle</u>?

That is a <u>blue</u> triangle.

| Section C | Make a question |

Is this <u>circle</u> <u>green</u>?

Yes, it is. / No, it isn't. It's <u>blue</u>.

Is that <u>rectangle</u> <u>orange</u>?

Yes, it is. / No, it isn't. It's <u>purple</u>.

| Section D | Learn a verb |

find – finding – found – found bulmak

I can't **find** my keys.

The teacher is **finding** many mistakes in my homework.

I **found** my grandfather's watch.

He still hasn't **found** his workbook.

| Section E | Learn an idiom |

Be out of shape

Meaning: To be unfit or overweight.

"He can't climb this mountain. He *is* really *out of shape*!"

| Section F | Write |

Trace and fill in the words

1. What color is this rectangle?

This is a yellow rectangle.

2. What color is that oval?

_____ is a green oval.

3. What _____ is _____ diamond?

This is a _____ diamond.

4. _____ color _____ that _____?

_____ _____ a _____ heart.

5. Is this circle purple?

Yes, it is.

6. _____ that octagon blue?

No, _____ _____. It's pink.

7. Is this _____ _____?

Yes, _____ _____.

8. _____ that _____ red?

No, _____ _____. It's _____.

| Section G | Let's have fun |

Shapes!

1. What color is this rectangle?   [blue]

　<u>This is a blue rectangle.</u>

2. What color is this star?   [red]

　_____.

3. What color is this circle?   [gray]

　_____.

4. What color is this oval?   [purple]

　_____.

5. What color is this diamond?   [black]

　_____.

6. What color is this square?   [blue]

　_____.

7. What color is this pentagon?   [green]

　_____.

8. What color is this triangle?   [pink]

　_____.

Test 3   Lesson 9 - 12

Write the answer next to the letter "A"

A: ___ **1.** What ___ you like to do? I like to ___ piano.

a. does, do   b. is, play   c. are, go   d. do, play

A: ___ **2.** Don't ___ like to play cards? Yes, I ___.

a. we, can   b. you, do   c. he, am   d. you, can

A: ___ **3.** He ___ comic books.

a. read   b. reading   c. see   d. reads

A: ___ **4.** "I think I can find a cheaper price. I'm going to ___ around."

a. buy   b. play   c. shop   d. cost

A: ___ **5.** How ___ pizza is there? There is ___ pizza.

a. many, big   b. much, a lot of   c. small, many   d. much, all

A: ___ **6.** Is ___ a lot of coffee? No, ___ isn't.

a. there, there   b. this, lot   c. them, she   d. it, he

A: ___ **7.** My grandmother ___ a lot of soda.

a. want   b. wanting   c. wants   d. doesn't

A: ___ **8.** "I need that job to put ___ on the table."

a. food   b. money   c. meat   d. milk

A: ___ **9.** What ___ you want? I don't ___ a banana.

a. do, try   b. can't, want   c. can, have   d. don't, want

A: ___ **10.** ___ there seven cherries? No, there ___.

a. Is, isn't   b. Our, aren't   c. Are, aren't   d. Have, hasn't

A: ___ **11.** We ___ eight pineapples.

a. needing   b. needs   c. need   d. is need

A: ___ **12.** "He's not a nice guy. He's really a bad ___."

a. tomato   b. orange   c. lemon   d. apple

A: ___ **13.** What color is ___ oval? That ___ a purple oval.

a. that, is   b. this, are   c. an, can   d. purple, has

A: ___ **14.** Is this ___ blue? Yes, it ___.

a. circle, can   b. heart, does   c. square, is   d. star, blue

A: ___ **15.** I can't ___ an orange octagon.

a. finding   b. found   c. find   d. be found

A: ___ **16.** "He really needs to get healthy. He's really ___ shape."

a. into   b. taking   c. losing   d. out of

Answers on page 206

Lesson 13: At the supermarket

Süpermarket

> What do you want to buy?
> I want to buy some bread.

Section A — Words

1. **milk**
   Süt
2. **juice**
   Meyve suyu
3. **meat**
   Et
4. **drinks**
   İçecek
5. **vegetables**
   Sebze
6. **ice cream**
   Dondurma
7. **fruit**
   Meyve
8. **bread**
   Ekmek
9. **fish**
   Balık
10. **pizza**
    Pizza

Section B — Make a sentence

What do you want to buy?

I want to buy some <u>milk</u>.

What don't you want to buy?

I don't want to buy any <u>ice cream</u>.

Learn: some, any

| Section C | Make a question |

Do you want to buy some <u>juice</u>?
Yes, I do. / No, I don't.

Do you want to buy some <u>fruit</u>?
Yes, I do. / No, I don't.

| Section D | Learn a verb |

get – getting – got – gotten almak

I **get** my bread at the supermarket.

He is **getting** some bananas from the fruit market.

Last night, she **got** a pizza for dinner.

We haven't **gotten** any vegetables yet.

| Section E | Learn an idiom |

A rip off

Meaning: Something is too expensive.

"The supermarket around the corner is *a rip off*."

| Section F | Write |

Trace and fill in the words

1. What do you want to buy?

I want to buy some fruit.

2. What don't you want _____ buy?

I don't want to buy any bread.

3. What _____ you want to _____?

I want to _____ some _____.

4. What _____ you _____ to buy?

I don't want to _____ any _____.

5. Do you want to buy some fish?

Yes, I _____.

6. Do you want to buy some milk?

No, I don't.

7. Do you _____ to buy _____ _____?

Yes, I _____.

8. Do you want to _____ some _____?

No, I _____.

Section G Let's have fun

At the supermarket!

Read the conversation

Max: What do you want to buy?

Julie: I want to buy some milk.

Max: What don't you want to buy?

Julie: I don't want to buy any meat.

Max: What do you want to buy?

Julie: I want to buy some fruit.

Max: What do you want to buy?

Julie: I want to buy some bread.

Max: What don't you want to buy?

Julie: I don't want to buy any fish.

Max: What do you want to buy?

Julie: I want to buy some vegetables.

Circle the things Julie wants

meat   milk   fruit   fish   vegetables
ice cream   bread   pizza   drinks   juice

Write the things she wants in the shopping cart

1. _____
2. _____
3. _____
4. _____

Lesson 14: At the ice cream shop

Dondurma dükkanında

> Which flavor do you like?
> I like mint flavor.

Section A — Words

1. **chocolate**
   Çikolata
2. **strawberry**
   Çilek
3. **mint**
   Nane
4. **raspberry**
   Ahududu
5. **cherry**
   Vişne
6. **vanilla**
   Vanilya
7. **coffee**
   Kahve
8. **almond**
   Badem
9. **caramel**
   Karame
10. **coconut**
    Hindistan cevizi

Section B — Make a sentence

Which flavor do you like?

I like <u>chocolate</u> flavor.

I don't like <u>almond</u> flavor.

Which flavor does he like?

He likes <u>vanilla</u> flavor.

He doesn't like <u>raspberry</u> flavor.

Section C — Make a question

Do you like <u>strawberry</u> ice cream?
Yes, I do. / No, I don't.

Does she like <u>mint</u> ice cream?
Yes, she does. / No, she doesn't.

Section D — Learn a verb

have/has – having – had – had sahip olmak

She **has** coffee ice cream in her refrigerator.

I am **having** mint ice cream instead.

My sister **had** almond ice cream last time.

My father hasn't **had** caramel ice cream yet.

Section E — Learn an idiom

Flavor of the month

Meaning: Something is suddenly popular for a short time.

"This song is just the *flavor of the month*."

Section F — Write

Trace and fill in the words

1. Which flavor do you like?

I like coconut flavor.

2. Which flavor does he like?

He _____ chocolate flavor.

3. Which _____ do you _____?

I like _____ _____.

4. Which _____ does she _____?

She _____ _____ _____.

5. Do you like vanilla ice cream?

No, I don't.

6. Does she like coffee ice cream?

Yes, she does.

7. Do you _____ _____ ice cream?

Yes, I _____.

8. Does he _____ _____ ice cream?

No, _____ _____.

68

Section G Let's have fun

At the ice cream shop!

| don't   raspberry   do   like   you   flavor   she   does |

1. Which _____ do you like? I _____ chocolate flavor.

2. Which flavor _____ you like? I like _____ flavor.

3. Which flavor _____ she like? _____ likes mint flavor.

4. Do _____ like vanilla flavor? No, I _____.

Do or Does?

1. What flavor _____ she like?

2. What flavor _____ they like?

3. What flavor _____ he like?

4. What flavor _____ you like?

5. _____ you like strawberry flavor?

6. _____ he like vanilla flavor?

7. _____ they like vanilla flavor?

8. _____ she like vanilla flavor?

9. Yes, they _____.

10. No, she _____ not.

Lesson 15: In the refrigerator

Buzdolabında

> What do you want to eat?
> I want to eat rice.

Section A — Words

1. **rice**
   Pirinç
2. **salad**
   Salata
3. **toast**
   Tost
4. **soup**
   Çorba
5. **dumplings**
   Hamur köftesi
6. **tea**
   Çay
7. **cola**
   Kola
8. **eggs**
   Yumurta
9. **water**
   Su
10. **ice**
    Buz

Section B — Make a sentence

What do you want to <u>eat</u>?

I want to eat <u>rice</u>.

I don't want to eat <u>dumplings</u>.

What does he want to <u>drink</u>?

He wants to drink <u>tea</u>.

He doesn't want to drink <u>cola</u>.

Section C — Make a question

Do you want to <u>eat</u> <u>salad</u>?
Yes, I do. / No, I don't.

Does she want to <u>drink</u> <u>juice</u>?
Yes, she does. / No, she doesn't.

Section D — Learn a verb

sell – selling – sold – sold satmak

They **sell** eggs at the supermarket.

He was **selling** delicious dumplings at the market last night.

Last week, they **sold** me some cheap rice.

The supermarket has never **sold** ice.

Section E — Learn an idiom

Be as cold as ice

Meaning: To describe someone who is very unfriendly.

"The teacher *was as cold as ice* after she caught me cheating on the science test."

Section F — Write

Trace and fill in the words

1. What do you want to drink?

I want to drink water.

2. What does he want to eat?

He _____ to eat soup.

3. What _____ you want to _____?

I want to eat _____.

4. What _____ she _____ to drink?

She wants to _____ _____.

5. Do you want to eat toast?

Yes, I do.

6. Does he _____ to drink tea?

No, he doesn't.

7. Do you _____ to drink _____?

Yes, I _____.

8. Does _____ want to eat _____?

No, she _____.

Section G — Let's have fun

In the refrigerator!

1	2	3	4	5	6	7	8	9	10	11	12	13
a	b	c	d	e	f	g	h	i	j	k	l	m
14	15	16	17	18	19	20	21	22	23	24	25	26
n	o	p	q	r	s	t	u	v	w	x	y	z

Write the words using the code above

1. 19-15-21-16 __ __ __ __
2. 20-15-1-19-20 __ __ __ __ __
3. 19-1-12-1-4 __ __ __ __ __
4. 18-9-3-5 __ __ __ __
5. 23-1-20-5-18 __ __ __ __ __
6. 3-15-12-1 __ __ __ __

This man's refrigerator has no food! Help him write a shopping list!

Shopping list

1. dumplings
2. _____
3. _____
4. _____
5. _____
6. _____
7. _____
8. _____

Lesson 16: Jobs

Meslekler

> What is her job?
> She is a salesclerk.

Section A — Words

1. **doctor**
   Doktor
2. **cook**
   Aşçı
3. **nurse**
   Hemşire
4. **police officer**
   Polis memuru
5. **taxi driver**
   Taksi şoförü
6. **teacher**
   Öğretmen
7. **farmer**
   Çiftçi
8. **salesclerk**
   Satıcı
9. **firefighter**
   İtfaiyeci
10. **builder**
    İnşaatçı

Section B — Make a sentence

What is her job?

She is a <u>doctor</u>.

She isn't a <u>nurse</u>.

What is his job?

He is a <u>teacher</u>.

He isn't a <u>salesclerk</u>.

Section C — Make a question

Is he a <u>farmer</u>?
Yes, he is. / No, he isn't.

Are they <u>teacher</u>s?
Yes, they are. / No, they aren't.

Section D — Learn a verb

work – working – worked – worked çalışmak

I **work** on a farm every day.

She wasn't **working** at the hospital last year.

My mother **worked** at the police station yesterday.

He hasn't **worked** for two years.

Section E — Learn an idiom

Keep up the good work

Meaning: To encourage someone to keep doing well.

"You're doing a great job. *Keep up the good work.*"

Section F — Write

Trace and fill in the words

1. What is his job?

He is a cook.

2. What is _____ job?

She is a teacher.

3. What _____ his _____?

_____ is a _____.

4. What is _____ job?

She _____ a _____.

5. Is she a builder?

No, she isn't.

6. Are they doctors?

No, they aren't.

7. Is _____ a _____?

Yes, she _____.

8. Are we _____?

Yes, _____ _____.

Section G | Let's have fun

Jobs!

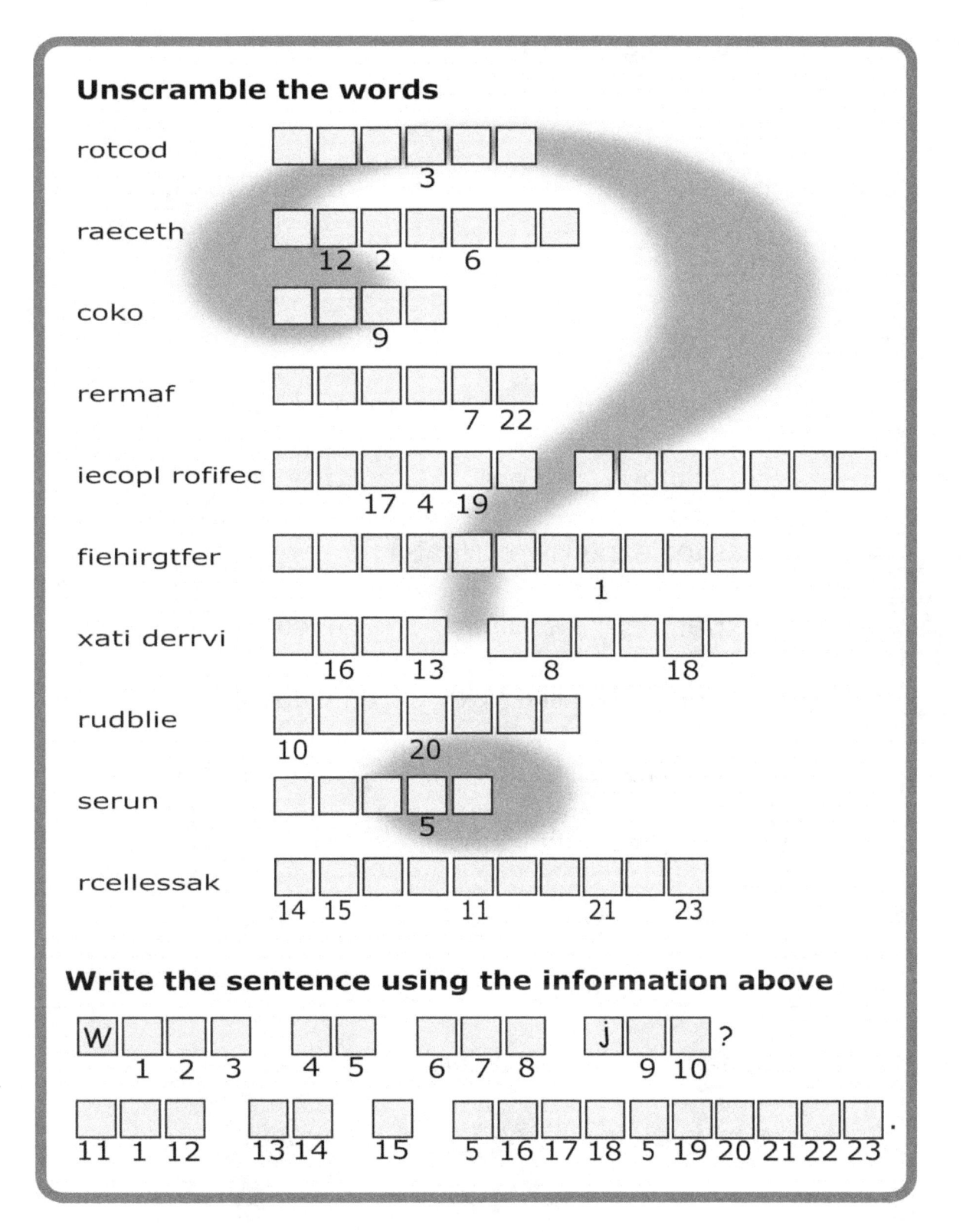

Unscramble the words

rotcod ☐☐☐☐☐☐
             3

raeceth ☐☐☐☐☐☐☐
         12 2   6

coko ☐☐☐☐
        9

rermaf ☐☐☐☐☐☐
           7 22

iecopl rofifec ☐☐☐☐☐☐ ☐☐☐☐☐☐☐
                17 4 19

fiehirgtfer ☐☐☐☐☐☐☐☐☐☐
                    1

xati derrvi ☐☐☐☐ ☐☐☐☐☐☐
             16 13   8   18

rudblie ☐☐☐☐☐☐☐
         10   20

serun ☐☐☐☐☐
         5

rcellessak ☐☐☐☐☐☐☐☐☐☐
            14 15   11   21   23

Write the sentence using the information above

☐W☐☐☐ ☐☐ ☐☐☐ ☐j☐ ?
 1 2 3 4 5 6 7 8 9 10

☐☐☐ ☐☐ ☐ ☐☐☐☐☐☐☐☐☐ .
11 1 12 13 14 15 5 16 17 18 5 19 20 21 22 23

Test 4   Lesson 13 - 16

Write the answer next to the letter "A"

A: ___ **1.** What does he want to ___? He ___ to buy some milk.

a. buys, want   b. buy, have   c. buys, wants   d. buy, wants

A: ___ **2.** Do you ___ to buy some ___? Yes, I do.

a. wants, meat   b. want, bread   c. want, apple   d. wants, drinks

A: ___ **3.** She ___ the vegetables at the supermarket.

a. get   b. getting   c. got   d. is get

A: ___ **4.** "That was too expensive. What a rip ___."

a. of   b. over   c. off   d. curl

A: ___ **5.** Which flavor ___ he like? He ___ mint flavor.

a. do, like   b. can, like   c. does, like   d. does, likes

A: ___ **6.** ___ you like chocolate ice cream? Yes, I ___.

a. Does, does   b. Can, does   c. Do, like   d. Do, do

A: ___ **7.** They didn't ___ almond ice cream.

a. have   b. has   c. having   d. had

A: ___ **8.** "That new book is just the ___ of the month."

a. taste   b. word   c. ice cream   d. flavor

A: ___ 9. What ___ she want to drink? She wants to ___ cola.

a. do, try　　　b. does, drink　　　c. can, have　　d. don't, want

A: ___ 10. Do ___ want to eat salad? No, I ___.

a. he, doesn't　b. you, don't　　c. you, not like　　d. we, haven't

A: ___ 11. They are ___ coffee.

a. sell　　　　b. sells　　　　c. selling　　　　d. sold

A: ___ 12. "She wasn't friendly. She was as ___ as ice."

a. melted　　　b. cold　　　　c. dry　　　　d. mean

A: ___ 13. What is ___ job? She ___ a taxi driver.

a. she, is　　　b. hers, can　　c. she's, be　　d. her, is

A: ___ 14. ___ they teachers? No, they ___.

a. Are, don't　b. Do, don't　　c. Have, haven't　　d. Are, aren't

A: ___ 15. They ___ at a school.

a. work　　　　b. works　　　c. working　　　d. has worked

A: ___ 16. "You're doing well. Keep ___ the good work."

a. into　　　　b. on　　　　c. going　　　　d. up

Answers on page 206

Lesson 17: Names

İsimler

What's her name?
Her name is Helen.

| Section A | Words |

1. John
2. Matthew
3. Jason
4. Helen
5. Mary
6. Kevin
7. Tom
8. Emily
9. Jessica
10. Susan

| Section B | Make a sentence |

What's <u>your</u> name?
My name is <u>John</u>.

What's <u>her</u> name?
Her name is <u>Susan</u>.

Learn: my, your, his, her

Note: What's = What is

Section C | Make a question

Is <u>his</u> name <u>Jason</u>?
Yes, it is. / No, it isn't.

Is <u>her</u> name <u>Emily</u>?
Yes, it is. / No, it isn't.

Section D | Learn a verb

call – calling – called – called aramak

You can **call** him Jason.

I will be **calling** you tomorrow at 9:30 A.M.

Kevin **called** Mary yesterday.

Helen hasn't **called** Matthew back yet.

Section E | Learn an idiom

A household name

Meaning: To describe someone famous who everyone knows.

"The actor became *a household name* after he won an Oscar for his performance."

| Section F | Write |

Trace and fill in the words

1. What's your name?

My name is Susan.

2. What's his name?

His name _____ Tom.

3. What's _____ name?

My _____ is _____.

4. What's _____ _____?

Her name _____ _____.

5. Is his name John?

Yes, it is.

6. Is her name Jessica?

No, it isn't.

7. Is _____ name _____?

Yes, it _____.

8. Is _____ _____ Kevin?

No, _____ isn't.

| Section G | Let's have fun |

Names!

1 M **2** T **3** S **4** J **5** K

Write their names

1. __ __ __ __

2. __ __ __

3. __ __ __ __ __

4. __ __ __ __

5. __ __ __ __

What's your name?

_____

Answer the questions

1. What is her name?

   Her name is Mary.

2. What is his name?

   _____

3. What is her name?

   _____

4. What is his name?

   _____

5. What is his name?

   _____

Lesson 18: More places

Daha çok yer

> Where did you go yesterday?
> I went to school.

Section A — Words

1. **the library**
   Kütüphane
2. **school**
   Okul
3. **the hospital**
   Hastane
4. **the train station**
   Tren istasyonu
5. **the police station**
   Karakol
6. **the office**
   Ofis
7. **the factory**
   Fabrika
8. **the clinic**
   Klinik
9. **the bus stop**
   Otobüs durağı
10. **the fire station**
    İtfaiye merkezi

Section B — Make a sentence

Where did you go <u>yesterday</u>?

I went to <u>the library</u>.

Where did they go <u>last week</u>?

They went to <u>the office</u>.

Learn: yesterday, last week, last night, last month

Note: didn't = did not

Section C — Make a question

Did she go to <u>school</u> <u>last night</u>?
Yes, she did. / No, she didn't.

Did you go to <u>the factory</u> <u>yesterday</u>?
Yes, I did. / No, I didn't.

Section D — Learn a verb

go – going – went – gone gitmek

I will **go** to the library after school.

When I was **going** to the office, I saw my friend.

Matthew **went** to the clinic this morning.

Mary hasn't **gone** to school yet.

Section E — Learn an idiom

Heart is in the right place

Meaning: To mean well and try to do the right thing.

"He makes a lot of mistakes, but his *heart is in the right place*."

| Section F | Write |

Trace and fill in the words

1. Where did you go yesterday?

I went to the police station.

2. Where _____ they go last night?

They went to _____ clinic.

3. Where _____ we _____ last week?

_____ went to the _____.

4. Where did _____ go _____?

She _____ to the _____.

5. Did he go to the bus stop yesterday?

Yes, he did.

6. Did you _____ to the train station last night?

No, I _____.

7. Did _____ go to the _____ last week?

Yes, _____ _____.

8. Did she _____ to the _____ last night?

No, _____ _____.

Section G | Let's have fun

More places!

Library

1. Where did you go yesterday?

I went to the library.

→ Did you go to the library yesterday?
- ✓ Yes, I did.
- ○ No, I didn't.

Police station

2. Where did they go last week?

→ Did they go to school last week?
- ○ Yes, they did.
- ○ No, they didn't.

School

3. Where did he go last night?

→ Did he go to the hospital last night?
- ○ Yes, he did.
- ○ No, he didn't.

Factory

4. Where did she go yesterday?

→ Did she go to the factory yesterday?
- ○ Yes, she did.
- ○ No, she didn't.

Fire station

5. Where did you go last week?

→ Did you go to the clinic last week?
- ○ Yes, I did.
- ○ No, I didn't.

Lesson 19: Meats

Etler

> What did he eat for lunch?
> He ate chicken.

Section A — Words

1. **beef**
   Sığır eti
2. **pork**
   Domuz
3. **bacon**
   Pastırma
4. **fish**
   Balık
5. **salami**
   Salam
6. **chicken**
   Tavuk
7. **lamb**
   Kuzu
8. **ham**
   Jambon
9. **sausage**
   Sosis
10. **shrimp**
    Karides

Section B — Make a sentence

What did he eat for <u>lunch</u>?

He ate <u>beef</u>.

He didn't eat <u>chicken</u>.

Learn: breakfast, lunch, dinner

Section C — Make a question

Did they eat <u>ham</u> for <u>breakfast</u>?
Yes, they did. / No, they didn't.

Did you eat <u>fish</u> for <u>dinner</u>?
Yes, I did. / No, I didn't.

Section D — Learn a verb

eat – eating – ate – eaten yemek

I **eat** bacon for breakfast every Sunday.

They're not **eating** meat.

We **ate** a sandwich with cheese and salami yesterday.

I had never **eaten** German sausages until I went there.

Section E — Learn an idiom

Beef up

Meaning: To strengthen something or somebody.

"We need to *beef up* our efforts if we are going to do well this year."

| Section F | Write |

Trace and fill in the words

1. What did she eat for lunch?

She ate ham. She didn't eat fish.

2. What did they eat for dinner?

They ate pork. They didn't _____ shrimp.

3. What _____ he eat _____ lunch?

_____ ate _____. He didn't _____ beef.

4. _____ did you _____ for breakfast?

I _____ fish. _____ didn't eat _____.

5. Did we eat sausage for lunch?

Yes, we _____.

6. Did you eat lamb for dinner?

No, I _____.

7. Did _____ eat _____ for lunch?

Yes, he _____.

8. Did they _____ bacon for _____?

No, _____ _____.

Section G | Let's have fun

Meats!

Find the words!

```
f e p l x e m s x h e m d b o h z a l u
e p r n y l o q u y m x y r w g r p g d
i c r l y o i q d z m a u a p f q b s g
r v b k v y b n e z i x x q d r e c b h
r y u o r w l j g d s n z u u s l l z z
l h b e e f k w v q n b j e g f b w c m
c i b k b s q x b g m o i g n k n d r p
f q x b q a e k m f j o c b l s p k h n
m x j t o u n z z m f f s a l a m i y y
v i r m i a k e s k r g e k b u m z a e
w n p w n k q z r v h p h e s s n b l p
q o h n s t q u c n w u z l r a d f u v
a p s i g e l b o b q f x w s g n d e w
l b k p j c g n n c x o i z q e t e r i
s g n s x v w q l o x h k y k b q q y y
j k a x e h x a s z y p a c k r e v t r
j o w n g q v f i s h r i m p n o f m p
o a d h o b i e t h o h c q z n c p b m
y k o b m l v h v i c r q i k b c o f i
f i q a m x g l q k z w s n a w t n w w
```

~~beef~~   shrimp
pork   bacon
ham   sausage
fish   lamb
chicken   salami

Lesson 20: Vegetables

Sebzeler

> What will you cook tonight?
> I will cook pumpkin.

Section A — Words

1. **pumpkin**
   Balkabağı
2. **potato**
   Patates
3. **carrot**
   Havuç
4. **asparagus**
   Kuşkonmaz
5. **broccoli**
   Brokoli
6. **corn**
   Mısır
7. **cabbage**
   Lahana
8. **spinach**
   Ispanak
9. **mushroom**
   Mantar
10. **onion**
    Soğan

Section B — Make a sentence

What will he cook <u>tonight</u>?

He will cook <u>pumpkin</u>.

What won't she cook <u>tomorrow</u>?

She won't cook <u>onion</u>.

Learn: tonight, tomorrow, later, next week

Note: won't = will not

Section C — Make a question

Will we cook <u>carrot</u> <u>later</u>?
Yes, we will. / No, we won't.

Will you cook <u>asparagus</u> <u>tomorrow</u>?
Yes, I will. / No, I won't.

Section D — Learn a verb

cook – cooking – cooked – cooked pişirmek

She always **cooks** onions with the potatoes.

Mary will be **cooking** dinner for us tonight.

John **cooked** a delicious meal for us last weekend.

I've **cooked** cabbage and mushroom a lot lately.

Section E — Learn an idiom

Carrot on a stick

Meaning: A reward that is promised upon completion of a task.

"The coach gave his players a *carrot on a stick* and promised to take them all out for dinner if they win the game."

| Section F | Write |

Trace and fill in the words

1. What will he cook tonight?

He will cook corn.

2. What won't she cook tomorrow?

She won't _____ spinach.

3. What _____ he _____ later?

_____ will _____ onion. He won't cook _____.

4. What will _____ cook tonight?

She _____ cook _____.

5. Will they cook carrot tomorrow?

Yes, they _____.

6. Will you cook asparagus tomorrow?

No, I _____.

7. Will she _____ mushroom _____?

Yes, _____ will.

8. Will _____ cook _____ tomorrow?

No, we _____.

Section G — Let's have fun

Vegetables!

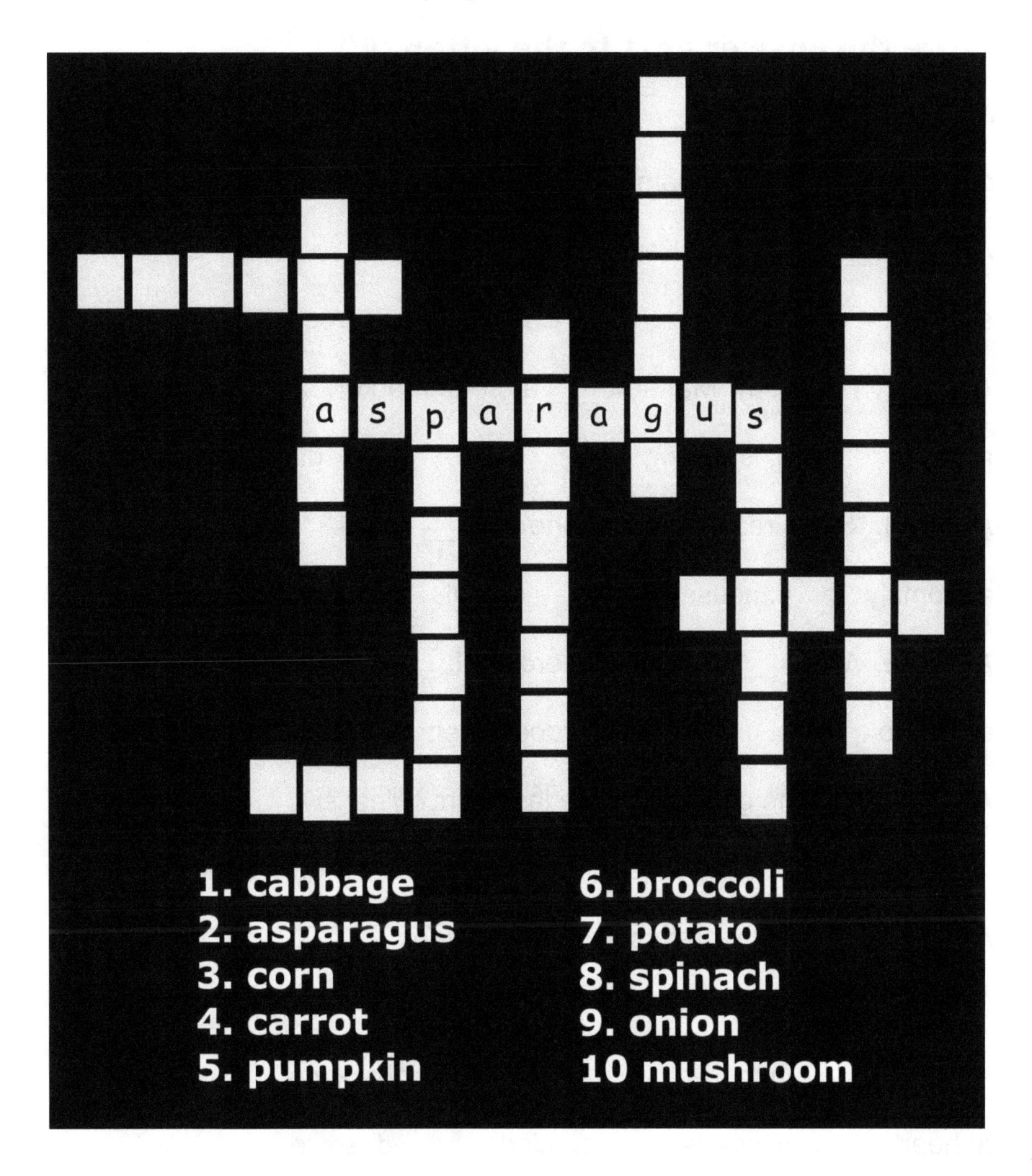

a s p a r a g u s

1. cabbage
2. asparagus
3. corn
4. carrot
5. pumpkin
6. broccoli
7. potato
8. spinach
9. onion
10 mushroom

Test 5   Lesson 17 - 20

Write the answer next to the letter "A"

A: ___ **1.** What's her ___? ___ name is Helen.

a. name, Her   b. name, She's   c. names, Her   d. name, She

A: ___ **2.** ___ his name Kevin? Yes, ___ is.

a. Is, it   b. Is, he   c. Can, it   d. Does, it

A: ___ **3.** Yesterday, Matthew ___ a green marker.

a. has   b. is having   c. had   d. did had

A: ___ **4.** "She's really famous. She's a ___ name."

a. homely   b. household   c. real   d. star

A: ___ **5.** Where ___ you go yesterday? I ___ to the clinic.

a. do, go   b. did, go   c. does, went   d. did, went

A: ___ **6.** ___ she go to the office last night? Yes, she ___.

a. Does, go   b. Can, does   c. Did, goes   d. Did, did

A: ___ **7.** I ___ to the train station every week.

a. gone   b. go   c. going   d. goes

A: ___ **8.** "He means well. His ___ is in the right place."

a. heart   b. words   c. mind   d. smile

A: ___ 9. What ___ he eat for dinner? He ___ eat pork.

a. does, didn't   b. is, is   c. didn't, didn't   d. did, was

A: ___ 10. ___ they eat sausage for lunch? No, they ___.

a. Were, weren't   b. Did, don't   c. Like, not like   d. Did, didn't

A: ___ 11. She has ___ all of the ham.

a. eat   b. ate   c. eaten   d. eating

A: ___ 12. "He wants to get stronger. He said he wants to beef ___."

a. out   b. up   c. on   d. in

A: ___ 13. What ___ he cook later? He will ___ broccoli.

a. is, cook   b. will, cooks   c. has, cook   d. will, cook

A: ___ 14. ___ we cook asparagus tonight? ___, we will.

a. Can, Can   b. Don't, Do   c. Will, Yes   d. Are, Yes

A: ___ 15. She will ___ vegetables tomorrow.

a. cook   b. cooks   c. cooking   d. cooked

A: ___ 16. "I think the reward is like a ___ on a stick."

a. potato   b. pumpkin   c. carrot   d. mushroom

Answers on page 206

Lesson 21: At school

Okulda

Where is the art room?
The art room is next to the gym.

Section A — Words

1. **classroom**
   Sınıf
2. **office**
   Ofis
3. **nurse's office**
   Revir
4. **gym**
   Spor salonu
5. **hall**
   Salon
6. **computer lab**
   Bilgisayar laboratuarı
7. **art room**
   Sanat odası
8. **music room**
   Müzik odası
9. **science lab**
   Bilim laboratuarı
10. **lunchroom**
    Yemek odası

Section B — Make a sentence

Where is the <u>classroom</u>?

The classroom is <u>across from</u> the <u>office</u>.

Where is the <u>computer lab</u>?

The computer lab is <u>between</u> the <u>gym</u> and the <u>hall</u>.

Learn: across from, next to, between

Section C — Make a question

Is the <u>art room</u> <u>next to</u> the <u>music room</u>?
Yes, it is. / No, it's <u>next to</u> the <u>science lab</u>.

Is the <u>nurse's office</u> <u>next to</u> the <u>office</u>?
Yes, it is. / No, it's <u>across from</u> the <u>computer lab</u>.

Section D — Learn a verb

put – putting – put – put koymak

You can **put** the guitar in the music room.

We are **putting** the chairs in the new office.

The students already **put** the books in the computer lab.

She hasn't **put** any food in the lunchroom yet.

Section E — Learn an idiom

Old school

Meaning: To do something the old-fashioned way.

"We're going to do this *old school* and use a hammer and nails."

Section F — Write

Trace and fill in the words

1. Where is the office?

The office is next to the lunchroom.

2. Where _____ the gym?

The gym is _____ the art room and the science lab.

3. Where _____ the _____ room?

The music room is across from the _____.

4. _____ is the _____ lab?

The science lab is _____ the lunchroom and the _____.

5. Is the art room next to the music room?

Yes, it is.

6. Is the computer lab _____ to the hall?

No, it's _____ the gym and the art room.

7. _____ the nurse's office next to the _____?

Yes, it is.

8. Is the hall across _____ the classroom?

No, it's _____ the _____ and the office.

Section G | Let's have fun

At school!

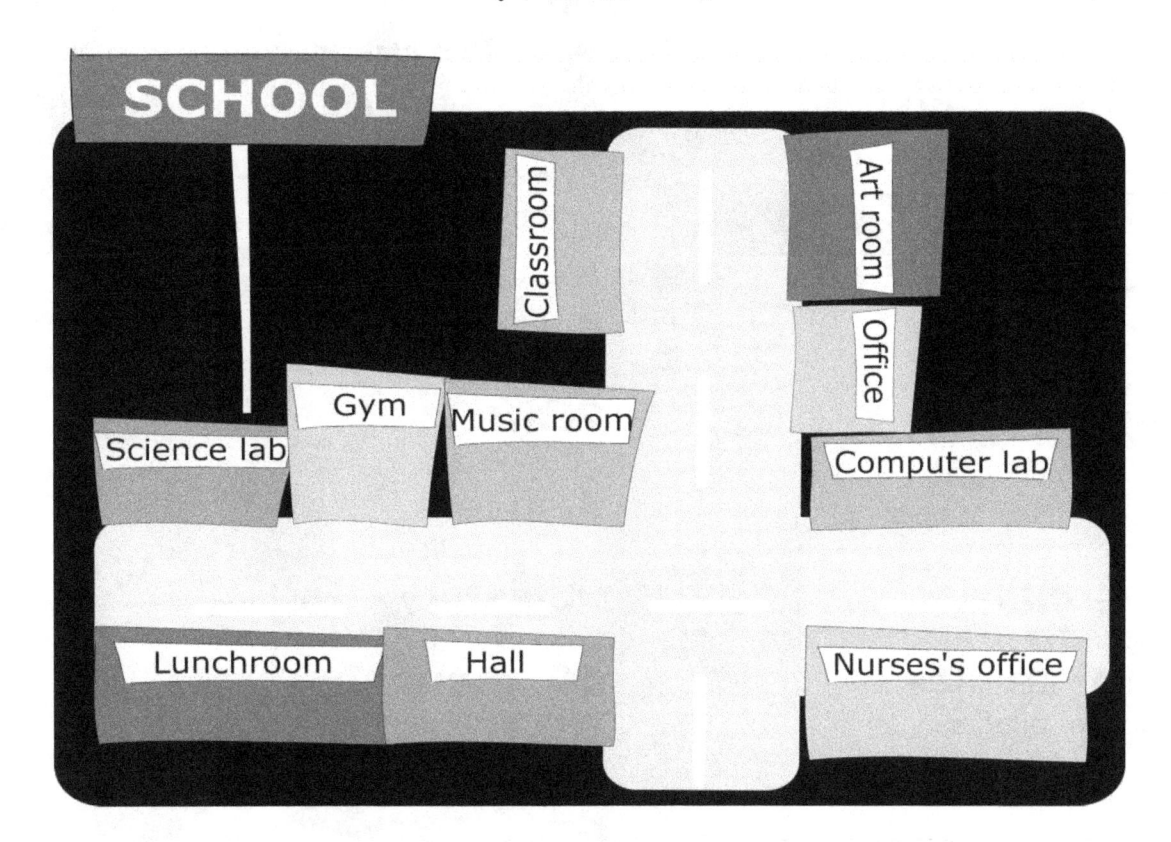

SCHOOL

- Classroom
- Art room
- Office
- Gym
- Music room
- Science lab
- Computer lab
- Lunchroom
- Hall
- Nurses's office

Answer the questions

1. Where is the gym?
   _____.

2. Where is the classroom?
   _____.

3. Where is the nurse's office?
   _____.

4. Is the lunchroom next to the hall?
   _____.

5. Is the science lab across from the office?
   _____.

Lesson 22: School subjects

Okul dersleri

What class do you have after math?
I have an art class after math.

Section A — Words

1. **science**
   Fen
2. **English**
   İngilizce
3. **P.E.**
   Beden eğitimi
4. **geography**
   Coğrafya
5. **social studies**
   Sosyal bilgiler
6. **math**
   Matematik
7. **art**
   Sanat
8. **music**
   Müzik
9. **history**
   Tarih
10. **computer**
    Bilgisayar

Section B — Make a sentence

What class do you have <u>after</u> <u>science</u>?

I have a <u>geography</u> class after science.

What class does he have <u>before</u> <u>science</u>?

He has a <u>history</u> class before science.

Learn: after, before / have, has

Section C — Make a question

Do you have a <u>math</u> class after <u>history</u>?
Yes, I do. / No, I have a <u>music</u> class.

Does he have a <u>math</u> class before <u>English</u>?
Yes, he does. / No, he has a <u>computer</u> class.

Section D — Learn a verb

do – doing – did – done yapmak

He couldn't **do** most of the questions on the math test.

They are **doing** the science project now.

John **did** really well on his English test last semester.

I will have already **done** the history homework by Sunday.

Section E — Learn an idiom

Cut class

Meaning: To miss class on purpose.

"Jenny *cut class* after she realized she didn't do her math homework."

Section F — Write

Trace and fill in the words

1. What class do you have after math?

I have an English class after math.

2. What class does she have before art?

She has a music _____ before art.

3. What _____ do you have _____ history?

I _____ a geography class before _____.

4. What class does _____ have after _____?

She _____ a science class _____ P.E.

5. Do you _____ a math class after history?

Yes, I _____.

6. Does he have a science _____ after English?

No, he _____ a computer class.

7. Do _____ have an art class before _____?

Yes, you _____.

8. Does _____ have a P.E. class _____ music?

No, she _____ an _____ class.

Section G   Let's have fun

School Subjects!

I have a geography class after science.
I have an English class before science.
I have a math class before English.
I have a history class after geography.
I have a computer class before math.

Fill out the School Schedule using the information above

School Schedule

9am _____

10am _____

11am _____

1pm science class

2pm _____

3pm _____

True or False? Circle the answer

1. You have a science class before geography.   **True**   **False**

2. You have a computer class after math.   **True**   **False**

3. You have a history class after geography.   **True**   **False**

4. You have an English class after science.   **True**   **False**

Lesson 23: Chores

Ev işleri

> What do you need to do today?
> I need to feed the pets.

Section A — Words

1. **wash the dishes**
   Bulaşık yıkamak
2. **feed the pets**
   Hayvanları beslemek
3. **vacuum the carpet**
   Halıyı süpürmek
4. **take out the trash**
   Çöpü atmak
5. **clean the bedroom**
   Yatak odasını temizlemek
6. **mop the floor**
   Yerleri silmek
7. **cook dinner**
   Yemek yapmak
8. **do the laundry**
   Çamaşır yıkamak
9. **iron the clothes**
   Kıyafetleri ütülemek
10. **make the beds**
    Yatakları toplamak

Section B — Make a sentence

What do you need to do <u>this morning</u>?

This morning, I need to <u>wash the dishes</u>.

What does he need to do <u>this afternoon</u>?

This afternoon, he needs to <u>mop the floor</u>.

Learn: this morning, this afternoon, this evening, today

Section C — Make a question

Do you need to <u>make the beds</u> <u>this morning</u>?
Yes, I do. / No, I don't.

Does he need to <u>iron the clothes</u> <u>this afternoon</u>?
Yes, he does. / No, he doesn't.

Section D — Learn a verb

know – knowing – knew – known bilmek

I don't **know** what to feed the pets.

There is no way of **knowing** which chores have been done.

Mary **knew** the trash hadn't been taken out yet.

I hadn't **known** at the time that nobody did the laundry.

Section E — Learn an idiom

All in a day's work

Meaning: A normal day without a change in routine.

"Taking out the trash before school is *all in a day's work*."

| Section F | Write |

Trace and fill in the words

1. What do you need to do this afternoon?

This afternoon, I need to do the laundry.

2. What does he _____ to do this morning?

This morning, he _____ to make the beds.

3. _____ do you need to do this _____?

This afternoon, _____ need to feed the _____.

4. What _____ she _____ to do today?

Today, _____ needs to do the _____.

5. Do you need to iron the clothes this evening?

Yes, I _____.

6. Does he need to _____ the beds this morning?

No, he _____.

7. Do _____ need to _____ the carpet today?

No, I _____.

8. Does she need to cook _____ this evening?

Yes, she _____.

Section G | Let's have fun

Chores!

Connect the sentences

What do you need to do this morning? • — • This morning, she needs to do the dishes.

What does he need to do this afternoon? • — • This morning, I need to wash the clothes.

What does she need to do this morning? • — • This evening, they need to cook dinner.

What do they need to do this evening? • — • This afternoon, we need to make the beds.

What do we need to do this afternoon? • — • This afternoon, he needs to feed the pets.

Unscramble the sentences

wash the / morning / need to / I / this / dishes

1. _____ .

she / the pets / needs to / this afternoon / feed

2. _____ .

to / the laundry / need / they / do / this evening

3. _____ .

this afternoon / the trash / he / needs to / take out

4. _____ .

Lesson 24: At the toy store

Oyuncak mağazasında

What are you playing with?
I'm playing with my ball.

Section A — Words

1. **doll**
   Oyuncak bebek
2. **teddy bear**
   Ayıcık
3. **car**
   Araba
4. **airplane**
   Uçak
5. **dinosaur**
   Dinozor
6. **robot**
   Robot
7. **ball**
   Top
8. **jump rope**
   Atlama ipi
9. **board game**
   Masa oyunu
10. **blocks**
    Bloklar

Section B — Make a sentence

What are you playing with?

I am playing with <u>my</u> <u>doll</u>.

What is he playing with?

He is playing with <u>his</u> <u>robot</u>.

Learn: my, your, his, her, their, our, its

Note: I'm = I am

Section C — Make a question

Are you playing with <u>your</u> <u>teddy bear</u>?
Yes, I am. / No, I'm not.

Is she playing with <u>her</u> <u>ball</u>?
Yes, she is. / No, she isn't.

Section D — Learn a verb

borrow – borrowing – borrowed – borrowed ödünç almak

You can **borrow** my ball.

She will be **borrowing** the board game for tonight.

I **borrowed** a book about cars from the library yesterday.

They haven't **borrowed** these books yet.

Section E — Learn an idiom

Like a kid with a new toy

Meaning: To be really happy with something.

"He was *like a kid with a new toy* when he drove the car for the first time."

Section F — Write

Trace and fill in the words

1. What are you playing with?

I am playing with my teddy bear.

2. What is she playing _____?

She _____ playing with her ball.

3. What are _____ playing _____?

We _____ _____ with our board game.

4. What is he _____ with?

_____ is playing with his _____.

5. Are you playing _____ your car?

Yes, I am.

6. Is he playing with _____ airplane?

No, he isn't.

7. _____ you _____ with your jump rope?

_____, I'm _____.

8. _____ she playing _____ her dinosaur?

Yes, _____ _____.

Section G — Let's have fun

Toys!

Circle the toys

1. cool   geography   bag   (doll)   sister

2. desk   blocks   math   father   milk

3. teddy bear   history   classroom   beef

4. pen   science   water   ball   gym

Write the word

1. _____

2. _____

3. _____

4. _____

Write the answer using the information above

1. What is she playing with? _____.

2. What is he playing with? _____.

3. Is she playing with her teddy bear? _____.

4. Is he playing with his robot? _____.

Test 6   Lesson 21 - 24

Write the answer next to the letter "A"

A: ___ 1. ___ is the office? It's ___ to the gym.

a. There, next   b. Where, next   c. How, near   d. This, next

A: ___ 2. ___ the hall across from the office? Yes, ___ is.

a. Does, it   b. Is, it   c. Are, they   d. Can, he

A: ___ 3. They will ___ the art room later.

a. find   b. found   c. finding   d. finds

A: ___ 4. "We did it the old-fashioned way. We did it old ___."

a. way   b. time   c. man   d. school

A: ___ 5. What class ___ you ___ after science?

a. are, have   b. does, has   c. do, have   d. can, has

A: ___ 6. ___ we have math class after art? Yes, we ___.

a. Can, are   b. Does, do   c. Do, do   d. Are, are

A: ___ 7. They ___ gym class earlier today.

a. has   b. having   c. are had   d. had

A: ___ 8. "She ___ class because she didn't do her homework."

a. put   b. cut   c. lost   d. made

A: ___ **9.** This morning, I ___ to ___ the pets.

a. need, feed   b. am, take   c. can, walk   d. need, make

A: ___ **10.** ___ we need to ___ the beds this morning?

a. Does, take   b. Are, open   c. Do, mop   d. Do, make

A: ___ **11.** He ___ to do the laundry before lunch.

a. needs   b. need   c. needing   d. is need

A: ___ **12.** "Cleaning the room after school is all in a day's ___."

a. time   b. work   c. travel   d. test

A: ___ **13.** What are you ___ with? I'm playing ___ my robot.

a. play, with   b. playing, with   c. plays, by   d. play, on

A: ___ **14.** Is he playing with ___ jump rope? Yes, he ___.

a. him, can   b. he, is   c. his, is   d. him, has

A: ___ **15.** She doesn't like to ___ with dinosaurs.

a. plays   b. playing   c. play   d. played

A: ___ **16.** "He was so happy, he was like a kid with a new ___."

a. car   b. bike   c. toy   d. ball

Answers on page 206

Lesson 25: In the kitchen

Mutfakta

> What was he cleaning?
> He was cleaning the stove.

Section A — Words

1. **refrigerator**
   Buzdolabı
2. **coffee maker**
   Kahve makinesi
3. **microwave oven**
   Mikrodalga fırın
4. **stove**
   Ocak
5. **blender**
   Karıştırıcı
6. **cupboard**
   Dolap
7. **rice cooker**
   Pilav pişirme makinesi
8. **dish rack**
   Bulaşıklık
9. **pan**
   Tava
10. **toaster**
    Tost makinesi

Section B — Make a sentence

What was he cleaning?

He was cleaning the <u>refrigerator</u>.

What were they cleaning?

They were cleaning the <u>cupboard</u>.

Note: weren't = were not, wasn't = was not

Section C — Make a question

Was she cleaning the <u>coffee maker</u>?
Yes, she was. / No, she wasn't.

Were they cleaning the <u>toaster</u>?
Yes, they were. / No, they weren't.

Section D — Learn a verb

clean – cleaning – cleaned – cleaned temizlemek

He **cleans** the gas stove every day.

We are **cleaning** the refrigerator.

My mother **cleaned** the toaster this morning.

I've already **cleaned** the blender, so you can use it now.

Section E — Learn an idiom

Too many cooks in the kitchen

Meaning: When too many people try to take control.

"We couldn't find a solution because there were *too many cooks in the kitchen*."

| Section F | Write |

Trace and fill in the words

1. What was she cleaning?

She was cleaning the cupboard.

2. What were they cleaning?

They were _____ the coffee maker.

3. What _____ he cleaning?

_____ was _____ the pan.

4. _____ were _____ cleaning?

They _____ cleaning the toaster.

5. Was he cleaning the microwave oven?

No, he wasn't.

6. Were we cleaning the gas stove?

No, we _____.

7. Was _____ cleaning the _____?

Yes, she _____.

8. _____ they _____ the blender?

Yes, _____ _____.

Section G — Let's have fun

In the kitchen!

Write the missing words

| wasn't   was   you   were   pan   cleaning   she   the |

1. What _____ he cleaning? He was _____ the microwave.

2. What _____ they cleaning? They were cleaning _____ stove.

3. What was _____ cleaning? She was cleaning the _____.

4. Were _____ cleaning the blender? No, I _____.

Was or Were?

1. What _____ she cleaning?

She _____ cleaning the blender.

2. What _____ they cleaning?

They _____ cleaning the toaster.

3. What _____ you cleaning?

I _____ cleaning the refrigerator.

4. _____ he cleaning the cupboard?

Yes, he _____.

5. _____ they cleaning the rice cooker?

No, they _____ not.

Lesson 26: In the toolbox

Alet çantası

> What were you using to fix the chair?
> I was using the electric drill.

Section A — Words

1. **hammer**
   Çekiç
2. **electric drill**
   Elektrikli matkap
3. **screwdriver**
   Tornavida
4. **paintbrush**
   Boya fırçası
5. **shovel**
   Kürek
6. **tape measure**
   Mezür
7. **axe**
   Balta
8. **pliers**
   Pense
9. **ladder**
   Merdiven
10. **wrench**
    İngiliz anahtarı

Section B — Make a sentence

What were you using to fix the <u>table</u>?

I was using the <u>hammer</u>.

What was she using to fix the <u>fence</u>?

She was using the <u>pliers</u>.

Learn: table, chair, fence, roof, door, cupboard

Section C — Make a question

Was he using the <u>electric drill</u> to <u>fix the chair</u>?
Yes, he was. / No, he wasn't.

Were they using the <u>ladder</u> to <u>fix the roof</u>?
Yes, they were. / No, they weren't.

Section D — Learn a verb

use – using – used – used kullanmak

She **uses** the shovel to do the gardening.

They were **using** the wrench last week.

My father **used** the screwdriver earlier today.

My brother has never **used** an electric drill.

Section E — Learn an idiom

Tools of the trade

Meaning: Things that are needed for a specific job.

"My cell phone, diary and calculator are all *tools of the trade*."

Section F — Write

Trace and fill in the words

1. What were you using to fix the table?

I was using the electric drill.

2. What was she _____ to fix the chair?

She _____ using the screwdriver.

3. What _____ you _____ to fix the door?

_____ was using the _____.

4. What was _____ using to _____ the roof?

He _____ _____ the ladder.

5. Was she using the pliers to fix the cupboard?

No, she wasn't.

6. Were they using the shovel to fix the fence?

No, _____ weren't.

7. Was _____ using the pliers to fix the _____?

Yes, he _____.

8. Were you using the hammer to fix the chair?

Yes, _____ _____.

Section G Let's have fun

In the toolbox!

Was or Were?

He _____ using the electric drill to fix the cupboard.

She _____ using the hammer to fix the fence.

They _____ using the tape measure to fix the door.

We _____ using the ladder to fix the roof.

I _____ using the pliers to fix the table.

John _____ using the screwdriver to fix the chair.

What was fixed?

1. _____   4. _____

2. _____   5. _____

3. _____   6. _____

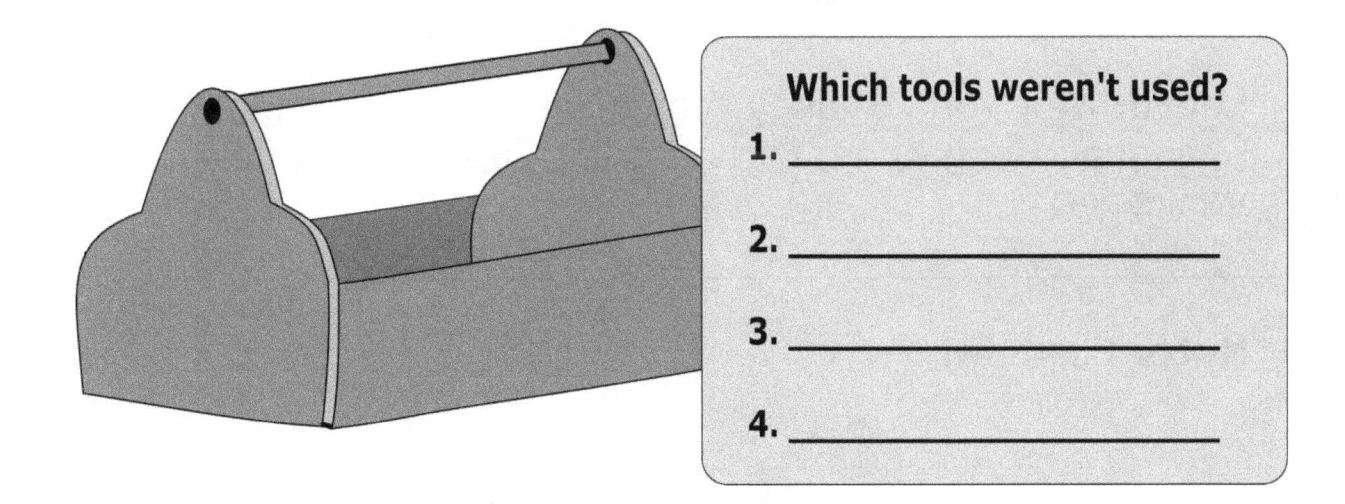

Which tools weren't used?

1. _____

2. _____

3. _____

4. _____

Lesson 27: Transportation

Ulaşım

> How will you be going to Rome?
> I will be taking a bus.

Section A — Words

1. **catch a bus**
   Otobüsü yakalamak
2. **take a taxi**
   Taksiye binmek
3. **take a ferry**
   Vapura binmek
4. **ride a motorcycle**
   Motorsiklet binmek
5. **take the subway**
   Metroya binmek
6. **take a train**
   Trene binmek
7. **drive a car**
   Araba sürmek
8. **ride a scooter**
   Mobilet sürmek
9. **ride a bicycle**
   Bisiklet sürmek
10. **take an airplane**
    Uçağa binmek

Section B — Make a sentence

How will you be going to <u>New York</u>?

I will be <u>catching a bus</u> there.

Learn: New York, Sydney, Vancouver, Rome, London, Shanghai, Hong Kong, Paris, Berlin, Cape town, Buenos Aires, Venice

Note: I'll = I will

Section C — Make a question

Will you be <u>taking a ferry</u> to <u>Hong Kong</u>?
Yes, I will be. / No, I'll be <u>taking an airplane</u>.

Will you be <u>riding a bicycle</u> to <u>Sydney</u>?
Yes, I will be. / No, I'll be <u>catching a bus</u>.

Section D — Learn a verb

take – taking – took – taken almak

You can **take** the subway to work.

She will be **taking** a taxi to the restaurant.

We **took** a ferry to the Hong Kong airport last year.

I hadn't **taken** an airplane until I went to Rome.

Section E — Learn an idiom

Lose one's train of thought

Meaning: To forget what you were thinking about.

"I'm sorry, I *lost my train of thought*. What were we talking about?"

Section F — Write

Trace and fill in the words

1. How will you be going to Sydney?

I will be taking a train there.

2. How will he be _____ to Vancouver?

He will _____ driving a car.

3. How _____ we be going to Rome?

_____ will be _____ a scooter there.

4. How will _____ be _____ to Paris?

They _____ be _____ an airplane.

5. Will you be riding a motorcycle to Berlin?

No, I'll be riding a bicycle.

6. Will _____ be _____ a ferry to Hong Kong?

No, they'll be taking an airplane.

7. Will _____ be _____ the subway to Venice?

No, he'll _____ catching a bus.

8. Will she _____ _____ a train to London?

Yes, _____ _____ _____.

Section G Let's have fun

Transportation!

Unscramble the words and write

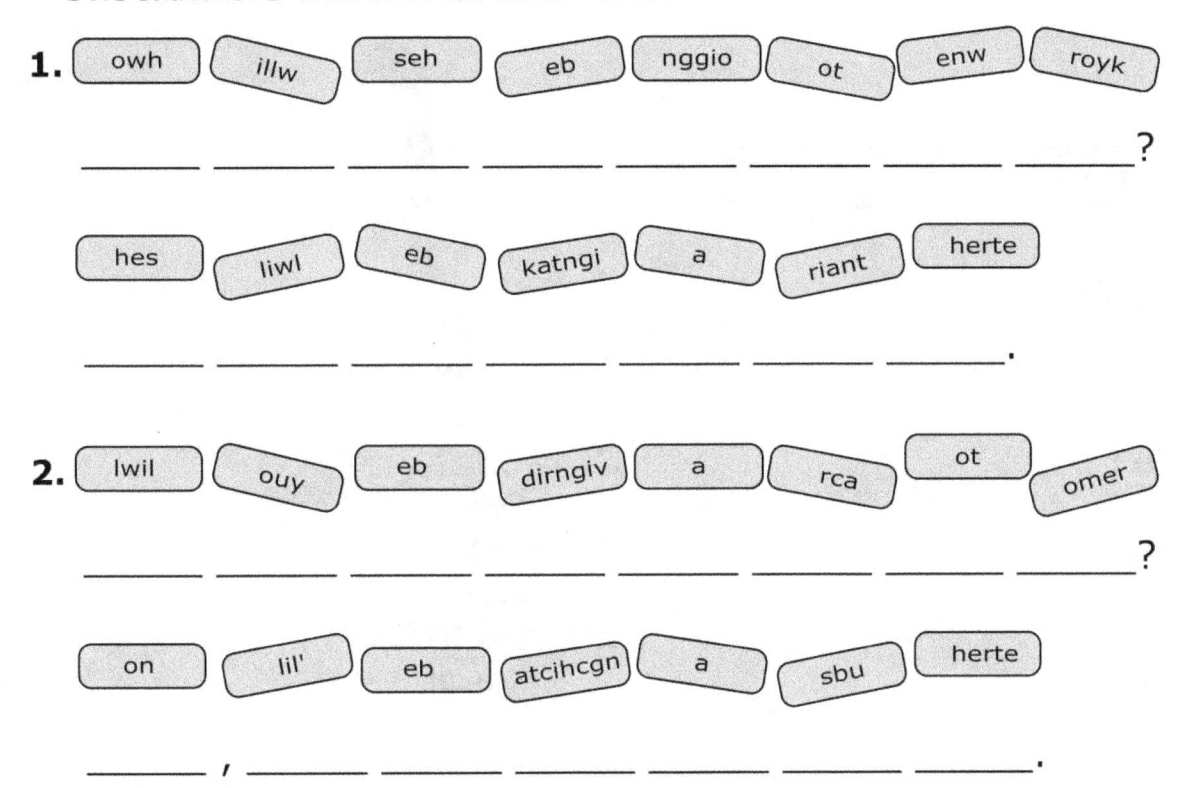

1. owh / illw / seh / eb / nggio / ot / enw / royk

   _____ _____ _____ _____ _____ _____ _____ _____?

   hes / liwl / eb / katngi / a / riant / herte

   _____ _____ _____ _____ _____ _____ _____.

2. lwil / ouy / eb / dirngiv / a / rca / ot / omer

   _____ _____ _____ _____ _____ _____ _____ _____?

   on / lil' / eb / atcihcgn / a / sbu / herte

   _____ , _____ _____ _____ _____ _____ _____.

Connect the words

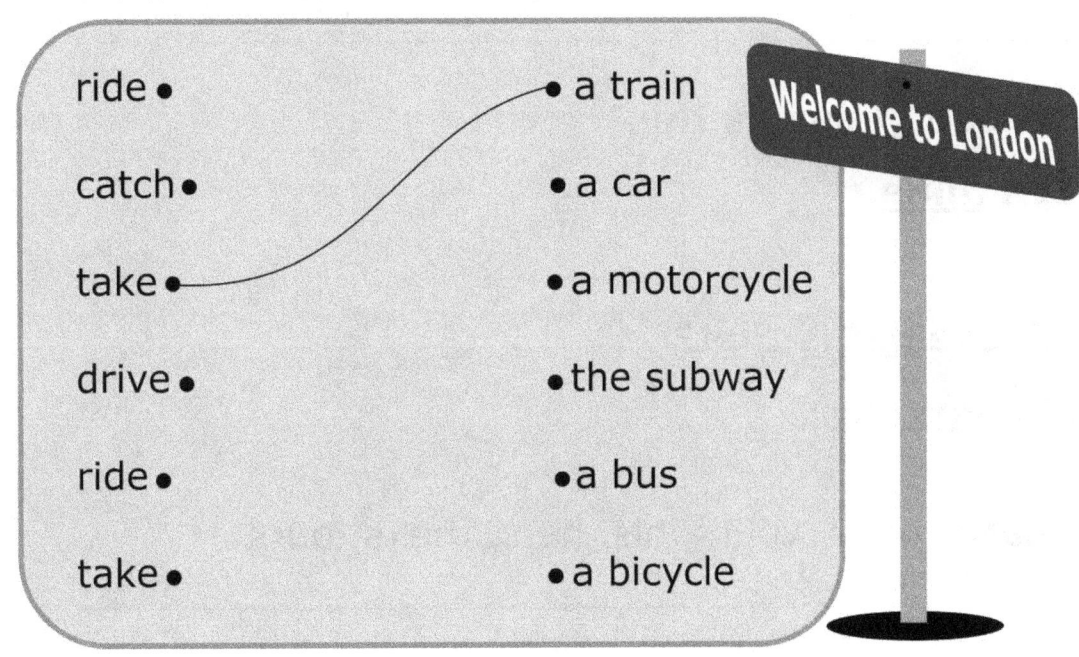

ride •   • a train

catch •   • a car

take •   • a motorcycle

drive •   • the subway

ride •   • a bus

take •   • a bicycle

Welcome to London

Lesson 28: Clothes

Giysiler

Whose jacket is that?
It's mine.

Section A — Words

1. **T-shirt**
   Tişört
2. **blouse**
   Bluz
3. **scarf**
   Atkı
4. **coat**
   Palto
5. **dress**
   Elbise
6. **hat**
   Şapka
7. **sweater**
   Süveter
8. **jacket**
   Ceket
9. **skirt**
   Etek
10. **necktie**
    Kravat

Section B — Make a sentence

Whose T-shirt is this?

It's mine.

Whose hat is that?

It's yours.

Learn: mine, yours, his, hers, theirs, ours

Section C — Make a question

Is this your <u>sweater</u>?
Yes, it is. / No, it isn't.

Is this her <u>blouse</u>?
Yes, it is. / No, it isn't.

Section D — Learn a verb

wear – wearing – wore – worn giymek

You should **wear** a jacket today.

I don't like **wearing** a necktie.

She **wore** a skirt to school yesterday.

My sister hasn't **worn** a dress for a long time.

Section E — Learn an idiom

Wear somebody out

Meaning: To make someone tired.

"My boss completely *wore me out* today."

Section F — Write

Trace and fill in the words

1. Whose hat is this?

It's mine.

2. Whose blouse _____ that?

It's hers.

3. Whose sweater _____ this?

_____ his.

4. _____ scarf _____ that?

_____ ours.

5. Is this your jacket?

No, _____ isn't.

6. Is this your coat?

_____, it is.

7. _____ this his jacket?

No, _____ _____.

8. _____ that her _____?

Yes, _____ _____.

Section G | Let's have fun

Clothes!

- skirt
- T-shirt
- necktie
- jacket

Write the answer

1. Whose skirt is this? _____.

2. Whose T-shirt is that? _____.

3. Whose necktie is this? _____.

4. Whose jacket is that? _____.

Complete the words

j__ck__t

bl__u__e

__o__t

sk__r__

d__e__s

swe__t__r

n__c__t__e

Is or Are?

1. _____ this your sweater?

Yes, it _____.

2. _____ that her T-shirt?

No, it _____ not.

3. _____ these his shoes?

Yes, they _____.

4. _____ those their jackets?

No, they _____ not.

Test 7   Lesson 25 - 28

Write the answer next to the letter "A"

A: ___ 1. What ___ he cleaning? He was ___ the blender.

a. is, clean   b. can, cleans   c. was, cleaning   d. is, cleaned

A: ___ 2. ___ they cleaning the cupboard? Yes, ___ were.

a. Are, we   b. Can, there   c. Were, they   d. Do, they

A: ___ 3. They ___ the stove yesterday morning.

a. clean   b. cleaned   c. cleans   d. is cleaning

A: ___ 4. "It's difficult because there are too many ___ in the kitchen."

a. cooks   b. cook   c. cooking   d. cooked

A: ___ 5. She was ___ a hammer to fix the fence.

a. use   b. using   c. uses   d. used

A: ___ 6. Was he ___ the axe to fix the tree? No, he ___.

a. using, wasn't   b. use, can't   c. uses, doesn't   d. used, isn't

A: ___ 7. He ___ the pliers every Thursday.

a. use   b. using   c. uses   d. was use

A: ___ 8. "These important things are all my ___ of the trade."

a. work   b. stuff   c. jobs   d. tools

A: ___ 9. How will he be ___ to New York?

a. go b. goes c. went d. going

A: ___ 10. ___ you be ___ a taxi to Sydney? Yes, I will be.

a. Can, take b. Are, riding c. Will, taking d. Do, takes

A: ___ 11. They ___ a ferry to Hong Kong last night.

a. took b. taken c. taking d. takes

A: ___ 12. "I wasn't thinking clearly, I lost my ___ of thought."

a. taxi b. mind c. train d. take

A: ___ 13. ___ blouse is this? It's ___.

a. Who, my b. Whose, mine c. Wear, on d. Who is, my

A: ___ 14. Is that ___ jacket? Yes, ___ is.

a. she, it b. her, it c. him, this d. his, they

A: ___ 15. She was ___ a skirt at school yesterday.

a. wear b. wore c. wears d. wearing

A: ___ 16. "Doing my homework was tiring. It wore me ___."

a. over b. on c. in d. out

Answers on page 206

Lesson 29: More clothes

Daha fazla giysi

Whose jeans are these?
They're mine.

Section A — Words

1. **pants**
   Pantolon
2. **shorts**
   Şort
3. **shoes**
   Ayakkabı
4. **dresses**
   Elbise
5. **shirts**
   Gömlek
6. **jeans**
   Kot
7. **socks**
   Çorap
8. **gloves**
   Eldiven
9. **pajamas**
   Pijama
10. **boots**
    Bot

Section B — Make a sentence

Whose pants are these?

They're mine.

Whose jeans are those?

They're hers.

Note: They're = They are

Section C — Make a question

Are these <u>shoes</u> <u>yours</u>?
Yes, they are. / No, they aren't.

Are those <u>socks</u> <u>his</u>?
Yes, they are. / No, they aren't.

Section D — Learn a verb

lend – lending – lent – lent ödünç vermek

I will **lend** my shirt to you.

He is **lending** me his gloves.

My mother **lent** her eraser to me.

I have **lent** my shovel to him before.

Section E — Learn an idiom

Fits like a glove

Meaning: Something is the right size.

"The new shirt you bought me *fits like a glove*."

Section F — Write

Trace and fill in the words

1. Whose jeans are these?

   They're mine.

2. Whose shorts _____ those?

   _____ hers.

3. Whose socks are _____?

   _____ his.

4. _____ shoes _____ those?

   _____ hers.

5. Are these gloves yours?

   No, they aren't.

6. _____ _____ dresses hers?

   _____, they _____.

7. _____ _____ bags his?

   Yes, _____ _____.

8. _____ those _____ mine?

   No, _____ _____.

Section G — Let's have fun

More clothes!

- dresses
- skirts
- shoes
- pants

Write the answer

1. Whose dresses are those? _____.
2. Whose pants are these? _____.
3. Whose skirts are those? _____.
4. Whose shoes are these? _____.

Connect the words

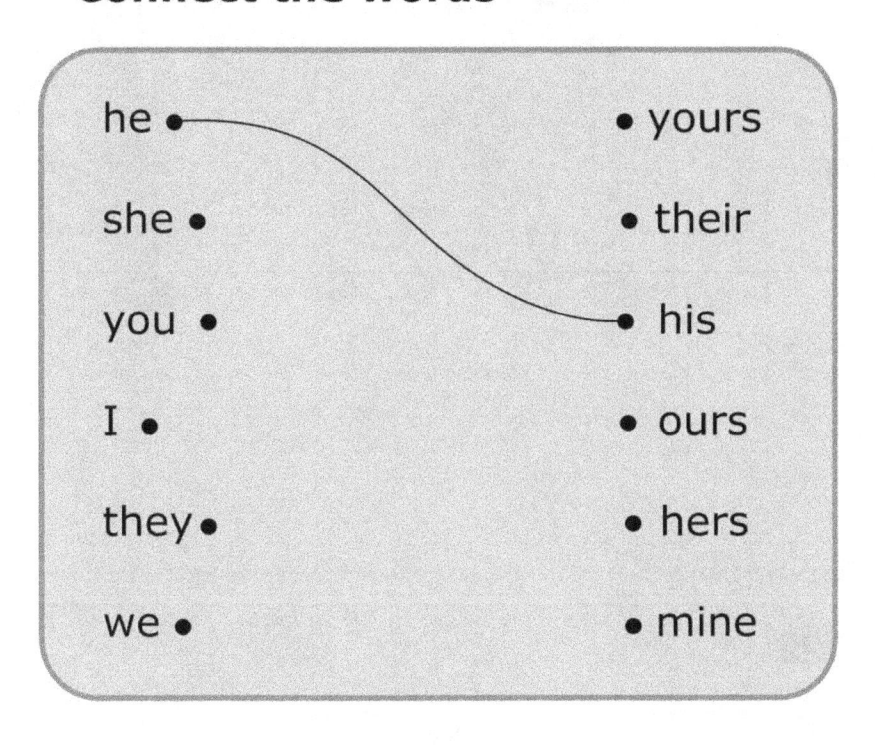

- he — yours
- she — their
- you — his
- I — ours
- they — hers
- we — mine

Complete the words

p___ nts

sh___rt___

s___o___s

sk___rt

dre___s___s

g___ov___s

bo___ts

Lesson 30: In the living room

Oturma odasında

Where is the coffee table?
It's in front of the sofa.

Section A — Words

1. **bookcase**
   Kitaplık
2. **television**
   Televizyon
3. **clock**
   Saat
4. **coffee table**
   Sehpa
5. **armchair**
   Koltuk
6. **painting**
   Tablo
7. **TV stand**
   Televizyon büfesi
8. **rug**
   Kilim
9. **sofa**
   Kanepe
10. **vase**
    Vazo

Section B — Make a sentence

Where is the <u>bookcase</u>?

It's <u>next to</u> the <u>sofa</u>.

Where are the <u>book</u>s?

They're <u>under</u> the <u>vase</u>.

Learn: in front of, behind, next to, on, under

| Section C | Make a question |

Is there a <u>vase</u> on the <u>coffee table</u>?
Yes, there is. / No, there isn't.

Are there <u>pen</u>s behind the <u>TV stand</u>?
Yes, there are. / No, there aren't.

| Section D | Learn a verb |

move – moving – moved – moved hareket etmek

After dinner, I will **move** the coffee table.

They are **moving** the armchair next to the sofa.

Dad **moved** the television to the bedroom last night.

We still haven't **moved** the bookcase to the living room.

| Section E | Learn an idiom |

A race against the clock

Meaning: To not have too much time left to complete a task.

"It's *a race against the clock* to finish this project."

Section F — Write

Trace and fill in the words

1. Where is the television?

It's in front of the sofa.

2. Where _____ the paintings?

They're next _____ the armchair.

3. _____ is the _____?

_____ behind the _____.

4. _____ _____ the vases?

_____ in front of the _____.

5. Is there a cup on the bookcase?

No, there isn't.

6. Are _____ pencils on the coffee table?

No, there aren't.

7. _____ _____ a notebook on the _____?

Yes, _____.

8. _____ _____ books _____ the rug?

Yes, _____ _____.

Section G Let's have fun

In the living room!

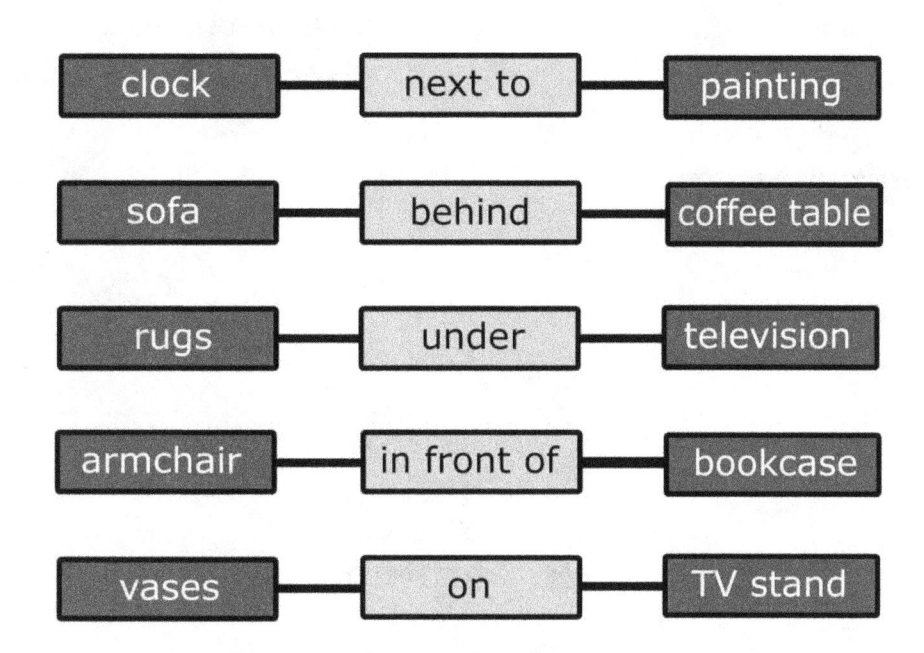

clock	— next to —	painting
sofa	— behind —	coffee table
rugs	— under —	television
armchair	— in front of —	bookcase
vases	— on —	TV stand

Answer the questions

1. Where is the clock?
_____.

2. Where is the sofa?
_____.

3. Where are the rugs?
_____.

4. Where is the armchair?
_____.

5. Where are the vases?
_____.

Choose the correct answer

1. Is there a clock next to the painting?

   ☑ Yes, there is.   ○ No, there isn't.

2. Is there a sofa behind the coffee table?

   ○ Yes, there is.   ○ No, there isn't.

3. Are there rugs under the bookcase?

   ○ Yes, there are.   ○ No, there aren't.

4. Is there an armchair in front of the sofa?

   ○ Yes, there is.   ○ No, there isn't.

5. Are there vases on the TV stand?

   ○ Yes, there are.   ○ No, there aren't.

Lesson 31: In the bathroom

Banyoda

What is above the sink?
There is a mirror above the sink.

Section A — Words

1. **mirror**
   Ayna
2. **bath towel**
   Banyo havlusu
3. **shower**
   Duş
4. **toilet paper**
   Tuvalet kağıdı
5. **bath mat**
   Banyo paspası
6. **shelf**
   Raf
7. **sink**
   Lavabo
8. **toilet**
   Klozet
9. **bathtub**
   Küvet
10. **soap**
    Sabun

Section B — Make a sentence

What is <u>beside</u> the <u>bathtub</u>?
There is a <u>bath mat</u> beside the bathtub.

What are <u>on</u> the <u>shelf</u>?
There are some <u>towel</u>s on the shelf.

There isn't any <u>toilet paper</u> in the bathroom.
There aren't any <u>bath towel</u>s in the bathroom.

Section C — Make a question

Is there a <u>shelf</u> <u>below</u> the <u>mirror</u>?
Yes, there is. / No, there isn't.

Is there <u>toilet paper</u> <u>beside</u> the <u>toilet</u>?
Yes, there is. / No, there isn't.

Section D — Learn a verb

wash – washing – washed – washed yıkamak

She **washes** the sink every day.

He was **washing** his hands with the new soap.

Kevin **washed** the bath towel this morning.

I won't have **washed** the bath mat by tomorrow.

Section E — Learn an idiom

Throw in the towel

Meaning: To give up or quit.

"After trying three times, he decided to *throw in the towel*."

Section F — Write

Trace and fill in the words

1. What is below the mirror?

There is a sink below the mirror.

2. What _____ beside the bath mat?

There is a bathtub _____ the bath mat.

3. _____ is _____ the toilet?

There _____ a shelf beside the _____.

4. What _____ above _____ shower?

_____ is a shelf _____ the _____.

5. Is there a showerhead above the bathtub?

No, _____ isn't.

6. Is there a mirror above _____ toilet?

Yes, there is.

7. Is _____ a bath towel next to the _____?

_____, _____ isn't.

8. _____ _____ a sink beside the _____?

_____, _____ is.

Section G Let's have fun

In the bathroom!

There is a mirror above the sink.
There are some bath towels on the shelf.
There aren't any towels in the bathroom.
There is a toilet beside the bathtub.
There isn't any soap in the bathroom.
There is a bath mat under the sink.

Read the information above. Choose the correct answer

1. Is there a mirror above the sink? ✓Yes, there is   ○No, there isn't

2. Are there bath towels on the shelf? ○Yes, there are ○No, there aren't

3. Are there any towels in the bathroom? ○Yes, there are ○No, there aren't

4. Is there a toilet beside the bathtub? ○Yes, there is ○No, there isn't

5. Is there any soap in the bathroom? ○Yes, there is ○No, there isn't

6. Is there a bath mat under the sink? ○Yes, there is ○No, there isn't

Complete the words

m__rr __r   t__il __t

b__th__ub   to__l__t p__per

s__ow__r   sh__l__

s__a__   b__t__ to__el

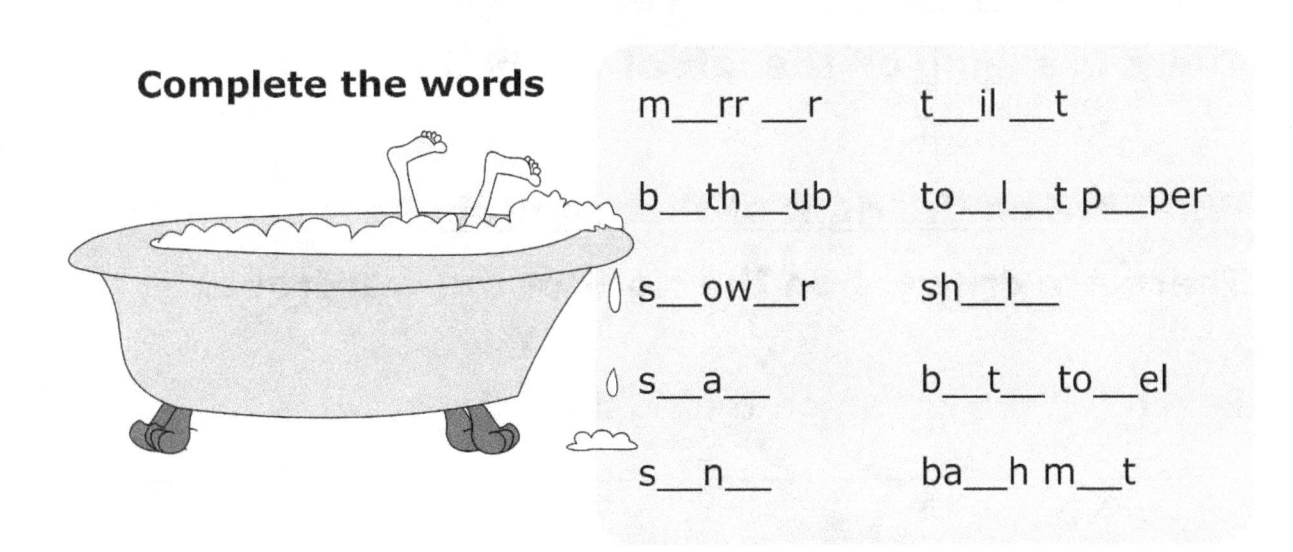

s__n__   ba__h m__t

Lesson 32: In the bedroom

Yatak odasında

> What is on the left of the bed?
> There is a lamp on the left of the bed.

Section A — Words

1. **bed**
   Yatak
2. **pillow**
   Yastık
3. **mattress**
   Döşek
4. **blanket**
   Battaniye
5. **drawers**
   Çekmece
6. **lamp**
   Lamba
7. **alarm clock**
   Çalar saat
8. **wardrobe**
   Gardırop
9. **bed sheets**
   Yatak çarşafı
10. **nightstand**
    Komodin

Section B — Make a sentence

What is <u>on the left of</u> the <u>bed</u>?

There is a <u>lamp</u> on the left of the bed.

What are <u>on the right of</u> the <u>wardrobe</u>?

There are <u>drawers</u> on the right of the wardrobe.

Learn: on the left of, on the right of

Section C — Make a question

Is there a <u>nightstand</u> <u>on the left of</u> the <u>bed</u>?
Yes, there is. / No, there isn't.

Are there <u>pillows</u> <u>on the left of</u> the <u>blanket</u>?
Yes, there are. / No, there aren't.

Section D — Learn a verb

change – changing – changed – changed değiştirmek

My brother needs to **change** his bed sheets soon.

We will be **changing** our mattress for a harder one.

I **changed** my pillow last night and slept much better.

I haven't **changed** the light bulb in this lamp for two years.

Section E — Learn an idiom

Get up on the wrong side of the bed

Meaning: To describe somebody who is in a bad mood.

"Mom's in a really bad mood. I think she *got up on the wrong side of the bed*."

| Section F | Write |

Trace and fill in the words

1. What is on the right of the bed?

There is a pillow on the right of the bed.

2. What is on the _____ of the nightstand?

_____ is a book on the left of the _____.

3. _____ is on the right of the _____?

_____ is a chair on the _____ of the wardrobe.

4. _____ _____ on the left of the bed?

There _____ a pillow on the left of the _____.

5. Is _____ a nightstand on the right of the bed?

No, there isn't.

6. _____ there blankets on the left of the mattress?

Yes, _____ are.

7. _____ there a _____ on the right of the drawers?

No, _____ _____.

8. Are there _____ on the left of the _____?

Yes, _____ _____.

Section G — Let's have fun

In the bedroom!

Write the answers

| alarm clock | bed | drawers |

1. What is on the left of the bed?

   _____.

2. Are the drawers on the right of the bed?

   _____.

| blanket | mattress | pillow |

1. What is on the right of the mattress?

   _____.

2. Is the pillow on the left of the mattress?

   _____.

| bed sheets | wardrobe | lamp |

1. What is on the left of the wardrobe?

   _____.

2. Is the lamp on the left of the wardrobe?

   _____.

Test 8 Lesson 29 - 32

Write the answer next to the letter "A"

A: ___ 1. ___ jeans are those? Those jeans are ___.

a. Whose, hers b. Who, her c. Wear, on d. Whose, her

A: ___ 2. ___ those gloves his? Yes, ___ are.

a. Are, there b. Are, they c. Were, them d. Do, they

A: ___ 3. Can you ___ me your boots?

a. lent b. lending c. lend d. has lent

A: ___ 4. "The new shirt fits perfectly. It fits like a ___."

a. hat b. sock c. boot d. glove

A: ___ 5. Where ___ the books? ___ under the vase.

a. is, They b. do, It's c. are, They're d. put, It's

A: ___ 6. Is ___ a vase on the coffee table? No, there ___.

a. it, wasn't b. there, isn't c. there, doesn't d. he, isn't

A: ___ 7. He hasn't ___ that new television yet.

a. move b. moving c. moves d. moved

A: ___ 8. "We don't have much time. We have to race against the ___."

a. clock b. watch c. car d. team

A: ___ **9.** There ___ a bath mat ___ the bathtub.

a. are, above   b. have, on   c. be, in   d. is, beside

A: ___ **10.** Are ___ towels beside the mirror? No, there ___.

a. them, can't   b. there, aren't   c. have, hasn't   d. it, isn't

A: ___ **11.** He ___ the sink every Saturday afternoon.

a. wash   b. washing   c. washes   d. is wash

A: ___ **12.** "After failing many times, I decided to throw in the ___."

a. towel   b. quit   c. anger   d. ball

A: ___ **13.** There ___ drawers on the ___ of the wardrobe.

a. have, top   b. is, side   c. can, right   d. are, left

A: ___ **14.** Is ___ a lamp on the left of the bed? Yes, there ___.

a. it, have   b. there, is   c. they're, are   d. his, can

A: ___ **15.** We will ___ the blankets tomorrow.

a. changes   b. changing   c. change   d. changed

A: ___ **16.** "He's grumpy. I think he got up on the wrong side of the ___."

a. bed   b. lamp   c. happy   d. clock

Answers on page 206

Lesson 33: Around the house

Evin etrafında

What will he be doing this weekend?
He will be fixing the gate.

Section A — Words

1. **work in the garage**
   Garajda çalışmak
2. **fix the mailbox**
   Posta kutusunu tamir etmek
3. **fix the gate**
   Kapıyı tamir etmek
4. **work in the garden**
   Bahçede çalışmak
5. **clean the pool**
   Havuzu temizlemek
6. **work in the yard**
   Avluda çalışmak
7. **fix the fence**
   Çitleri tamir etmek
8. **clean the balcony**
   Balkonu temizlemek
9. **clean the outdoor furniture**
   Dış mekan mobilyalarını temizlemek
10. **clean the barbecue**
    Izgarayı temizlemek

Section B — Make a sentence

What will he be doing <u>this weekend</u>?

He will be <u>working in the garage</u>.

What won't she be doing <u>this weekend</u>?

She won't be <u>fixing the mailbox</u>.

Note: won't be = will not be, he'll = he will, she'll = she will

Section C — Make a question

Will he be <u>working in the garden</u> <u>tomorrow</u>?
Yes, he will be. / No, he won't be.

Will you be <u>cleaning the barbecue</u> <u>tomorrow</u>?
Yes, I will be. / No, I won't be.

Section D — Learn a verb

fix – fixing – fixed – fixed tamir etmek

He **fixes** the fence every year.

My father is **fixing** the gate right now.

My uncle **fixed** our mailbox after the big storm last week.

I still haven't **fixed** the grammar mistakes in my report.

Section E — Learn an idiom

On the house

Meaning: To get something for free.

"The waiter apologized and gave him the meal *on the house*."

Section F — Write

Trace and fill in the words

1. What will she be doing this weekend?

She will be working in the yard.

2. What will _____ be _____ this weekend?

He _____ be fixing the fence.

3. What _____ they be doing this _____?

_____ will be cleaning the balcony.

4. _____ will _____ be doing this _____?

He _____ _____ fixing the gate.

5. Will he be working in the garden tomorrow?

No, he won't _____.

6. Will we _____ cleaning the pool tomorrow?

Yes, _____ will _____.

7. _____ you be working in the garage _____?

Yes, _____ _____ _____.

8. Will they _____ cleaning the barbecue _____?

No, _____ _____ _____.

154

Section G — Let's have fun

Around the house!

doing	weekend	this		
be	will	the	working	

Write the words

What _____ she be doing this weekend?

She will _____ cleaning the balcony.

What will they be _____ this _____?

They will be fixing _____ fence.

What will you be doing _____ weekend?

I will be _____ in the yard.

don't, doesn't, didn't, won't, isn't, aren't, wasn't, weren't?

do not = __don't__   were not = _____

did not = _____   are not = _____

will not = _____   does not = _____

is not = _____   was not = _____

Lesson 34: Hobbies

Hobiler

What do you enjoy doing on the weekend?
I enjoy going hiking.

Section A — Words

1. **do gardening**
   Bahçecilik yapmak
2. **go hiking**
   Dağ yürüyüşüne çıkmak
3. **take photographs**
   Fotoğraf çekmek
4. **play video games**
   Video oyunları oynamak
5. **listen to music**
   Müzik dinlemek
6. **go camping**
   Kampa gitmek
7. **play chess**
   Satranç oynamak
8. **watch movies**
   Film izlemek
9. **go fishing**
   Balık tutmak
10. **sing karaoke**
    Karaoke yapmak

Section B — Make a sentence

What do you enjoy doing on the weekend?

I enjoy <u>doing gardening</u> on the weekend.

What does he enjoy doing on the weekend?

He enjoys <u>going camping</u> on the weekend.

Section C — Make a question

Do you enjoy <u>going hiking</u> on the weekend?
Yes, I do. / No, I enjoy <u>playing chess</u>.

Does he enjoy <u>watching movies</u> on the weekend?
Yes, he does. / No, he enjoys <u>going fishing</u>.

Section D — Learn a verb

enjoy – enjoying – enjoyed – enjoyed zevk almak

He **enjoys** doing the gardening in spring.

My aunt is **enjoying** the book you lent her.

I really **enjoyed** the movie we watched last night.

You would have **enjoyed** the video game we played today.

Section E — Learn an idiom

Face the music

Meaning: To face the consequences of one's actions.

"You need to own up to your mistake and *face the music*."

Section F — Write

Trace and fill in the words

1. What do you enjoy doing on the weekend?

I enjoy going camping on the weekend.

2. What does _____ enjoy doing on the _____?

She _____ going hiking on the weekend.

3. _____ do they enjoy _____ on the weekend?

_____ enjoy singing karaoke on the _____.

4. What _____ he enjoy _____ on the _____?

_____ _____ playing chess on the _____.

5. Do you enjoy playing video games on the weekend?

No, I enjoy listening to music.

6. _____ he enjoy taking photographs on the weekend?

_____, _____ does.

7. _____ they _____ going hiking on the _____?

No, _____ enjoy _____ _____.

8. _____ she enjoy _____ chess on the _____?

Yes, _____ _____.

Section G Let's have fun

Hobbies!

Connect the words

listen •   • hiking

take •   • movies

go •   • chess

play •   • karaoke

watch •   • photographs

sing •   • to music

Enjoy or Enjoys?

1. He _____ listening to music on the weekend.

2. They _____ watching movies on the weekend.

3. We _____ going hiking on the weekend.

4. My brother _____ playing chess on the weekend.

5. She _____ taking photographs on the weekend.

6. I _____ playing video games on the weekend.

Answer the questions

1. What do you enjoy doing on the weekend?
_____.

2. What does your friend enjoy doing on the weekend?
_____.

Lesson 35: Countries

Ülkeler

Which countries have you been to?
I have been to Brazil and Mexico.

Section A — Words

1. **Japan**
   Japonya
2. **Canada**
   Kanada
3. **Brazil**
   Brezilya
4. **Australia**
   Avustralya
5. **South Africa**
   Güney Afrika
6. **China**
   Çin
7. **Mexico**
   Meksika
8. **Argentina**
   Arjantin
9. **New Zealand**
   Yeni Zelanda
10. **Kenya**
    Kenya

Section B — Make a sentence

Which countries have you been to?

I have been to <u>Japan</u> and <u>China</u>.

Which countries has she been to?

She has been to <u>Canada</u> and <u>Mexico</u>.

Note: haven't = have not / hasn't = has not

Section C — Make a question

Have you been to <u>Brazil</u>?
Yes, I have. / No, I haven't.

Has he been to <u>Argentina</u>?
Yes, he has. / No, he hasn't.

Section D — Learn a verb

write – writing – wrote – written yazmak

I always **write** homework on the weekend.

She is **writing** a new book about South Africa.

My father **wrote** a letter to his friend in Japan last week.

He has already **written** four emails to the factory in China.

Section E — Learn an idiom

Second to none

Meaning: To describe something that is the best.

"The mountains in Canada are *second to none* for skiing."

Section F — Write

Trace and fill in the words

1. Which countries have you been to?

I have been to Canada and Mexico.

2. Which _____ has he been to?

He has _____ to Brazil and Argentina.

3. _____ countries _____ we been to?

We _____ been to _____ and _____.

4. Which _____ has she _____ _____?

_____ _____ been to _____ and _____.

5. Have you been to New Zealand?

Yes, I have.

6. Has _____ been _____ Australia?

_____, she hasn't.

7. _____ they _____ to China?

Yes, _____ _____.

8. _____ he _____ _____ Kenya?

No, _____ _____.

162

Section G Let's have fun

Countries!

Write the missing words

| hasn't | they | has | been |
| to | countries | Which | haven't |

1. Which _____ have you been to?

I have _____ to Japan and China.

2. _____ countries has he been to?

He _____ been to Mexico and Canada.

3. Has she been _____ South Africa?

No, she _____.

4. Have _____ been to New Zealand?

No, they _____.

Has or Have?

1. _____ she been to Canada?

Yes, she _____.

2. _____ they been to Mexico?

No, they _____ not.

3. Which countries _____ you been to?

I _____ been to Argentina and Brazil.

4. Which countries _____ he been to?

He _____ been to Kenya and China.

Lesson 36: Landscapes

Manzaralar

> What had you prepared for yesterday's math class?
> I had prepared a video about lakes.

Section A — Words

1. **river**
   Nehir
2. **beach (es)**
   Kumsal
3. **mountain**
   Dağ
4. **volcano (es)**
   Yanardağ
5. **forest**
   Orman
6. **lake**
   Göl
7. **waterfall**
   Şelale
8. **island**
   Ada
9. **ocean**
   Okyanus
10. **jungle**
    Orman

Section B — Make a sentence

What had you prepared for yesterday's <u>geography</u> class?
I had prepared a <u>poster</u> about <u>river</u>s.

What had they prepared for yesterday's <u>Chinese</u> class?
They had prepared an <u>article</u> about <u>lake</u>s.

Learn: poster, speech, video, article, presentation

Note: hadn't = had not

Section C — Make a question

Had you prepared anything for yesterday's <u>English</u> class?
Yes, I had prepared a <u>speech</u>. / No, I hadn't.

Had you prepared anything for yesterday's <u>science</u> class?
Yes, I had prepared a <u>video</u>. / No, I hadn't.

Section D — Learn a verb

prepare – preparing – prepared – prepared hazırlamak

I'll **prepare** some food for you to take to the mountains.

She'll be **preparing** some drinks for the picnic at the lake.

The teacher always **prepared** a quiz for the students before.

I wish I had **prepared** more for the geography test.

Section E — Learn an idiom

A drop in the ocean

Meaning: To only make a tiny impact.

"We donated money to the victims of the tsunami, but I'm afraid it is just *a drop in the ocean*."

| Section F | Write |

Trace and fill in the words

1. What had you prepared for yesterday's geography class?

I had prepared an article about beaches.

2. What had he _____ for yesterday's _____ class?

He _____ prepared a speech _____ waterfalls.

3. What had they _____ for _____ _____ class?

They _____ _____ a video about mountains.

4. What had you _____ for _____ geography class?

_____ _____ _____ a poster about islands.

5. Had he prepared anything for yesterday's math class?

No, he hadn't.

6. Had you prepared _____ for yesterday's art class?

Yes, I _____ _____ a poster.

7. Had she _____ anything for _____ science class?

No, _____ _____ .

8. Had he prepared anything for yesterday's English class?

Yes, _____ had _____ a _____ .

Section G Let's have fun

Landscapes!

Unscramble the words and write

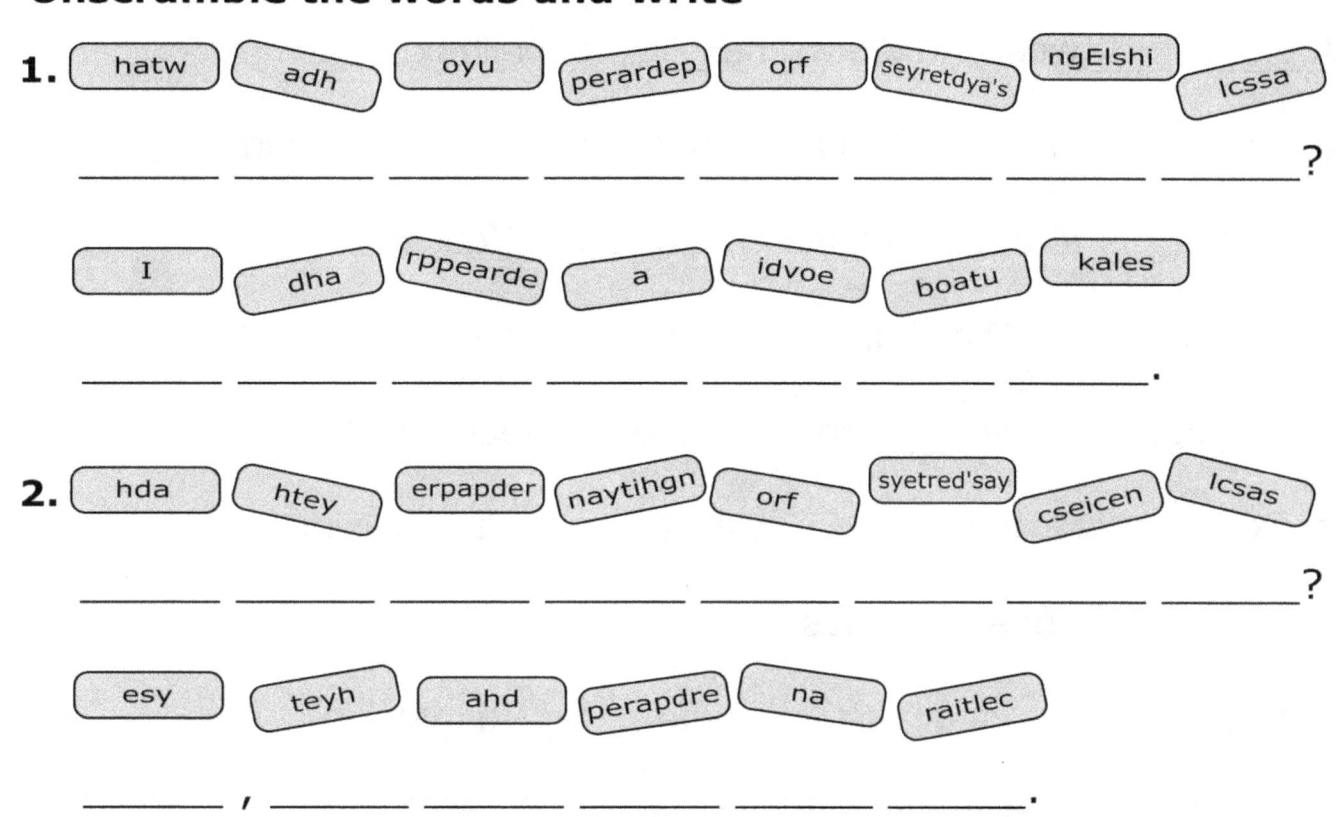

1. hatw | adh | oyu | perardep | orf | seyretdya's | ngElshi | lcssa

   ___ ___ ___ ___ ___ ___ ___ ___?

   I | dha | rppearde | a | idvoe | boatu | kales

   ___ ___ ___ ___ ___ ___ ___.

2. hda | htey | erpapder | naytihgn | orf | syetred'say | cseicen | lcsas

   ___ ___ ___ ___ ___ ___ ___ ___?

   esy | teyh | ahd | perapdre | na | raitlec

   ___ , ___ ___ ___ ___ ___.

Complete the words

r__v__r   j__ng__e

v__l__a__o   i__la__d

m__un__a__n   f__r__ __t

be__c__   w__te__f__l__

o__e__n   l__k__

Test 9   Lesson 33 - 36

Write the answer next to the letter "A"

A: ___ **1.** ___ weekend, he will be ___ the mailbox.

a. On, clean   b. This, fixing   c. That, work   d. In, cleaning

A: ___ **2.** ___ she be fixing the gate tonight? Yes, she ___.

a. Can, is   b. Won't, fix   c. Will, will be   d. Will, fix

A: ___ **3.** My mother ___ the barbecue last year.

a. fix   b. is fixing   c. fixed   d. will fixing

A: ___ **4.** "This one's free. It's on the ___."

a. house   b. yard   c. gate   d. garage

A: ___ **5.** He ___ fishing on the weekend.

a. enjoy going   b. is enjoy go   c. enjoys go   d. enjoys going

A: ___ **6.** ___ he enjoy watching movies? No, he ___ playing chess.

a. Do, does   b. Is, isn't   c. Does, doesn't   d. Does, enjoys

A: ___ **7.** She is ___ her new barbecue.

a. enjoying   b. enjoy   c. enjoys   d. enjoyed

A: ___ **8.** "You should admit your mistake and face the ___."

a. sunshine   b. music   c. trouble   d. smile

A: ___ **9.** Which countries ___ you ___ to?

a. have, go b. did, went c. do, be d. have, been

A: ___ **10.** ___ she been to Japan? No, she ___.

a. Has, hasn't b. Have, don't c. Is, hasn't d. Is, can't

A: ___ **11.** He has ___ nine messages this week.

a. write b. wrote c. written d. writes

A: ___ **12.** "Her English is the best. It's second to ___."

a. all b. none c. best d. win

A: ___ **13.** They had ___ a speech for last week's geography class.

a. prepare b. prepared c. preparing d. prepares

A: ___ **14.** ___ he prepared anything for English class? No, he ___.

a. Had, hadn't b. Is, isn't c. Does, don't d. Has, haven't

A: ___ **15.** The teacher always ___ easy tests for his students.

a. prepare b. preparing c. prepares d. are preparing

A: ___ **16.** "It had a very small effect. It was just a drop in the ___."

a. line b. ball c. water d. ocean

Answers on page 206

Lesson 37: Everyday life

Günlük yaşam

When will you have woken up by?
I will have woken up by six o'clock.

Section A | Words

1. **woken up**
   Uyandım
2. **brushed my teeth**
   Dişimi fırçaladım
3. **done homework**
   Ödevimi yaptım
4. **cooked dinner**
   Yemek yaptım
5. **taken out the trash**
   Çöpü attım
6. **eaten breakfast**
   Kahvaltı ettim
7. **gone to school**
   Okula gittim
8. **taken a shower**
   Duş aldım
9. **gone to sleep**
   Uyudum
10. **gone shopping**
    Alışverişe gittim

Section B | Make a sentence

When will you have woken up by?

I will have woken up by seven o'clock.

When will he have eaten breakfast by?

He will have eaten breakfast by half past eight.

Learn: o'clock, half past, a quarter past, a quarter to

Section C — Make a question

Will you have <u>taken a shower</u> by <u>nine o'clock</u>?
Yes, I will have. / No, I won't have.

Will they have <u>done homework</u> by <u>a quarter to six</u>?
Yes, they will have. / No, they won't have.

Section D — Learn a verb

wake – waking – woke – woken uyanmak

I **wake** up at seven o'clock every day.

The baby is **waking** up now.

You **woke** up late this morning.

I haven't **woken** up this early for years.

Section E — Learn an idiom

Hit the nail on the head

Meaning: To say something that is correct.

"I agree with what you said. You really *hit the nail on the head*."

Section F — Write

Trace and fill in the words

1. When will you have woken up by?

I will have woken up by a quarter past seven.

2. When will he have _____ his teeth by?

He _____ have brushed his teeth by half past nine.

3. When _____ you _____ gone to school _____?

I will _____ gone to _____ by ten _____.

4. When will _____ have _____ homework by?

She will _____ done _____ by _____ o'clock.

5. Will they have cooked dinner by six o'clock?

No, they won't _____.

6. Will _____ have gone to sleep by _____ past ten?

Yes, we _____ _____.

7. _____ she _____ gone shopping by nine o'clock?

No, _____ _____ have.

8. _____ you have brushed _____ teeth by one o'clock?

Yes, _____ _____ _____.

Section G | Let's have fun

Everyday life!

Unscramble the sentences

o'clock / gone / have / we / will / shopping / by / four

1. _____.

two / taken / have / they / will / a shower / by / half past

2. _____.

I / the trash / won't / one o'clock / have / by / taken out

3. _____.

o'clock / cooked dinner / have / he / won't / by / six

4. _____.

Connect the words

brushed • — • out the trash

gone • • dinner

taken • • my teeth

done • • a shower

cooked • • homework

taken • • to sleep

Lesson 38: Languages

Diller

How long have you been learning German?
I have been learning German for one year.

Section A — Words

1. **English**
   İngilizce
2. **German**
   Almanca
3. **Portuguese**
   Portekizce
4. **Japanese**
   Japonca
5. **Vietnamese**
   Vietnamca
6. **Spanish**
   İspanyolca
7. **French**
   Fransızca
8. **Chinese**
   Çince
9. **Hindi**
   Hintçe
10. **Arabic**
    Arapça

Section B — Make a sentence

How long have you been learning English?

I have been learning English for three years.

How long has he been studying Spanish?

He has been studying Spanish for five months.

Learn: learning, studying, speaking

Section C — Make a question

Have they been <u>studying</u> <u>French</u> for a long time?
Yes, they have been. / No, they haven't been.

Has she been <u>learning</u> <u>Japanese</u> for a long time?
Yes, she has been. / No, she hasn't been.

Section D — Learn a verb

speak – speaking – spoke – spoken konuşmak

He **speaks** three languages.

She is **speaking** to him in Japanese.

I **spoke** with my teacher about the German homework.

We haven't **spoken** to each other for over five years.

Section E — Learn an idiom

Speak the same language

Meaning: To share the same understanding and be in agreement.

"I agree with everything you are saying. I think we're *speaking the same language*."

Section F — Write

Trace and fill in the words

1. How long have you been _____ German?

   I have been learning German for three years.

2. How _____ has _____ been studying French?

   She has _____ studying _____ for six years.

3. How _____ have we _____ learning _____?

   _____ have been _____ English for three years.

4. _____ long have _____ been _____ Hindi?

   They _____ been learning _____ for one year.

5. _____ they been speaking Arabic for a long time?

   Yes, they have _____.

6. Has he been _____ Japanese for a long time?

   No, _____ hasn't _____.

7. Have _____ been _____ Arabic for a long time?

   Yes, I _____ _____.

8. Has she _____ studying _____ for a long time?

   No, _____ _____ _____.

Section G | Let's have fun

Languages!

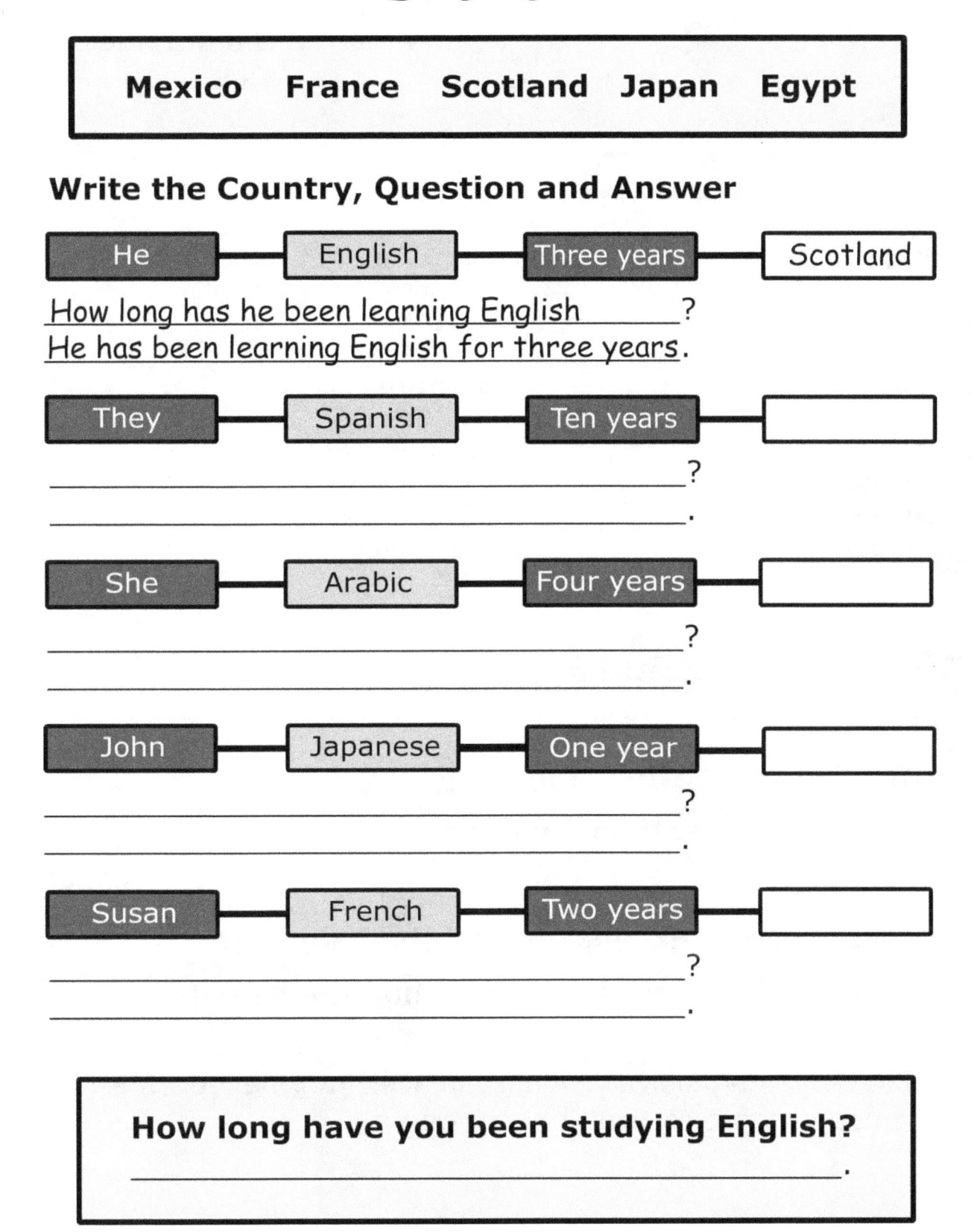

| Mexico | France | Scotland | Japan | Egypt |

Write the Country, Question and Answer

[He] — [English] — [Three years] — [Scotland]

How long has he been learning English ?
He has been learning English for three years.

[They] — [Spanish] — [Ten years] — [ ]

_____ ?
_____ .

[She] — [Arabic] — [Four years] — [ ]

_____ ?
_____ .

[John] — [Japanese] — [One year] — [ ]

_____ ?
_____ .

[Susan] — [French] — [Two years] — [ ]

_____ ?
_____ .

How long have you been studying English?
_____ .

Lesson 39: Pets

Evcil hayvanlar

> What is faster than a mouse?
> A rabbit is faster than a mouse.

Section A — Words

1. **dog**
   Köpek
2. **fish**
   Balık
3. **bird**
   Kuş
4. **rabbit**
   Tavşan
5. **guinea pig**
   Kobay faresi
6. **cat**
   Kedi
7. **turtle**
   Kaplumbağa
8. **mouse**
   Fare
9. **hamster**
   Hamster
10. **snake**
    Yılan

Section B — Make a sentence

What is <u>bigger</u> than a <u>mouse</u>?

A <u>dog</u> is bigger than a mouse.

What is <u>more expensive</u> than the <u>hamster</u>?

The <u>rabbit</u> is more expensive than the hamster.

Learn: faster, slower, bigger, smaller, more expensive, cheaper, more colorful, better, worse

Section C — Make a question

Is a <u>turtle</u> <u>slower</u> than a <u>guinea pig</u>?
Yes, it is. / No, it's not. It's <u>faster</u>.

Is the <u>bird</u> <u>more expensive</u> than the <u>snake</u>?
Yes, it is. / No, it's not. It's <u>cheaper</u>.

Section D — Learn a verb

feed – feeding – fed – fed beslemek

You need to **feed** the dog every morning.

He is **feeding** the turtle some leaves.

I **fed** the mouse some cheese and it happily ate it.

My sister hasn't **fed** the pets today.

Section E — Learn an idiom

The teacher's pet

Meaning: A student whom the teacher favors.

"Her classmates are jealous of her because she is *the teacher's pet.*"

Section F — Write

Trace and fill in the words

1. What is bigger than a mouse?

A rabbit is _____ than a mouse.

2. What is more _____ _____ the dog?

The fish is _____ colorful than the _____.

3. _____ _____ slower than a _____?

A turtle is _____ _____ a cat.

4. What is less _____ _____ the snake?

_____ bird is _____ expensive than the _____.

5. Is the bird faster _____ the guinea pig?

Yes, _____ _____.

6. Is the rabbit more _____ than the dog?

No, _____ _____. It's cheaper.

7. _____ the turtle slower than the _____?

_____, _____ is.

8. Is the cat slower _____ the hamster?

No, it's _____. It's _____.

Section G | Let's have fun

Pets!

Write the animals

Animal	Speed	Size
_____	48 km/h	30 cm
_____	0.4 km/h	40 cm
_____	13 km/h	9 cm
_____	5 km/h	15 cm

Answer the questions

1. What is bigger than a fish? _____.

2. What is faster than a mouse? _____.

3. Is the turtle faster than the fish? _____.

4. Is the mouse slower than the rabbit? _____.

5. What is bigger than a rabbit? _____.

6. What is smaller than a fish? _____.

7. Is the rabbit bigger than the turtle? _____.

8. Is the rabbit bigger than the fish? _____.

Lesson 40: Fast food

Hazır yemek

What is the sweetest food?
The sweetest food is the pancake.

Section A — Words

1. **doughnut**
   Tatlı çörek
2. **cheeseburger**
   Çizburger
3. **chicken nuggets**
   Tavuk nugget
4. **pancake**
   Krep
5. **taco**
   Tako
6. **french fries**
   Patates kızartması
7. **onion rings**
   Soğan halkası
8. **hot dog**
   Sosisli sandviç
9. **fried chicken**
   Kızarmış tavuk
10. **burrito**
    Burrito

Section B — Make a sentence

What is the <u>cheapest</u> food?

The cheapest food is the <u>doughnut</u>.

What is the <u>most expensive</u> food?

The most expensive food is the <u>burrito</u>.

Learn: most delicious, most expensive, cheapest, saltiest, sweetest, best, worst

Section C — Make a question

Is the <u>hot dog</u> the <u>most delicious</u>?
Yes, it is. / No, it's not.

Are the <u>french fries</u> the <u>cheapest</u>?
Yes, they are. / No, they aren't.

Section D — Learn a verb

try – trying – tried – tried denemek

He wants to **try** the cheeseburger at that restaurant.

I'm **trying** to decide whether to buy the taco or burrito.

My baby brother **tried** the pancake, but didn't like it.

We haven't **tried** the fried chicken here yet.

Section E — Learn an idiom

You are what you eat

Meaning: The food that you eat affects your health.

"Careful not to eat too much fast food. *You are what you eat.*"

Section F — Write

Trace and fill in the words

1. What is the cheapest food?

   The _____ food is the taco.

2. What is the best _____?

   The _____ food is the burrito.

3. _____ is the _____ delicious food?

   _____ most _____ food is the doughnut.

4. _____ _____ the worst food?

   _____ _____ food is _____ hot dog.

5. Is the most expensive food the cheeseburger?

   No, it _____. It's the cheapest.

6. _____ the saltiest food _____ french fries?

   Yes, _____ _____.

7. Is the most delicious _____ the fried chicken?

   Yes, _____ _____.

8. Is _____ worst _____ _____ pancake?

   No, it _____. It's _____ best.

Section G Let's have fun

Fast food!

Joe's Diner

doughnut	$2	french fries	$5
cheeseburger	$4	onion rings	$6
chicken nugget	$1	hot dog	$3
pancake	$6	fried chicken	$7
taco	$8	burrito	$9

Answer the questions

1. What is the most expensive food? _____.

2. What is the cheapest food? _____.

3. What is the saltiest food? _____.

4. What is the sweetest food? _____.

5. What is the most delicious food? _____.

6. Is the pancake the sweetest food? _____.

7. Is the taco the most delicious food? _____.

8. Are the french fries the saltiest food? _____.

Test 10   Lesson 37 - 40

Write the answer next to the letter "A"

A: ___ **1.** When ___ you have ___ to school by?

a. do, go   b. will, gone   c. can, went   d. will, go

A: ___ **2.** They will have ___ dinner by ___ six.

a. eat, o'clock   b. ate, past   c. eats, quarter   d. eaten, half past

A: ___ **3.** They haven't ___ with each other for two years.

a. spoken   b. spokes   c. speaking   d. speaks

A: ___ **4.** "You said it exactly right. You hit the ___ on the head."

a. hammer   b. work   c. nail   d. day

A: ___ **5.** How long ___ he ___ learning Arabic?

a. does, is   b. is, can   c. have, does   d. has, been

A: ___ **6.** No, ___ haven't been ___ Spanish for a long time.

a. I, learn   b. we, learned   c. they, learning   d. he, learns

A: ___ **7.** He ___ Chinese with the doctor last night.

a. spoke   b. is   c. was   d. speaks

A: ___ **8.** "I really agree with him. I think we ___ the same language."

a. speaks   b. speak   c. spoken   d. speaking

A: ___ **9.** What is ___ than a guinea pig?

a. cheaper   b. more cheap   c. more cheaper   d. cheapest

A: ___ **10.** Is the mouse ___ than the cat? No, it's ___.

a. slow, slower   b. big, smaller   c. slow, fast   d. slower, faster

A: ___ **11.** We haven't ___ the pets yet.

a. feed   b. fed   c. feeding   d. feeds

A: ___ **12.** "The teacher really loved him. He was the teacher's ___."

a. pets   b. petting   c. pet   d. best

A: ___ **13.** What is the ___ food on the menu?

a. more cheap   b. cheapest   c. most cheap   d. cheapen

A: ___ **14.** ___ the taco the ___ delicious?

a. Had, more   b. Is, more   c. Does, most   d. Is, most

A: ___ **15.** He usually ___ new food every weekend.

a. try   b. trying   c. tries   d. had try

A: ___ **16.** "You should eat healthier food. You ___ what you eat."

a. are   b. can   c. do   d. try

Answers on page 206

Lesson 41: At the cinema

Sinemada

> What was the romance movie like?
> It was romantic.

Section A — Words

1. **scary**
   Korkunç
2. **exciting**
   Heyecan verici
3. **informative**
   Bilgilendirici
4. **romantic**
   Romantik
5. **violent**
   Şiddetli
6. **boring**
   Sıkıcı
7. **interesting**
   İlginç
8. **funny**
   Komik
9. **enjoyable**
   Zevkli
10. **sad**
    Üzücü

Section B — Make a sentence

What was the <u>horror</u> movie like?

It was <u>scary</u>.

What was the <u>action</u> movie like?

It was <u>exciting</u>.

Learn: horror, comedy, action, romance, sci-fi, animation

Section C — Make a question

Was the <u>horror</u> movie as <u>exciting</u> as the <u>action</u> movie?
Yes, it was. / No, it wasn't.

Was the <u>sci-fi</u> movie as <u>funny</u> as the <u>comedy</u> movie?
Yes, it was. / No, it wasn't.

Section D — Learn a verb

teach – teaching – taught – taught öğretmek

The movie **teaches** us about looking after the environment.

My father will be **teaching** me how to swim.

My history teacher **taught** us interesting things this year.

The teacher hasn't **taught** us anything informative yet.

Section E — Learn an idiom

A tough act to follow

Meaning: Someone who did so well that it would be hard to do better.

"He was so funny in this movie. It will be *a tough act to follow*."

Section F | Write

Trace and fill in the words

1. What was the comedy movie like?

It was really funny.

2. What _____ the romance movie _____?

_____ was romantic.

3. _____ _____ the sci-fi movie like?

_____ _____ really exciting.

4. What _____ _____ animation movie _____?

_____ _____ enjoyable.

5. Was the _____ movie as funny as the comedy movie?

No, it _____.

6. Was the action movie as _____ as the horror movie?

Yes, _____ _____.

7. _____ the animation movie as sad as the sci-fi movie?

_____, _____ wasn't.

8. Was the horror _____ as violent as the action movie?

_____, it _____.

190

Section G | Let's have fun

At the cinema!

What was the comedy movie like?
It was funny.

What was the action movie like?
It was exciting.

What was the sci-fi movie like?
It was interesting.

What was the romance movie like?
It was boring.

True of False? Circle the answer

1. The comedy movie was funny.   True   False

2. The romance movie was informative.   True   False

3. The action movie was exciting.   True   False

4. The sci-fi movie was sad.   True   False

Complete the words

b__r__ng   i__fo__ma__i__e   e__jo__ab__e

i__t__r__s__in__   e__c__tin__   sc__r__

f__n__y   r__m__nt__c   v__o__en__

Lesson 42: Music

Müzik

How does she play the violin?
She plays the violin gracefully.

Section A — Words

1. **beautifully**
   Güzelce
2. **quietly**
   Sessizce
3. **slowly**
   Yavaşça
4. **gracefully**
   İncelikle
5. **well**
   İyi
6. **loudly**
   Yüksek sesle
7. **quickly**
   Hızla
8. **terribly**
   Korkunç
9. **correctly**
   Düzgünce
10. **badly**
    Kötüce

Section B — Make a sentence

How does he <u>sing the song</u>?

He sings the song <u>beautifully</u>.

How do they <u>play the guitar</u>?

They play the guitar <u>loudly</u>.

Learn: sing the song, play the piano, play the violin, play the cello, play the drums, play the guitar

Section C — Make a question

Does she <u>play the violin</u> <u>gracefully</u>?
Yes, she does. / No, she doesn't.

Do you <u>play the drums</u> <u>well</u>?
Yes, I do. / No, I don't.

Section D — Learn a verb

notice – noticing – noticed – noticed fark etmek

You will **notice** that my family speaks loudly.

I'm **noticing** more and more how well she speaks English.

I **noticed** you haven't done your homework correctly.

She hadn't **noticed** her friend looking at her.

Section E — Learn an idiom

Music to one's ears

Meaning: Something very pleasing to hear.

"It was *music to my ears* when I heard that the teacher cancelled the test!"

| Section F | Write |

Trace and fill in the words

1. How does _____ play the piano?

   She plays the _____ quickly.

2. _____ do we play the _____?

   _____ play the violin terribly.

3. How _____ he play _____ cello?

   He _____ the cello gracefully.

4. _____ _____ you play the drums?

   _____ _____ the drums well.

5. Does he play the trumpet correctly?

   Yes, _____ does.

6. _____ you sing the song beautifully?

   No, _____ don't.

7. _____ she _____ the cello correctly?

   Yes, _____ does.

8. _____ _____ play _____ guitar quietly?

   No, they _____.

Section G — Let's have fun

Music!

Write the correct verb

1. **play/plays?** He _____ the piano beautifully.

2. **sing/sings?** She _____ the song quietly.

3. **play/plays?** They _____ the violin badly.

4. **play/plays?** We _____ the guitar well.

Write the sentences

1. plays the piano - quick

   <u>She plays the piano quickly</u>.

2. sings the song - beautiful

   _____.

3. plays the trumpet - loud

   _____.

4. plays the cello - bad

   _____.

Lesson 43: Feelings

Duygular

> How have you been feeling lately?
> Lately, I've been feeling tired.

Section A — Words

1. **sad**
   Üzgün
2. **tired**
   Yorgun
3. **fine**
   İyi
4. **bored**
   Sıkkın
5. **energetic**
   Enerjik
6. **happy**
   Mutlu
7. **sick**
   Hasta
8. **angry**
   Kızgın
9. **excited**
   Heyecanlı
10. **frustrated**
    Sinirli

Section B — Make a sentence

How have you been feeling lately?

Lately, I've been feeling <u>sad</u>.

How are you now?

I'm <u>happy</u>.

Note: I've = I have / she's = she has / he's = he has
they've = they have / we've = we have / you've = you have

Section C — Make a question

Have you been feeling <u>tired</u> lately?
Yes, I have. / No, I haven't.

Are you <u>angry</u>?
Yes, I am. / No, I'm not.

Section D — Learn a verb

think – thinking – thought – thought düşünmek

I **think** she feels fine now. Thank you for your concern.

She's frustrated because she keeps **thinking** about work.

Peter **thought** about how excited his child was to see him.

I haven't **thought** about this before.

Section E — Learn an idiom

Mixed Feelings

Meaning: When you are not sure about how you feel about something.

"He had *mixed feelings* about moving to a new city."

Section F — Write

Trace and fill in the words

1. How have you been feeling lately?

Lately, I've been feeling tired.

2. How has she _____ feeling lately?

Lately, she's been _____ angry.

3. How _____ they been _____ lately?

Lately, they've _____ feeling bored.

4. How _____ he _____ feeling _____?

Lately, _____ been _____ _____.

5. Have you been feeling excited lately?

No, I haven't.

6. Has he been _____ energetic lately?

Yes, _____ _____.

7. Have _____ _____ feeling frustrated lately?

Yes, I _____.

8. _____ he been _____ sick _____?

No, _____ _____.

Section G | Let's have fun

Feelings!

Match the face with the word

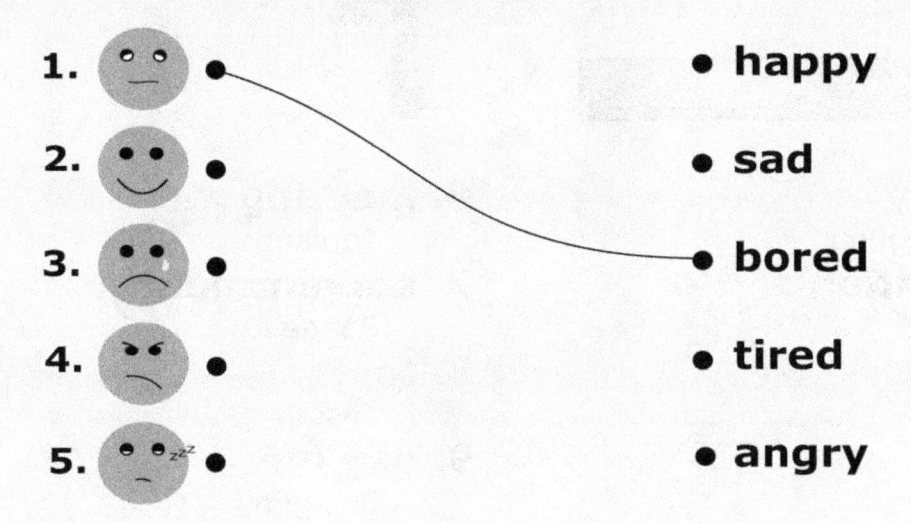

1. •   • happy
2. •   • sad
3. •   • bored
4. •   • tired
5. •   • angry

Answer the questions

1. How has he been feeling lately?
   <u>Lately, he's been feeling bored</u>.

2. How has she been feeling lately?
   _____.

3. How have they been feeling lately?
   _____.

4. Has she been feeling tired lately?
   _____.

5. Has he been feeling angry lately?
   _____.

How have you been feeling lately?

_____.

Lesson 44: The Calendar

Takvim

When is your competition?
My competition is on the 2nd of May.

Section A — Words

1. **birthday**
   Doğum günü
2. **competition**
   Yarışma
3. **class**
   Sınıf
4. **speech**
   Konuşma
5. **party**
   Parti
6. **meeting**
   Toplantı
7. **appointment**
   Randevu
8. **test**
   Test
9. **day off**
   Boş gün
10. **recital**
    Anlatış

Section B — Make a sentence

When is your <u>birthday</u>?

My birthday is on the <u>21st</u> of <u>February</u>.

Learn: January, February, March, April, May, June, July, August, September, October, November, December

1st 2nd 3rd 4th 5th 6th 7th 8th 9th 10th 11th 12th 13th 14th 15th 16th 17th 18th 19th 20th 21st 22nd 23rd 24th 25th 26th 27th 28th 29th 30th 31st

| Section C | Make a question |

Is your <u>meeting</u> on the <u>12th</u> of <u>November</u>?
Yes, it is. / No, it isn't.

Was your <u>party</u> on the <u>10th</u> of <u>June</u>?
Yes, it was. / No, it wasn't.

| Section D | Learn a verb |

organize – organizing – organized – organized düzenlemek

She will **organize** a meeting for this Friday.

Fran is **organizing** a person to help me with the recital.

The teacher **organized** a speech competition at school.

She has **organized** many parties for the company.

| Section E | Learn an idiom |

Make a date

Meaning: To arrange a meeting with someone.

"We should *make a date* and discuss this further."

Section F Write

Trace and fill in the words

1. When is your appointment?

My appointment is on the 22nd of September.

2. When _____ his competition?

His _____ is on the 31st of October.

3. When is their test?

_____ _____ is on the 11th of _____.

4. When _____ _____ party?

Her _____ is _____ _____ 12th of _____.

5. Is your recital on the 15th of November?

No, _____ isn't.

6. Was his speech _____ the 18th of _____?

No, it _____.

7. Is her day off _____ the _____ of _____?

Yes, _____ _____.

8. Was their class _____ the _____ _____ May?

_____, it _____.

Section G | Let's have fun

The calendar!

May

Monday	Tuesday	Wednesday	Thursday	Friday	Saturday	Sunday
	1st	2nd	3rd	4th Meeting	5th	6th
7th	8th Recital	9th	10th	11th	12th	13th
14th	15th	16th	17th Birthday	18th	19th	20th
21st	22nd Test	23rd	24th	25th	26th Party	27th
28th Day off	29th	30th	31st			

Answer the questions

1. When is your birthday?

   _____.

2. When is your test?

   _____.

3. Is your party on the 26th of May?

   _____.

4. Was your test on the 22nd of April?

   _____.

Test 11   Lesson 41 - 44

Write the answer next to the letter "A"

A: ___ 1. ___ was the horror movie ___? It was scary.

a. How, like   b. When, see   c. Where, like   d. What, like

A: ___ 2. Was the comedy as funny ___ the action movie?

a. movie   b. watch   c. like   d. as

A: ___ 3. His mother ___ how to swim.

a. teach him   b. taught him   c. teaches he   d. learn him

A: ___ 4. "Her speech was great. It will be a tough ___ to follow."

a. day   b. act   c. song   d. beat

A: ___ 5. She ___ the piano ___ every Saturday night.

a. plays, well   b. play, quickly   c. playing, slowly   d. play, bad

A: ___ 6. Does he ___ the drums ___ for this song?

a. play, correctly   b. play, good   c. plays, well   d. plays, badly

A: ___ 7. He hadn't ___ his friend speaking Chinese to him.

a. notice   b. notices   c. noticed   d. noticing

A: ___ 8. "It's such good news! It's ___ to my ears."

a. singing   b. dancing   c. sound   d. music

A: ___ 9. Lately, she ___ been ___ happy.

a. have, feeling　　b. is, felt　　c. has, feeling　　d. does, feels

A: ___ 10. ___ you been feeling ___ lately? No, I haven't been.

a. Do, tired　　b. Can, tired　　c. Have, tired　　d. Have, tire

A: ___ 11. Todd wasn't ___ excited during gym class yesterday.

a. feeling　　b. feel　　c. feels　　d. felt

A: ___ 12. "He wasn't sure what to do. He had ___ feelings."

a. mixing　　b. mixed　　c. mix　　d. mixes

A: ___ 13. When is ___ birthday? His birthday is on ___ 10th of May.

a. him, it　　b. he's, a　　c. he's, one　　d. his, the

A: ___ 14. Is ___ recital on the 15th of November? No, it ___.

a. her, isn't　　b. his, doesn't　　c. your, can't　　d. my, won't

A: ___ 15. Fran is ___ a group of people to help us.

a. organize　　b. organizing　　c. organizes　　d. organized

A: ___ 16. "Let's arrange a meeting. We should make a ___."

a. meet　　b. test　　c. date　　d. try

Answers on page 206

Answers Test 1 - 11

Test 1
1. a 2. c 3. a 4. d 5. d 6. c 7. c 8. b 9. d 10. b 11. b 12. a 13. a 14. a
15. c 16. d

Test 2
1. b 2. c 3. c 4. d 5. a 6. b 7. d 8. b 9. d 10. a 11. c 12. c 13. d 14. c
15. b 16. d

Test 3
1. d 2. b 3. d 4. c 5. b 6. a 7. c 8. a 9. d 10. c 11. c 12. d 13. a 14. c
15. c 16. d

Test 4
1. d 2. b 3. c 4. c 5. d 6. d 7. a 8. d 9. b 10. b 11. c 12. b 13. d 14. d
15. a 16. d

Test 5
1. a 2. a 3. c 4. b 5. d 6. d 7. b 8. a 9. c 10. d 11. c 12. b 13. d 14. c
15. a 16. c

Test 6
1. b 2. b 3. a 4. d 5. c 6. c 7. d 8. b 9. a 10. d 11. a 12. b 13. b 14. c
15. c 16. c

Test 7
1. c 2. c 3. b 4. a 5. b 6. a 7. c 8. d 9. d 10. c 11. a 12. c 13. b 14. b
15. d 16. d

Test 8
1. a 2. b 3. c 4. d 5. c 6. b 7. d 8. a 9. d 10. b 11. c 12. a 13. d 14. b
15. c 16. a

Test 9
1. b 2. c 3. c 4. a 5. d 6. d 7. a 8. b 9. d 10. a 11. c 12. b 13. b 14. a
15. c 16. d

Test 10
1. b 2. d 3. a 4. c 5. d 6. c 7. a 8. b 9. a 10. d 11. b 12. c 13. b 14. d
15. c 16. a

Test 11
1. d 2. d 3. b 4. b 5. a 6. a 7. c 8. d 9. c 10. c 11. a 12. b 13. d 14. a
15. b 16. c

Preston Lee's Conversation ENGLISH

Lesson 1 - 40

For Turkish Speakers

CONTENTS

Lesson 1: My family Ailem — Page 212

Lesson 2: My pencil case Kalem kutum — Page 216

Lesson 3: In the classroom Sınıfta — Page 220

Lesson 4: The weather Hava durumu — Page 224

Lesson 5: Places Yerler — Page 228

Lesson 6: Sports Spor — Page 232

Lesson 7: At the zoo Hayvanat bahçesinde — Page 236

Lesson 8: Colors Renkler — Page 240

Lesson 9: Activities Aktiviteler — Page 244

Lesson 10: Food & Drinks Yiyecek ve içecekler — Page 248

Lesson 11: At the fruit market Manavda — Page 252

Lesson 12: Shapes Şekiller — Page 256

Lesson 13: At the supermarket Süpermarket — Page 260

Lesson 14: At the ice cream shop Dondurma dükkanında — Page 264

Lesson 15: In the refrigerator Buzdolabında — Page 268

Lesson 16: Jobs Meslekler — Page 272

Lesson 17: Names İsimler — Page 276

Lesson 18: More places Daha çok yer — Page 280

Lesson 19: Meats Etler — Page 284

Lesson 20: Vegetables Sebzeler — Page 288

Lesson 21: At school Okulda — Page 292

Lesson 22: School subjects Okul dersleri — Page 296

Lesson 23: Chores Ev işleri — Page 300

Lesson 24: At the toy store Oyuncak mağazasında — Page 304

Lesson 25: In the kitchen Mutfakta — Page 308

Lesson 26: In the toolbox Alet çantası — Page 312

Lesson 27: Transportation Ulaşım — Page 316

Lesson 28: Clothes Giysiler — Page 320

Lesson 29: More clothes Daha fazla giysi — Page 324

Lesson 30: In the living room Oturma odasında — Page 328

Lesson 31: In the bathroom Banyoda — Page 332

Lesson 32: In the bedroom Yatak odasında — Page 336

Lesson 33: Around the house Evin etrafında — Page 340

Lesson 34: Hobbies Hobiler — Page 344

Lesson 35: Countries Ülkeler — Page 348

Lesson 36: Landscapes Manzaralar — Page 352

Lesson 37: Everyday life Günlük yaşam — Page 356

Lesson 38: Languages Diller — Page 360

Lesson 39: Pets Evcil hayvanlar — Page 364

Lesson 40: Fast food Hazır yemek — Page 368

Answers — Page 372

Lesson 1: My family

Ailem

> Who is she?
> She is my baby sister.

Learn the words

1. **mother**
   Anne
2. **grandmother**
   Büyükanne
3. **sister**
   Kız kardeş
4. **baby sister**
   Bebek kız kardeş
5. **aunt**
   Yenge

6. **father**
   Baba
7. **grandfather**
   Büyükbaba
8. **brother**
   Erkek kardeş
9. **baby brother**
   Bebek erkek kardeş
10. **uncle**
    Amca

Learn a verb

see – seeing – saw – seen görmek

Peter: I haven't seen your brother for a long time. How is he?

Learn an idiom

Like one of the family

Meaning: To be like a person in one's family.

"Our dog is treated *like one of the family*."

Conversation

Peter: Hey, Mary. What are you doing this weekend?

Mary: I'm going to my aunt's birthday party.

Peter: Great! Will many people be there?

Mary: No, just the family will be there.

Peter: I thought your grandfather was in hospital?

Mary: That's right. My grandfather won't be going to the party.

Peter: How is your grandfather feeling now?

Mary: My grandmother said he's feeling better.

Peter: Did you get your aunt a gift?

Mary: No. My brother and I are still deciding what to get her.

Peter: I haven't seen your brother for a long time. How is he?

Mary: He's fine. He's playing tennis with my sister now.

Peter: I didn't know he plays tennis.

Mary: He has been learning for six months.

Peter: My mother plays tennis really well.

Mary: I saw her at the park. She was with your baby sister.

Peter: They were walking the dog.

Mary: Your dog is so cute. It really loves your baby sister.

Peter: I know. It's like one of the family.

Mary: Hey, Peter. Is he your father?

Peter: No, he isn't.

Mary: Who is he?

Peter: He is my uncle. I better go. Have fun at the party!

Learn the English

Fill in the blanks

Peter: Hey, Mary. What _____ you doing this _____?

Mary: I'm _____ to my aunt's _____ party.

Peter: How is _____ grandfather _____ now?

Mary: My grandmother _____ he's feeling _____.

Peter: I haven't seen your brother for a long _____. How is he?

Mary: He's fine. He's _____ tennis with my sister _____.

Peter: I _____ know he _____ tennis.

Answer the questions

1. What is Mary doing this weekend?

_____

2. Where is Mary's grandfather?

_____

3. What is Mary's brother doing now?

_____

4. How long has Mary's brother been playing tennis?

_____

5. Who did Mary see at the park?

_____

Test

Write the answer next to the letter "A"

A: ___ **1.** Mary's ___ is having a birthday party this weekend.

a. uncle   b. mother   c. aunt   d. sister

A: ___ **2.** Mary's ___ won't be going to the party.

a. grandfather   b. father   c. brother   d. uncle

A: ___ **3.** Does Mary have a gift for her aunt?

a. Yes, she does.   b. No, she doesn't.   c. Yes, she is.   d. No, she isn't.

A: ___ **4.** Mary's brother is playing ___ with her ___.

a. soccer, sister   b. tennis, sister   c. golf, aunt   d. tennis, mother

A: ___ **5.** How long has Mary's brother been learning tennis?

a. Six days.   b. Six weeks.   c. Seven months.   d. Six months.

A: ___ **6.** Peter's dog is like one of the ___.

a. animals   b. family   c. people   d. friends

A: ___ **7.** The dog really loves Peter's ___.

a. mother   b. father   c. baby sister   d. aunt

A: ___ **8.** Who did Mary see?

a. Peter's father.   b. Peter's uncle.   c. Peter's brother.   d. Peter's aunt.

Answers on page 372

Lesson 2: My pencil case

Kalem kutum

> What is this?
>
> It is an eraser.

Learn the words

1. **a pencil**
   Kalem
2. **an eraser**
   Silgi
3. **glue**
   Tutkal
4. **a pencil sharpener**
   Kalemtıraş
5. **whiteout**
   Daksil
6. **a pen**
   Dolma kalem
7. **a ruler**
   Cetvel
8. **tape**
   Bant
9. **a marker**
   Keçeli kalem
10. **a crayon**
    Pastel boya

Learn a verb

buy – buying – bought – bought satın almak

Kevin: Sorry. Here's my ruler. I bought it yesterday.

Learn an idiom

Cross your fingers

Meaning: To wish for luck.

"*Cross your fingers* and hope this marker has ink."

Conversation

Jessica: Hi, Kevin. I forgot my pencil case.

Kevin: We have art class now. You will need it.

Jessica: I know. Can I borrow your pencils?

Kevin: I'm using crayons to draw my picture. I didn't bring pencils.

Jessica: Okay. I want to draw a house, so I'll need a ruler.

Kevin: That's fine. You can use mine. Here you go.

Jessica: What is this?

Kevin: It's a ruler.

Jessica: No, it isn't. It's an eraser.

Kevin: Sorry. Here's my ruler.

Jessica: What are you going to draw?

Kevin: I don't know what I should draw.

Jessica: The teacher wants us to draw our home.

Kevin: I think I'm going to draw the classroom.

Jessica: Is the classroom your home?

Kevin: No, but it feels like it. We are here all day, every day!

Jessica: I'm not sure if the teacher will like that.

Kevin: She'll think it's funny.

Jessica: Cross your fingers she won't be angry!

Kevin: I want to stick pictures on my paper. Look at these pictures.

Jessica: They look good. Do you have any tape?

Kevin: No, I don't, but I bought some glue last Friday.

Jessica: Hey, Kevin. That's whiteout, not glue!

Learn the English

Unscramble the sentences

1. to / picture / my / I'm / draw / crayons / using

_____

2. our / wants / teacher / to / draw / The / home / us

_____

3. stick / on / to / I / paper / want / my / pictures

_____

Answer the questions

1. What class are they in?

_____

2. What did Jessica forget to bring?

_____

3. Why does Jessica want to use a ruler?

_____

4. What does Kevin want to draw?

_____

5. Does Kevin have any tape?

_____

Test

Write the answer next to the letter "A"

A: ___ **1.** Jessica ___ her pencil case.

a. forgets   b. forgot   c. forget   d. forgotten

A: ___ **2.** Kevin and Jessica are in ___ class now.

a. math   b. art   c. science   d. English

A: ___ **3.** Will Kevin draw a house?

a. Yes, he will.   b. No, he doesn't.   c. Yes, he does.   d. No, he won't.

A: ___ **4.** Jessica wanted to borrow a ___ from Kevin.

a. eraser   b. ruler   c. whiteout   d. marker

A: ___ **5.** Kevin wants to use ___ to draw his picture.

a. markers   b. pencils   c. pens   d. crayons

A: ___ **6.** The teacher wants the students to draw their ___.

a. apartment   b. house   c. home   d. classroom

A: ___ **7.** Kevin ___ some ___ last Friday.

a. bought, glue   b. bought, tape   c. buys, glue   d. buys, tape

A: ___ **8.** Kevin will use ___ to stick the pictures on the paper.

a. eraser   b. whiteout   c. tape   d. glue

Answers on page 372

Lesson 3: In the classroom

Sınıfta

> What are these?
> These are old books.

Learn the words

1. **chair**
   Sandalye
2. **blackboard**
   Karatahta
3. **poster**
   Afiş
4. **globe**
   Küre
5. **clock**
   Saat
6. **desk**
   Sıra
7. **whiteboard**
   Beyaz tahta
8. **bookshelf**
   Kitaplık
9. **computer**
   Bilgisayar
10. **book**
    Kitap

Learn a verb

look – looking – looked – looked bakmak

Susan: I was looking at your classroom before. It looks great.

Learn an idiom

Class clown

Meaning: A student who often makes everyone laugh in the classroom.

"Peter is the *class clown*. Even the teacher laughs sometimes."

Conversation

Matthew: Hi, Susan. Did you have fun on your holidays?

Susan: Yes, I did. I traveled to Canada for two weeks.

Matthew: That sounds excellent! How was it?

Susan: It was so much fun! I learned how to ski.

Matthew: My holidays were boring. I'm happy school has started.

Susan: I'm not happy to be back at school!

Matthew: Why? I thought you loved school.

Susan: I like school, but I'm angry about my new classroom.

Matthew: Really? Why?

Susan: It has a really old computer and there's no whiteboard.

Matthew: That's too bad. My classroom has new desks and chairs.

Susan: I was looking at your classroom before. It looks great.

Matthew: I'm lucky this year. Last year, the clock was broken.

Susan: Your bookshelf also has many new books.

Matthew: Doesn't your classroom have new books?

Susan: No, they're all old, but we do have a new globe.

Matthew: What happened to the other globe?

Susan: The teacher said John knocked it off her desk.

Matthew: The teacher must have been really angry at him!

Susan: He didn't mean to push it. He was dancing like a robot.

Matthew: John really is the class clown.

Susan: That's true. He can be so funny sometimes.

Matthew: We better go to class. We'll talk at lunch.

Learn the English

Find the mistakes and write the sentence correctly

Susan: It has a really new computer and there's no blackboard.

_____

Matthew: I'm lucky this week. Last year, the globe was broken.

_____

Susan: No, they're all new, but we do have an old bookshelf.

_____

Answer the questions

1. How long was Susan in Canada for?

_____

2. What did Susan learn how to do?

_____

3. Is Susan happy to be back at school?

_____

4. What was broken in Matthew's classroom last year?

_____

5. What was John dancing like?

_____

Test

Write the answer next to the letter "A"

A: ___ **1.** Susan ___ to ___ for two weeks.

a. travel, Canada   b. traveled, Canada   c. will travel, USA   d. travel, USA

A: ___ **2.** Matthew thinks his holidays ___ boring.

a. are   b. is   c. were   d. was

A: ___ **3.** Susan ___ angry about her new classroom.

a. feels   b. feel   c. feeling   d. fell

A: ___ **4.** Susan's new classroom doesn't have a ___.

a. computer   b. poster   c. blackboard   d. whiteboard

A: ___ **5.** "I ___ looking at your classroom. It ___ great."

a. were, looking   b. am, looks   c. was, look   d. was, looks

A: ___ **6.** When was the clock in Matthew's classroom broken?

a. Two years ago.   b. Last year.   c. This year.   d. Last month.

A: ___ **7.** Susan's ___ classroom has ___ books.

a. new, old   b. old, new   c. big, old   d. old, big

A: ___ **8.** The teacher ___ John knocked it ___ her desk.

a. says, off   b. said, of   c. say, of   d. said, off

Answers on page 372

Lesson 4: The weather

Hava durumu

How is the weather on Friday?
It is sunny.

Learn the words

1. **snowy**
   Karlı
2. **sunny**
   Güneşli
3. **rainy**
   Yağmurlu
4. **windy**
   Rüzgarlı
5. **cloudy**
   Bulutlu
6. **hot**
   Sıcak
7. **cold**
   Soğuk
8. **warm**
   Ilık
9. **cool**
   Serin
10. **freezing**
    Çok Soğuk

Learn a verb

feel – feeling – felt – felt hissetmek

Tom: It's surrounded by trees. We won't feel the wind there.

Learn an idiom

It's raining cats and dogs

Meaning: It's raining heavily.

"You can't play outside right now. *It's raining cats and dogs.*"

Conversation

Tom: Do you want to play basketball with me on Saturday?

John: Sure. Where do you want to play?

Tom: We can play at the park.

John: Which park?

Tom: The big park that is next to the swimming pool.

John: If we want to play outside, we better check the weather.

Tom: How is the weather on Saturday?

John: It is cold and rainy.

Tom: Are you sure? It's been sunny all week.

John: Yes, I think it's going to rain cats and dogs.

Tom: How about on Sunday? Will it be warm enough to play?

John: Let me check.

Tom: I'm okay with cold weather as long as it's not freezing.

John: The weather is cloudy on Sunday, but no rain.

Tom: Sounds good. Let's play basketball on Sunday.

John: It might be windy at the park.

Tom: It's fine. We'll play on basketball court 2.

John: Why that one?

Tom: It's surrounded by trees. We won't feel the wind there.

John: Great! What time do you want to meet?

Tom: Let's get there early when nobody is playing.

John: I can arrive at eight o'clock.

Tom: Perfect! I'll see you at the big park at eight.

Learn the English

Put the sentences in order

John: Which park? ____

Tom: We can play at the park. ____

Tom: How is the weather on Saturday? ____

John: Sure. Where do you want to play? ____

Tom: Do you want to play basketball with me on Saturday? ____

John: If we want to play outside, we better check the weather. ____

John: It is cold and rainy. ____

Tom: The big park that is next to the swimming pool. ____

Answer the questions

1. Which sport does Tom want to play?

_____

2. How is the weather on Saturday?

_____

3. Which park does Tom want to play basketball at?

_____

4. Why does Tom want to play on basketball court 2?

_____

5. What time will they meet at the park?

_____

Test

Write the answer next to the letter "A"

A: ___ **1.** What ___ the boys want to play? They ___ to play basketball.

a. does, wants   b. do, want   c. will, want   d. will, wants

A: ___ **2.** They will play basketball at the big park next to the ___.

a. swimming pool   b. school   c. park   d. home

A: ___ **3.** Will they play basketball on Saturday?

a. Yes, they will.   b. No, they won't.   c. Yes, they did.   d. No, they don't.

A: ___ **4.** The weather is ___ on Saturday.

a. sunny and hot   b. cold and windy   c. sunny and warm   d. cold and rainy

A: ___ **5.** The weather is ___ on Sunday, but no ___.

a. windy, rain   b. cold, rain   c. cloudy, rain   d. freezing, snow

A: ___ **6.** They will play on basketball court 2 because of the ___.

a. cold   b. rain   c. wind   d. sun

A: ___ **7.** Basketball court 2 is surrounded by ___.

a. walls   b. a fence   c. a tree   d. trees

A: ___ **8.** The boys will meet at ___ on ___.

a. Saturday, eight   b. eight, Saturday   c. Sunday, eight   d. eight, Sunday

Answers on page 372

Lesson 5: Places

Yerler

> Where is he going?
> He is going to the gym.

Learn the words

1. **park**
   Park
2. **beach**
   Plaj
3. **night market**
   Akşam pazarı
4. **store**
   Mağaza
5. **supermarket**
   Süpermarket
6. **restaurant**
   Restoran
7. **swimming pool**
   Yüzme havuzu
8. **department store**
   Alışveriş merkezi
9. **cinema**
   Sinema
10. **gym**
    Spor salonu

Learn a verb

walk – walking – walked – walked yürümek

Peter: We first walked around the supermarket. That was boring.

Learn an idiom

Have a change of heart

Meaning: To change your mind about something.

"I've *had a change of heart* about this place. Let's go to another restaurant."

Conversation

Peter: Hi, Kevin. What did you do last weekend?

Kevin: I went swimming.

Peter: Where did you go swimming?

Kevin: At first, Dad wanted to go to the beach, but it was too cold.

Peter: I agree. The water would have been freezing at the beach!

Kevin: Dad decided to take me to the swimming pool instead.

Peter: Do you mean the swimming pool next to the big park?

Kevin: Yes, that's right.

Peter: Mary is going to that swimming pool now.

Kevin: I like that one because it has warm water.

Peter: Last week, you said you were going to see a movie, right?

Kevin: I had a change of heart about going to the cinema.

Peter: Really? Why?

Kevin: Because I haven't been exercising much lately.

Peter: That's true. I haven't seen you at the gym for a long time.

Kevin: How about you? What did you do on the weekend?

Peter: I went shopping with Mom.

Kevin: Was that fun?

Peter: Yes and no.

Kevin: What do you mean?

Peter: We first walked around the supermarket. That was boring.

Kevin: And then?

Peter: Later, we went to the night market. That was a lot of fun.

Learn the English

Fill in the blanks

Kevin: Dad _____ to take me to the swimming pool _____.

Peter: Do you mean the _____ pool next to the big _____?

Kevin: I had a _____ of heart about going to the _____.

Peter: Mary is _____ to that swimming pool _____.

Kevin: How _____ you? What did you do on the _____?

Peter: I _____ shopping with _____.

Peter: We first walked around the _____. That was _____.

Answer the questions

1. What did Kevin do last weekend?

_____

2. Where did Kevin's father first want to go?

_____

3. Why did Kevin have a change of heart about seeing a movie?

_____

4. Where is Mary going now?

_____

5. What did Peter think about walking around the supermarket?

_____

Test

Write the answer next to the letter "A"

A: ___ **1.** Kevin and his father ___ to the beach because it was too cold.

a. don't go   b. didn't go   c. doesn't go   d. didn't went

A: ___ **2.** "The water would ___ freezing at the beach!"

a. have   b. had been   c. being   d. have been

A: ___ **3.** The swimming pool is ___ the big park.

a. near   b. in front of   c. next to   d. behind

A: ___ **4.** Mary ___ to that swimming pool now.

a. going   b. is going   c. goes   d. gone

A: ___ **5.** Kevin ___ that swimming pool because the water is ___.

a. like, warm   b. likes, warm   c. like, cold   d. likes, cold

A: ___ **6.** Kevin ___ a movie last weekend.

a. saw   b. had seen   c. didn't see   d. didn't saw

A: ___ **7.** Kevin ___ a change of ___ about seeing a movie.

a. has, mind   b. had, mind   c. has, heart   d. had, heart

A: ___ **8.** Peter first walked around the ___.

a. supermarket   b. night market   c. beach   d. swimming pool

Answers on page 372

Lesson 6: Sports

Spor

What are you playing?
I am playing golf.

Learn the words

1. **basketball**
   Basketbol
2. **soccer**
   Futbol
3. **badminton**
   Badminton
4. **golf**
   Golf
5. **hockey**
   Hokey
6. **cricket**
   Kriket
7. **tennis**
   Tenis
8. **baseball**
   Beyzbol
9. **volleyball**
   Voleybol
10. **football**
    Amerikan futbolu

Learn a verb

play – playing – played – played oynamak

Mary: I've been playing soccer since I was four years old.

Learn an idiom

A good sport

Meaning: Someone who can accept losing or be made fun of.

"We made fun of Johnny, but he was *a good sport* and laughed with us."

Conversation

Jason: Hi, Mary. What are you doing today?

Mary: I'm playing badminton.

Jason: Who are you going to play with?

Mary: Susan is coming later. You can play with us if you like.

Jason: No, I can't. Kevin and Tom want to play tennis today.

Mary: I think tennis is more difficult than badminton.

Jason: I agree. Tennis needs a lot more practice.

Mary: That's true. Golf also is a really difficult sport.

Jason: I didn't know you played golf.

Mary: I've been having golf lessons for about twelve months.

Jason: I prefer team sports.

Mary: What's your favorite sport?

Jason: My favorite sport is volleyball.

Mary: Volleyball is fun, but I think soccer is better.

Jason: I'm not very good at soccer. I can't control the ball well.

Mary: That's surprising. You're an excellent basketball player.

Jason: I guess I'm not good at using my feet.

Mary: I've been playing soccer since I was four years old.

Jason: I saw you play soccer last Sunday. You scored three goals.

Mary: I remember that game. The other team wasn't very good.

Jason: Yes. They lost badly, but they were good sports.

Mary: Hey, there's Susan. I'll see you later.

Jason: Have fun playing badminton!

Learn the English

Unscramble the sentences

1. more / practice / lot / needs / a / Tennis

_____

2. golf / I / played / didn't / know / you

_____

3. tennis / I / think / than / difficult / more / badminton / is

_____

Answer the questions

1. Who is Mary going to play badminton with?

_____

2. What is Jason doing today?

_____

3. How long has Mary been having golf lessons?

_____

4. Which sport is Jason excellent at?

_____

5. How many goals did Mary score in the soccer game?

_____

Test

Write the answer next to the letter "A"

A: ___ **1.** "I think tennis is ___ than badminton."

a. most difficult   b. more difficult   c. difficult   d. difficulter

A: ___ **2.** "I've been having golf lessons ___ about twelve months."

a. for   b. of   c. on   d. in

A: ___ **3.** Mary thinks golf is a ___ sport.

a. really difficult   b. real difficult   c. really easy   d. real easy

A: ___ **4.** Jason is not very ___ soccer.

a. good for   b. bad for   c. good at   d. bad at

A: ___ **5.** Did Mary score four goals at the soccer game last Sunday?

a. No, she don't.   b. Yes, she did.   c. No, she did.   d. No, she didn't.

A: ___ **6.** Mary ___ been playing soccer since she was four years old.

a. is   b. have   c. has   d. had

A: ___ **7.** Jason's favorite sport is ___.

a. basketball   b. volleyball   c. soccer   d. golf

A: ___ **8.** Jason can't control the ball ___.

a. well   b. good   c. badly   d. bad

Answers on page 372

Lesson 7: At the zoo

Hayvanat bahçesinde

How many lions are there?
There are two lions.

Learn the words

1. **monkey**
   Maymun
2. **lion**
   Aslan
3. **tiger**
   Kaplan
4. **rhino**
   Gergedan
5. **bear**
   Ayı
6. **penguin**
   Penguen
7. **giraffe**
   Zürafa
8. **elephant**
   Fil
9. **kangaroo**
   Kanguru
10. **crocodile**
    Timsah

Learn a verb

like – liking – liked – liked beğenmek

Helen: That's right. I really like kangaroos. They are so amazing.

Learn an idiom

Let the cat out of the bag

Meaning: To let someone know a secret.

"He *let the cat out of the bag* about the surprise party."

Conversation

Helen: Thanks for coming with me to the zoo today.

Emily: I love the zoo!

Helen: Me, too. I haven't been there for two years.

Emily: They have new animals now.

Helen: Really? Which new animals do they have?

Emily: I heard they have giraffes now.

Helen: How many giraffes do they have?

Emily: There are four giraffes. One of them is a baby giraffe.

Helen: That's so cute!

Emily: Last time I went, I thought the penguins were the cutest.

Helen: Are penguins your favorite animal?

Emily: No, my favorite animal is a lion. The zoo doesn't have any.

Helen: That's too bad.

Emily: Your favorite animal is a kangaroo, right?

Helen: That's right. I really like kangaroos. They are so amazing.

Emily: I didn't want to let the cat out of the bag, but guess what?

Helen: What?

Emily: There are two baby kangaroos at the zoo now.

Helen: Wow! I'm so excited to see them.

Emily: I wanted to make it a surprise and not tell you.

Helen: You know baby kangaroos are called joeys, right?

Emily: That's right! I forgot. Which animal should we see first?

Helen: The monkeys are funny. Let's go see them first.

Learn the English

Find the mistakes and write the sentence correctly

Emily: No, my favorite animal is a tiger. The zoo doesn't have any.

_____

Helen: The bears are funny. Let's go see them later.

_____

Emily: There are three giraffes. Two of them are baby giraffes.

_____

Answer the questions

1. Where are the girls going?

_____

2. What is Helen's favorite animal?

_____

3. Which animal does Emily think is the cutest?

_____

4. What are baby kangaroos called?

_____

5. Which animal does Helen think is funny?

_____

Test

Write the answer next to the letter "A"

A: ___ **1.** Helen ___ to the zoo for two years.

a. haven't been   b. hasn't been   c. have been   d. has been

A: ___ **2.** There are four giraffes and one of ___ is a baby.

a. it   b. they   c. animal   d. them

A: ___ **3.** Emily thinks ___ are the cutest animals.

a. penguins   b. giraffes   c. monkeys   d. kangaroos

A: ___ **4.** The zoo ___ any lions.

a. doesn't have   b. don't have   c. have   d. has

A: ___ **5.** Helen thinks kangaroos ___.

a. amazing   b. is amazing   c. are amazing   d. amazingly

A: ___ **6.** Helen ___ likes kangaroos.

a. real   b. very   c. really   d. does

A: ___ **7.** Baby kangaroos ___ called ___.

a. is, joeys   b. is, joey   c. are, joey   d. are, joeys

A: ___ **8.** They want to see the monkeys ___.

a. first   b. last   c. later   d. now

Answers on page 372

Lesson 8: Colors

Renkler

> What is your favorite color?
> My favorite color is red.

Learn the words

1. **red**
   Kırmızı
2. **blue**
   Mavi
3. **orange**
   Turuncu
4. **pink**
   Pembe
5. **black**
   Siyah
6. **yellow**
   Sarı
7. **green**
   Yeşil
8. **purple**
   Mor
9. **brown**
   Kahverengi
10. **white**
    Beyaz

Learn a verb

draw – drawing – drew – drawn çizmek

Susan: I'm not sure about what I should draw.

Learn an idiom

Feeling blue

Meaning: Feeling unhappy.

"He's *feeling blue* today because he lost the game."

Conversation

Susan: What are you drawing?

Jessica: I'm drawing my family.

Susan: Why do you want to draw your family?

Jessica: It's for Thanksgiving. I'm making a thank you card.

Susan: That's a great idea. Where did you get the pink paper?

Jessica: I bought it at the bookstore.

Susan: Is pink your favorite color?

Jessica: No, it isn't. My favorite color is purple.

Susan: Why didn't you buy purple paper?

Jessica: I wanted to, but the store didn't have any purple paper.

Susan: That's a shame.

Jessica: I'm feeling a little blue. I wanted to use purple paper.

Susan: Is that your mom? I didn't know she has black hair.

Jessica: She changed her hair color from brown a week ago.

Susan: I like her red dress. You draw really well.

Jessica: Thank you. I like to draw.

Susan: I'm not sure about what I should draw.

Jessica: What are you thankful for?

Susan: I really like our new house. Maybe I should draw that.

Jessica: You'll need a lot of different colors for the front yard.

Susan: I know! Mom planted a lot of colorful flowers.

Jessica: The yellow flowers are my favorite.

Susan: Mine, too. They are called carnations.

Learn the English

Put the sentences in order

Jessica: I'm drawing my family. ___

Susan: What are you drawing? ___

Jessica: No, it isn't. My favorite color is purple. ___

Susan: Is pink your favorite color? ___

Jessica: It's for Thanksgiving. I'm making a thank you card. ___

Susan: That's a great idea. Where did you get the pink paper? ___

Jessica: I bought it at the bookstore. ___

Susan: Why do you want to draw your family? ___

Answer the questions

1. What is Jessica drawing a picture of?

_____

2. What color paper did Jessica buy?

_____

3. Where did Jessica buy the paper at?

_____

4. What color hair did Jessica's mother have before?

_____

5. What is Susan thankful for?

_____

Test

Write the answer next to the letter "A"

A: ___ **1.** Jessica is ___ a picture ___ her family.

a. draw, of   b. drawing, of   c. drawing, for   d. draws, for

A: ___ **2.** Susan ___ Jessica's thank you card is a great idea.

a. thought   b. think   c. thinking   d. thinks

A: ___ **3.** Did Jessica want to use pink paper?

a. No, she did.   b. No, she didn't.   c. Yes, she did.   d. No, she doesn't.

A: ___ **4.** Susan ___ know Jessica's mother has black hair.

a. isn't   b. don't   c. didn't   d. doesn't

A: ___ **5.** Susan thinks Jessica ___ very ___.

a. draw, well   b. draw, good   c. draws, well   d. draws, good

A: ___ **6.** Susan didn't know what ___.

a. to draw   b. will draw   c. draw   d. drawing

A: ___ **7.** Susan is thankful ___ her new house.

a. with   b. of   c. for   d. to

A: ___ **8.** Susan's mother planted ___ colorful flowers.

a. a lot   b. many   c. a few   d. a little

Answers on page 372

Lesson 9: Activities

Aktiviteler

What do you like to do?
I like to read books.

Learn the words

1. **play piano**
   Piyano çalmak
2. **read books**
   Kitap okumak
3. **play video games**
   Video oyunu oynamak
4. **surf the internet**
   İnternette gezinmek
5. **take photos**
   Fotoğraf çekmek
6. **watch TV**
   Televizyon izlemek
7. **sing songs**
   Şarkı söylemek
8. **study English**
   İngilizce çalışmak
9. **play cards**
   Kart oynamak
10. **go shopping**
    Alışverişe gitmek

Learn a verb

read – reading – read – read okumak

Matthew: I like to read books, but I'm feeling lazy. Let's watch TV.

Learn an idiom

Shop around

Meaning: To shop at different stores to find the best price.

"You should *shop around* before you buy this piano."

Conversation

Matthew: What did you do last weekend?

John: I was playing video games.

Matthew: Which game were you playing?

John: I was playing the new hockey game.

Matthew: Awesome. I wanted to buy it, but it's too expensive.

John: You can shop around online. It's cheaper on the internet.

Matthew: Cool. I will surf the internet tonight.

John: What did you do last weekend?

Matthew: I studied English on Saturday.

John: Was that fun?

Matthew: Yes, it was. I like to study English.

John: Where do you study English?

Matthew: There's an English class I attend near the train station.

John: I know that place. My sister plays piano next door.

Matthew: I didn't know she plays piano.

John: She's been playing piano for three years.

Matthew: How about you?

John: I don't like to play piano. It's too difficult.

Matthew: What do you want to do now?

John: We can play cards or read books.

Matthew: I like to read books, but I'm feeling lazy. Let's watch TV.

John: Sure, but only for thirty minutes. I have to go shopping.

Matthew: That's fine. I have to take photos for art class later.

Learn the English

Fill in the blanks

Matthew: Which _____ were you _____?

John: I _____ playing the _____ hockey game.

John: What _____ you do _____ weekend?

Matthew: I _____ English _____ Saturday.

John: I know that _____. My sister plays _____ next door.

Matthew: I _____ know she _____ piano.

John: I _____ like to play piano. It's too _____.

Answer the questions

1. What was John doing last weekend?

_____

2. Why couldn't Matthew buy the hockey game?

_____

3. Where is Matthew's English class?

_____

4. How long has John's sister been playing piano?

_____

5. How long will they watch TV for?

_____

Test

Write the answer next to the letter "A"

A: ___ **1.** Last weekend, John ___ playing video games.

a. are   b. is   c. were   d. was

A: ___ **2.** The hockey game is ___ to buy on the ___.

a. cheaper, internet   b. cheap, online   c. expensive, internet   d. cheap, shop

A: ___ **3.** Matthew ___ the internet tonight.

a. surf   b. will surf   c. surfs   d. surfing

A: ___ **4.** Matthew attends an English class near the ___ station.

a. radio   b. police   c. fire   d. train

A: ___ **5.** John's sister has a piano class ___ to Matthew's English class.

a. near   b. by   c. next   d. beside

A: ___ **6.** Is playing piano too difficult for John?

a. Yes, it has.   b. Yes, it does.   c. Yes, it has been.   d. Yes, it is.

A: ___ **7.** What will John do after they watch TV?

a. Go shopping.   b. Play cards.   c. Read books.   d. Take photos.

A: ___ **8.** Which class does Matthew have to take photos for?

a. English class.   b. Piano class.   c. Art class.   d. History class.

Answers on page 372

Lesson 10: Food & Drinks

Yiyecek ve içecekler

How much tea is there?
There is a lot of tea.

Learn the words

1. **cake**
   Pasta
2. **cheese**
   Peynir
3. **milk**
   Süt
4. **tea**
   Çay
5. **soda**
   Soda
6. **pizza**
   Pizza
7. **water**
   Su
8. **juice**
   Meyve suyu
9. **coffee**
   Kahve
10. **pie**
    Turta

Learn a verb

want – wanting – wanted – wanted istemek

Helen: Do you want something to drink while we wait for the pizza?

Learn an idiom

Put food on the table

Meaning: To make money for the household expenses.

"I need this job to *put food on the table*."

Conversation

Helen: What do you want to eat for lunch Kevin?

Kevin: I'm not sure. What do you have?

Helen: Let me check what's in the refrigerator.

Kevin: I haven't eaten all day, so I'm pretty hungry.

Helen: There's an apple pie in the refrigerator.

Kevin: Okay. How much pie is there?

Helen: There is only a little pie.

Kevin: Perhaps we should order a pizza. What do you think?

Helen: I think that's a good idea.

Kevin: What flavor pizza do you like?

Helen: I'm happy with a cheese pizza.

Kevin: That sounds good. Get some lemon soda as well.

Helen: We have some milk tea in the refrigerator.

Kevin: Oh, okay. Milk tea is fine. Is one pizza enough?

Helen: I think so. We have a chocolate cake for later.

Kevin: Was the cake baked by your mom?

Helen: Yes, it was.

Kevin: Your mom makes delicious cakes.

Helen: Do you want a drink while we wait for the pizza?

Kevin: Sure. Do you have any juice?

Helen: Sorry. Mom's working and hasn't gone shopping this week.

Kevin: No problem. Somebody has to put food on the table!

Helen: I'm starting to feel hungry now, too!

Learn the English

Unscramble the sentences

1. idea / a / that's / think / good / I

_____

2. have / later / We / cake / for / chocolate / a

_____

3. in / refrigerator / the / milk tea / We / some / have

_____

Answer the questions

1. Why is Kevin hungry?

_____

2. What flavor pizza did Helen order?

_____

3. What are they going to drink with the pizza?

_____

4. Who baked the chocolate cake?

_____

5. What does Kevin think about her mother's cakes?

_____

Test

Write the answer next to the letter "A"

A: ___ **1.** Kevin ___ eaten all day, ___ he's pretty hungry.

a. haven't, and   b. hasn't, so   c. has, but   d. have, therefore

A: ___ **2.** There ___ an apple pie in the refrigerator.

a. was   b. have   c. had   d. were

A: ___ **3.** How ___ pie is ___ in the refrigerator?

a. much, that   b. many, there   c. much, there   d. many, here

A: ___ **4.** Who was happy with a cheese pizza?

a. Both children.   b. Helen.   c. Kevin.   d. Nobody.

A: ___ **5.** Did Helen order some lemon soda?

a. Yes, she is.   b. No, she didn't.   c. Yes, she does.   d. Yes, she did.

A: ___ **6.** Kevin ___ to drink lemon soda, but they had milk tea instead.

a. wants   b. want   c. wanted   d. wanting

A: ___ **7.** Helen's mother hasn't gone shopping because she is ___.

a. working   b. works   c. work   d. worked

A: ___ **8.** Helen's ___ puts ___ on the table in their family.

a. mother, money   b. father, money   c. father, food   d. mother, food

Answers on page 372

Lesson 11: At the fruit market

Manavda

What do you want?
I want an apple.

Learn the words

1. **orange**
   Portakal
2. **pear**
   Armut
3. **watermelon**
   Karpuz
4. **strawberry**
   Çilek
5. **cherry**
   Vişne
6. **lemon**
   Limon
7. **banana**
   Muz
8. **grape**
   Üzüm
9. **pineapple**
   Ananas
10. **apple**
    Elma

Learn a verb

need – needing – needed – needed gerekmek

Helen: There are two oranges, but I need them for tonight.

Learn an idiom

A bad apple

Meaning: The one bad person in a good group.

"He is *a bad apple* on this basketball team."

Conversation

Tom: Hi, Helen. Did you just get home?

Helen: Hey, Tom. Yes, I just went shopping at the fruit market.

Tom: Wow! It looks like you got a lot of different things.

Helen: Yes, I'm going to prepare some fruit for dessert tonight.

Tom: Actually, I want to eat some fruit right now.

Helen: What do you want?

Tom: I want an apple. Is there an apple?

Helen: No, there isn't. The market didn't have any apples today.

Tom: I want an orange, then. Can I have an orange?

Helen: There are two oranges, but I need them for tonight.

Tom: That's okay. I'll wait until later. Who is coming tonight?

Helen: I invited John, Susan, and Emily.

Tom: Is Mary going to come for dinner, too?

Helen: I think she's a bad apple, so I didn't ask her.

Tom: Okay. What other fruit do you need for tonight?

Helen: I need a watermelon and two bananas.

Tom: Are there two bananas? I don't see any here.

Helen: Yes, they're under the grapes and the pears.

Tom: I don't want a pear. I like cherries more.

Helen: I bought a lemon and a pineapple, too.

Tom: Hmmm...There's only one other thing I need.

Helen: Oh? What do you need?

Tom: I need some strawberry ice cream.

Learn the English

Find the mistakes and write the sentence correctly

Helen: There are two apples, but I want them for tomorrow.

_____

Tom: Are there four pineapples? I don't have any there.

_____

Tom: I don't need a lemon. I like oranges better.

_____

Answer the questions

1. Where did Helen just go shopping?

_____

2. What is Helen going to prepare?

_____

3. Why didn't Helen buy any apples?

_____

4. Who did Helen invite for dinner?

_____

5. Where are the bananas?

_____

Test

Write the answer next to the letter "A"

A: ___ **1.** Helen just went shopping at the ___.

a. supermarket   b. fruit market   c. night market   d. store

A: ___ **2.** Helen is going to prepare some ___ for dessert tonight.

a. ice cream   b. pie   c. fruit   d. cake

A: ___ **3.** Does Tom eat an orange?

a. Yes, he does.   b. No, he doesn't.   c. Yes, he can.   d. No, he isn't.

A: ___ **4.** How many apples did Helen buy today?

a. None.   b. One.   c. Two.   d. Three.

A: ___ **5.** Helen thinks Mary is a bad ___.

a. grape   b. pineapple   c. orange   d. apple

A: ___ **6.** Tom doesn't see any ___.

a. cherries   b. grapes   c. pears   d. bananas

A: ___ **7.** Tom likes ___ better than pears.

a. cherries   b. grapes   c. pineapples   d. lemons

A: ___ **8.** What kind of dessert did Tom want?

a. Grapes.   b. Strawberries.   c. Ice cream.   d. Cherries.

Answers on page 372

Lesson 12: Shapes

Şekiller

> What color is this circle?
> This is a green circle.

Learn the words

1. **square**
   Kare
2. **circle**
   Çember
3. **star**
   Yıldız
4. **heart**
   Kalp
5. **octagon**
   Sekizgen
6. **triangle**
   Üçgen
7. **rectangle**
   dikdörtgen
8. **oval**
   Oval
9. **diamond**
   Elmas
10. **pentagon**
    Beşgen

Learn a verb

find – finding – found – found bulmak

Jason: I'm doing homework. I have to find shapes in this picture.

Learn an idiom

Be out of shape

Meaning: To be unfit or overweight.

"He can't climb this mountain. He *is* really *out of shape*!"

Conversation

Susan: What are you doing right now?

Jason: I'm doing homework. I have to find shapes in this picture.

Susan: What do you mean?

Jason: For example, this table is a blue oval.

Susan: Oh, I see! This stop sign is a red octagon!

Jason: That's right, and this painting is a green square.

Susan: Interesting! Look at this clock. Is this circle white?

Jason: No, it isn't. It's yellow. You're good at finding shapes.

Susan: It's pretty fun. What color is that door?

Jason: That door is a brown rectangle. Nice work!

Susan: What other homework do you have to do?

Jason: Well, I also have to draw some shapes and colors.

Susan: It says that you have to draw a heart and a star.

Jason: Those are easy, but I'm not very good at drawing.

Susan: That's because you like sports more than homework.

Jason: Well, I don't want to be out of shape.

Susan: Yes, but you also need to finish your homework on time.

Jason: Just help me find a diamond and a pentagon.

Susan: Okay, and then we can go outside. It's a sunny day.

Jason: I'll do this quickly, so then we can go to the park.

Susan: Wait, is this triangle black?

Jason: Yes, it is. Now, you're finding all of my mistakes.

Susan: Let's make sure you do it right.

Learn the English

Put the sentences in order

Jason: That door is a brown rectangle. Nice work! ____

Jason: Those are easy, but I'm not very good at drawing. ____

Susan: What other homework do you have to do? ____

Jason: Well, I don't want to be out of shape. ____

Susan: It's pretty fun. What color is that door? ____

Susan: It says that you have to draw a heart and a star. ____

Jason: Well, I also have to draw some shapes and colors. ____

Susan: That's because you like sports more than homework. ____

Answer the questions

1. What is Jason doing now?

_____

2. What shape is the table?

_____

3. What does Jason have to draw?

_____

4. Where do they want to go?

_____

5. How is the weather?

_____

Test

Write the answer next to the letter "A"

A: ___ **1.** Jason ___ to find shapes in the picture.

a. have   b. got   c. is   d. has

A: ___ **2.** The stop sign is a red ___.

a. octagon   b. circle   c. oval   d. pentagon

A: ___ **3.** Does Jason have other homework to do?

a. Yes, he will.   b. Yes, he does.   c. No, he won't.   d. No, he doesn't.

A: ___ **4.** Jason ___ very good at drawing.

a. doesn't   b. can't   c. isn't   d. hasn't

A: ___ **5.** Susan says he ___ sports more than drawing.

a. finds   b. liking   c. likes   d. like

A: ___ **6.** Jason doesn't want to be out of ___.

a. color   b. shape   c. oval   d. homework

A: ___ **7.** Susan is ___ all of Jason's mistakes.

a. finding   b. found   c. looking   d. look

A: ___ **8.** The ___ is ___.

a. heart, red   b. circle, white   c. square, blue   d. triangle, black

Answers on page 372

Lesson 13: At the supermarket

Süpermarket

What do you want to buy?
I want to buy some bread.

Learn the words

1. **milk**
   Süt
2. **juice**
   Meyve suyu
3. **meat**
   Et
4. **drinks**
   İçecek
5. **vegetables**
   Sebze
6. **ice cream**
   Dondurma
7. **fruit**
   Meyve
8. **bread**
   Ekmek
9. **fish**
   Balık
10. **pizza**
    Pizza

Learn a verb

get – getting – got – gotten almak

Max: No, I got some pizza yesterday.

Learn an idiom

A rip off

Meaning: Something is too expensive.

"The supermarket around the corner is *a rip off*."

Conversation

Max: I love shopping at different supermarkets.

Julie: You really like going out to buy different food and drinks.

Max: Yes, I like to shop around for the lowest prices.

Julie: I hope I can help. What do you want to buy first?

Max: First, I want to buy some vegetables.

Julie: Do you want to buy some fruit, too?

Max: No, I don't want to buy any fruit here.

Julie: Oh? Why don't you want to buy any fruit?

Max: The fruit at this place is a rip off!

Julie: Okay, so you'll buy fruit at the next place?

Max: Yes, that's right. I also want to buy some bread.

Julie: That sounds good. Do you want to get some pizza?

Max: No, I got some pizza yesterday.

Julie: What else do you want to buy from here?

Max: I want to buy some fish and some meat.

Julie: Do you also want to buy some juice or drinks?

Max: I would like some drinks. I don't need any juice.

Julie: I also see some ice cream and milk over there.

Max: I don't want anything sweet, so I don't want any ice cream.

Julie: Do you want to buy some milk?

Max: No, I don't. I know a better place to buy milk.

Julie: You really are a good shopper. You know all the best places.

Max: Well, eating is one of my favorite hobbies!

Learn the English

Fill in the blanks

Max: First, I want to _____ some _____.

Julie: _____ you want to buy some _____, too?

Max: No, I _____ want to buy _____ fruit here.

Julie: Oh? _____ don't you _____ to buy any fruit?

Max: The fruit at this _____ is a rip _____!

Julie: Okay, so _____ buy fruit at the _____ place?

Max: Yes, that's _____. I also want to buy some _____.

Answer the questions

1. What does Max love doing?

_____

2. Does Max want to buy some fruit?

_____

3. When did Max buy some pizza?

_____

4. What is one of Max's favorite hobbies?

_____

5. Why doesn't Max want ice cream?

_____

Test

Write the answer next to the letter "A"

A: ___ **1.** Max really ___ going out to ___ food and drinks.

a. likes, buys   b. like, get   c. like, eat   d. likes, buy

A: ___ **2.** Max shops ___ for the lowest prices.

a. off   b. on   c. over   d. around

A: ___ **3.** Julie asked Max if he wanted to buy ___.

a. fish   b. fruit   c. meat   d. bread

A: ___ **4.** They didn't buy ___ because it was a rip ___.

a. bread, over   b. fruit, off   c. pizza, around   d. juice, on

A: ___ **5.** When did Max get pizza?

a. Last week.   b. First.   c. Yesterday.   d. On Monday.

A: ___ **6.** Max also wanted to buy some ___ and ___.

a. bread, juice   b. pizza, milk   c. vegetables, ice cream   d. fish, meat

A: ___ **7.** Max said he knew a ___ place to buy milk.

a. better   b. favorite   c. sweet   d. cheaper

A: ___ **8.** What did Max say was one of his favorite hobbies?

a. Buying.   b. Shopping.   c. Eating.   d. Getting.

Answers on page 372

Lesson 14: At the ice cream shop

Dondurma dükkanında

Which flavor do you like?
I like mint flavor.

Learn the words

1. **chocolate**
   Çikolata
2. **strawberry**
   Çilek
3. **mint**
   Nane
4. **raspberry**
   Ahududu
5. **cherry**
   Vişne
6. **vanilla**
   Vanilya
7. **coffee**
   Kahve
8. **almond**
   Badem
9. **caramel**
   Karame
10. **coconut**
    Hindistan cevizi

Learn a verb

have/has – having – had – had sahip olmak

John: My friend said that the ice cream shop has many flavors.

Learn an idiom

Flavor of the month

Meaning: Something is suddenly popular for a short time.

"This song is just the *flavor of the month*."

Conversation

Bob: I went out with my brother last Tuesday to play volleyball.

John: That sounds fun. Where did you go to play?

Bob: After lunch, we went to the beach with some friends.

John: How many people went with you?

Bob: There were five people. My sister came with us, too.

John: I'm surprised your sister likes to play volleyball.

Bob: I think volleyball is just the flavor of the month for her.

John: What do you mean?

Bob: She'll like it for a short time, and then she'll change.

John: Ok. I also heard about a new ice cream shop near the beach.

Bob: Yes, we went there later. It's a small place beside a gym.

John: My friend said that the ice cream shop has many flavors.

Bob: Yes, it was really hard to choose. We all had different flavors.

John: Which flavor does your brother like?

Bob: He likes raspberry, but doesn't like cherry flavor.

John: That's interesting. Does your sister like the same flavors?

Bob: No, she doesn't. She likes caramel, almond and coffee.

John: Does the shop have chocolate, vanilla and strawberry?

Bob: Yes, it does. It also has mint and coconut. It's great.

John: Now, I really want to go there. I feel like having ice cream.

Bob: Me, too. Actually, I think I like ice cream a little too much.

John: Oh? So, which flavor do you like?

Bob: Well, it was too hard to choose, so I had every flavor.

Learn the English

Unscramble the sentences

1. like / brother / does / flavor / your / Which

___

2. likes / and / coffee / caramel / She / almond

___

3. little / think / much / I / a / I / cream / ice / like / too

___

Answer the questions

1. Which day did they go to the beach?

___

2. Who did they go to the beach with?

___

3. Where is the ice cream shop?

___

4. What does John feel like having now?

___

5. What flavor did Bob have?

___

Test

Write the answer next to the letter "A"

A: ___ **1.** They went to the beach last ___ to play volleyball.

a. weekend   b. Tuesday   c. night   d. lunch

A: ___ **2.** ___ people went with them.

a. four   b. five   c. family   d. beach

A: ___ **3.** Bob thinks volleyball is the ___ of the ___ for his sister.

a. taste, month   b. play, day   c. flavor, month   d. taste, day

A: ___ **4.** John ___ there is a ___ ice cream shop near the beach.

a. saw, different   b. thinks, fun   c. read, flavor   d. heard, new

A: ___ **5.** Who said there were many different flavors?

a. Kevin.   b. Bob.   c. John.   d. Bob's brother.

A: ___ **6.** His brother likes ___, but doesn't like ___ flavor.

a. raspberry, cherry   b. cherry, raspberry   c. caramel, cherry   d. mint, coconut

A: ___ **7.** ___ thinks he ___ ice cream a little too much.

a. Bob, like   b. John, eats   c. Bob, likes   d. Bob's sister, has

A: ___ **8.** Bob said it ___ hard to ___ a flavor.

a. is, chosen   b. has, choice   c. was, choosing   d. was, choose

Answers on page 372

Lesson 15: In the refrigerator

Buzdolabında

> What do you want to eat?
> I want to eat rice.

Learn the words

1. **rice**
   Pirinç
2. **salad**
   Salata
3. **toast**
   Tost
4. **soup**
   Çorba
5. **dumplings**
   Hamur köftesi
6. **tea**
   Çay
7. **cola**
   Kola
8. **eggs**
   Yumurta
9. **water**
   Su
10. **ice**
    Buz

Learn a verb

sell – selling – sold – sold satmak

Peter: A man was selling them at the night market last night.

Learn an idiom

Be as cold as ice

Meaning: To describe someone who is very unfriendly.

"The teacher *was as cold as ice* after she caught me cheating on the science test."

Conversation

Peter: That was a really fun soccer game this morning.

Mary: Yes, the weather today was great. It wasn't too hot.

Peter: I think Emily wasn't happy when you scored against her.

Mary: Yeah, after the game she was as cold as ice.

Peter: I called her after we got home. She'll be fine.

Mary: Are you hungry? What do you want to eat?

Peter: I don't want to eat anything hot, like soup.

Mary: I think we have other things. What's in the refrigerator?

Peter: We have rice, eggs, and dumplings.

Mary: Where did you get the dumplings from?

Peter: A man was selling them at the night market last night.

Mary: Do you want to eat dumplings?

Peter: No, I don't. I ate them last night. Do you want to eat toast?

Mary: No, I don't want to eat toast. Maybe I'll just have salad.

Peter: What do you want to drink?

Mary: I want to drink tea or cola. Do we have ice?

Peter: Yes, we have ice. I don't want to drink anything sweet.

Mary: There's water. Do you want to drink water?

Peter: Yes, I do. I need to drink water after playing sports today.

Mary: Your brother is at home too. What does he want to drink?

Peter: He doesn't like tea or soda. Maybe he wants to drink juice.

Mary: I'll ask him if he wants water, juice, or milk.

Peter: Wow! It's really difficult to get food and drinks for everyone.

Learn the English

Find the mistakes and write the sentence correctly

Peter: A boy was selling them at the cinema last night.

_____

Mary: No, I don't want to eat meat. Maybe I'll just have candy.

_____

Peter: He doesn't like milk or cola. Maybe she wants to drink tea.

_____

Answer the questions

1. When did they play soccer?

_____

2. What does Peter not want to eat?

_____

3. Where did Peter get the dumplings from?

_____

4. What does Mary want to drink?

_____

5. Who was as cold as ice?

_____

Test

Write the answer next to the letter "A"

A: ___ **1.** The weather was ___. It wasn't too ___.

a. hot, great   b. ice, cold   c. fun, hot   d. great, hot

A: ___ **2.** Emily wasn't ___ after the game.

a. hungry   b. friendly   c. eating   d. drinking

A: ___ **3.** Peter didn't want to eat anything ___.

a. cold   b. ice   c. difficult   d. hot

A: ___ **4.** He got the ___ at the night market.

a. dumplings   b. eggs   c. rice   d. toast

A: ___ **5.** Mary ___ want to eat toast.

a. don't   b. did   c. doesn't   d. do

A: ___ **6.** Peter needs to drink water after ___.

a. eating   b. dumplings   c. playing sports   d. selling

A: ___ **7.** Peter's brother doesn't like ___ or ___.

a. tea, soda   b. tea, juice   c. water, milk   d. soda, juice

A: ___ **8.** Peter said it's ___ to get food and drinks for everyone.

a. fun   b. difficult   c. great   d. sweet

Answers on page 372

Lesson 16: Jobs

Meslekler

What is her job?
She is a salesclerk.

Learn the words

1. **doctor**
   Doktor
2. **cook**
   Aşçı
3. **nurse**
   Hemşire
4. **police officer**
   Polis memuru
5. **taxi driver**
   Taksi şoförü
6. **teacher**
   Öğretmen
7. **farmer**
   Çiftçi
8. **salesclerk**
   Satıcı
9. **firefighter**
   İtfaiyeci
10. **builder**
    İnşaatçı

Learn a verb

work – working – worked – worked çalışmak

John: My aunt has a job working with food. She loves it.

Learn an idiom

Keep up the good work

Meaning: To encourage someone to keep doing well.

"You're doing a great job. *Keep up the good work*."

Conversation

Sam: I saw Matthew's father working yesterday in the city.

John: You saw his father? What's his job?

Sam: He's a police officer. He was driving a police car.

John: I thought his father was a firefighter. Is he a firefighter, too?

Sam: No, he was before, but he changed jobs.

John: I told the teacher I want to have a good job in the future.

Sam: Me too. He said to study, and to keep up the good work.

John: I think I want to be a doctor or a nurse.

Sam: You'll have to study hard. I want a job working with food.

John: My aunt has a job working with food. She loves it.

Sam: Is she a cook?

John: No, she isn't. She's a farmer. She sells many vegetables.

Sam: My brother has a job selling things right now, too.

John: Is he a salesclerk?

Sam: Yes, he is, but he wants to get a job as a builder this fall.

John: Mary's parents were builders before. Now they drive.

Sam: Are they taxi drivers?

John: Yes, they are. They work very hard every day.

Sam: I guess that's why Mary doesn't have to walk anywhere.

John: I think the important thing is to get a job that's interesting.

Sam: I agree. I don't want to feel bored at my job.

John: Maybe you should play video games less and study more.

Sam: That's probably a good idea. I'll start after this game!

Learn the English

Put the sentences in order

Sam: You should study hard. I want a job working with food. ____

Sam: My brother has a job selling things right now, too. ____

Sam: Is she a cook? ____

John: Is he a salesclerk? ____

John: I think I want to be a doctor or a nurse. ____

John: My aunt has a job working with food. She loves it. ____

Sam: Yes, he is, but he wants to get a job as a builder. ____

John: No, she isn't. She's a farmer. She sells vegetables. ____

Answer the questions

1. What is Matthew's father's job?

_____

2. What did John tell the teacher?

_____

3. Who has an aunt that works with food?

_____

4. What were Mary's parents before?

_____

5. Why does Sam want an interesting job?

_____

Test

Write the answer next to the letter "A"

A: ___ **1.** Sam saw Matthew's father ___ .

a. today   b. yesterday   c. this morning   d. Tuesday

A: ___ **2.** Matthew's father was ___ a police car.

a. drive   b. drove   c. drives   d. driving

A: ___ **3.** The teacher said to keep ___ the good work.

a. up   b. on   c. in   d. over

A: ___ **4.** John's ___ has a job ___ with food.

a. aunt, working   b. mother, cooking   c. uncle, work   d. father, selling

A: ___ **5.** Sam's ___ has a job ___ things.

a. aunt, working   b. brother, selling   c. father, driving   d. aunt, farming

A: ___ **6.** ___ parents work very hard every day.

a. Sam   b. Sam's   c. Mary's   d. Mary

A: ___ **7.** Who wants to get a job that's interesting?

a. Sam's aunt.   b. Matthew.   c. Mary.   d. John.

A: ___ **8.** Who should play video games less and study more?

a. John.   b. Mary.   c. Sam.   d. John's brother.

Answers on page 372

Lesson 17: Names

İsimler

Learn the words

1. John
2. Matthew
3. Jason
4. Helen
5. Mary
6. Kevin
7. Tom
8. Emily
9. Jessica
10. Susan

Learn a verb

call – calling – called – called aramak

Kevin: Sure, and we can also call some old friends to meet us.

Learn an idiom

A household name

Meaning: To describe someone famous who everyone knows.

"The actor became *a household name* after he won an Oscar for his performance."

Conversation

Kevin: Hey, what are you doing right now?

Ted: I'm looking at some old pictures of friends and family.

Kevin: That's interesting. Is this for homework?

Ted: It isn't homework. I just like things from a long time ago.

Kevin: Where did you find them? There are so many pictures.

Ted: I found an old box upstairs after I came home from the gym.

Kevin: This guy looks like you, but older. What's his name?

Ted: That's my uncle. His name is Jason. His friends call him J.

Kevin: The woman beside him, is her name Emily?

Ted: That's right, it's my Aunt Emily. She's my uncle's wife.

Kevin: Who's this other guy that's playing the piano?

Ted: That's another uncle. He was a household name before.

Kevin: He was a famous singer, right? What's his name?

Ted: His name is John. He wasn't a singer, he was a famous cook.

Kevin: Hey, here's our old school photo too.

Ted: This girl in the front, what's her name?

Kevin: Her name's Susan, she's at a different school now.

Ted: There's Tom, Helen, Mary, and Jessica. We look so young!

Kevin: Hey, look at the time. We should get something to eat.

Ted: Do you want to go to a restaurant for dinner?

Kevin: Sure, and we can also call some old friends to meet us.

Ted: Okay. Where do you want to go eat?

Kevin: How about your famous uncle cooks for us?

Learn the English

Fill in the blanks

Kevin: The woman _____ him, is her _____ Emily?

Ted: _____ right, it's my Aunt Emily. She's my _____ wife.

Kevin: Who's this _____ guy that's playing the _____?

Ted: That's another _____. He was a _____ name before.

Kevin: He was a _____ singer? _____ his name?

Ted: _____ name is John. He was a famous _____.

Kevin: Hey, _____'s our old _____ photo too.

Answer the questions

1. What is Ted doing right now?

_____

2. Where did he find the box of old pictures?

_____

3. When did he find the box?

_____

4. What did they call his uncle John before?

_____

5. What was the girl's name in the front of the school photo?

_____

Test

Write the answer next to the letter "A"

A: ___ **1.** Ted is looking at pictures of ___ and ___.

a. friends, family   b. animals, friends   c. aunts, uncles   d. sisters, brothers

A: ___ **2.** Are the pictures a part of Ted's homework?

a. No, they didn't.   b. Yes, they are.   c. Yes, they can.   d. No, they aren't.

A: ___ **3.** He ___ the pictures in an ___ box upstairs.

a. found, old   b. saw, orange   c. bought, open   d. got, ugly

A: ___ **4.** Before he looked at the pictures, he was at the ___.

a. school   b. restaurant   c. gym   d. household

A: ___ **5.** The person who looks like Ted is his ___.

a. father   b. aunt   c. uncle   d. grandfather

A: ___ **6.** Uncle John ___ a singer, he was a ___ cook.

a. was, great   b. wasn't, famous   c. isn't, bad   d. couldn't, household

A: ___ **7.** They want to go to a ___ and eat ___.

a. store, dinner   b. restaurant, dinner   c. park, lunch   d. school, snacks

A: ___ **8.** Who did Kevin want to call to meet them?

a. A famous singer.   b. Aunt Emily.   c. Old friends.   d. Old uncles.

Answers on page 372

Lesson 18: More places

Daha çok yer

> Where did you go yesterday?
> I went to school.

Learn the words

1. **the library**
   Kütüphane
2. **school**
   Okul
3. **the hospital**
   Hastane
4. **the train station**
   Tren istasyonu
5. **the police station**
   Karakol
6. **the office**
   Ofis
7. **the factory**
   Fabrika
8. **the clinic**
   Klinik
9. **the bus stop**
   Otobüs durağı
10. **the fire station**
    İtfaiye merkezi

Learn a verb

go – going – went – gone gitmek

Kevin: Yeah, she wasn't feeling well, so she went to a clinic.

Learn an idiom

Heart is in the right place

Meaning: To mean well and try to do the right thing.

"He makes a lot of mistakes, but his *heart is in the right place*."

Conversation

Jessica: Hi, Kevin. I saw your sister last week at the bus stop.

Kevin: Yeah, she wasn't feeling well, so she went to a clinic.

Jessica: She didn't look very well, and she was coughing.

Kevin: Later, she wasn't feeling better, so we went to the hospital.

Jessica: Is she okay? I heard that many people are sick now.

Kevin: Yes, I was in the library on Monday and it was empty.

Jessica: Maybe I should bring your sister some soup.

Kevin: Well, your heart is in the right place, but I think she's fine.

Jessica: It's okay. On my way to the office, I'll go to her house.

Kevin: That's very nice. There's a good soup place near the school.

Jessica: How are you feeling? You look a bit tired.

Kevin: This week was really busy. I had to go to many places.

Jessica: Where did you go yesterday?

Kevin: I went to the train station. I had to meet my aunt.

Jessica: Is she the one who works at the police station?

Kevin: Yes, that's right. Then we went to the factory.

Jessica: Why did you go to the factory?

Kevin: Her friend works there, so she wanted to say hello.

Jessica: It really sounds like you had a busy week!

Kevin: Yes, I think I've gone to almost every place I know.

Jessica: Did you also go to the fire station yesterday?

Kevin: How did you know that we went to the fire station, too?

Jessica: Well, it's the only place in the city you didn't say yet.

Learn the English

Unscramble the sentences

1. go / did / yesterday / you / Where

___

2. the / Is / at / one / the / works / who / she / police / station

___

3. to / you / go / the / yesterday / also / station / Did / fire

___

Answer the questions

1. When did Jessica see Kevin's sister?

___

2. Who wasn't feeling well last week?

___

3. When was Kevin at the library?

___

4. Where is a good place to get soup?

___

5. Why did Kevin go to the train station?

___

Test

Write the answer next to the letter "A"

A: ___ **1.** Last week, Kevin's sister was at the ___.

a. bus stop   b. library   c. school   d. police station

A: ___ **2.** Jessica's heart is in the right ___.

a. beat   b. clinic   c. place   d. feeling

A: ___ **3.** Jessica heard many people are ___ right now.

a. well   b. coughing   c. empty   d. sick

A: ___ **4.** When Kevin's sister wasn't feeling better, she went to the ___.

a. school   b. library   c. hospital   d. bus stop

A: ___ **5.** Kevin's ___ was really ___.

a. sister, tired   b. month, sick   c. day, tired   d. week, busy

A: ___ **6.** Kevin and his ___ went to the ___.

a. sister, school   b. aunt, factory   c. brother, bus stop   d. aunt, clinic

A: ___ **7.** Kevin's ___ works at the ___.

a. aunt, factory   b. aunt, police station   c. sister, clinic   d. sister, library

A: ___ **8.** Did Kevin and his aunt go to the fire station?

a. Yes, they did.   b. Yes, the will.   c. No, they didn't.   d. No, they won't.

Answers on page 372

Lesson 19: Meats

Etler

> What did he eat for lunch?
> He ate chicken.

Learn the words

1. **beef**
   Sığır eti
2. **pork**
   Domuz
3. **bacon**
   Pastırma
4. **fish**
   Balık
5. **salami**
   Salam
6. **chicken**
   Tavuk
7. **lamb**
   Kuzu
8. **ham**
   Jambon
9. **sausage**
   Sosis
10. **shrimp**
    Karides

Learn a verb

eat – eating – ate – eaten yemek

Matthew: Yes, I want to start eating well and doing more exercise.

Learn an idiom

Beef up

Meaning: To strengthen something or somebody.

"We need to *beef up* our efforts if we are going to do well this year."

Conversation

Helen: Hi, Matthew. You've been looking very healthy recently.

Matthew: Yes, I want to start eating well and do more exercise.

Helen: I didn't know you enjoyed sports and exercise.

Matthew: Yes, my new plan is to go to the gym and beef up.

Helen: So, you'll need to eat well, too. What did you eat for lunch?

Matthew: I ate well! I didn't eat salami or sausage. I ate chicken.

Helen: If you want to eat meat, I have lots at home.

Matthew: So, you like to eat meat. Did you have pork for lunch?

Helen: Yes, I did. I also ate ham and bacon for breakfast.

Matthew: That's a lot of meat. Maybe you can try eating a salad.

Helen: Oh, I ate some vegetables, too. I like eating a lot.

Matthew: What did you eat for dinner?

Helen: For dinner, I ate lamb and fish. I didn't eat beef.

Matthew: Why didn't you eat beef?

Helen: Well, I wanted to eat some cake for dessert.

Matthew: Wow. You really eat a lot of food every day.

Helen: Yes, that's right. Oh! I also ate shrimp as a snack last night.

Matthew: If you're eating this much food, how can you be healthy?

Helen: I didn't say I was healthy, I just said I like eating.

Matthew: Maybe you and I should try playing sports sometime.

Helen: That's a good idea, but I'm not sure I can.

Matthew: Why not? I think it's a good idea to be in shape.

Helen: I need lots of time to buy food at the supermarket.

Learn the English

Find the mistakes and write the sentence correctly

Matthew: Yes, I want to start eating more and doing less exercise.

_____

Helen: Yes, I did. I also ate fish and salad for lunch.

_____

Helen: Well, I wanted to eat some beef for dinner.

_____

Answer the questions

1. What is Matthew's new plan?

_____

2. When did Matthew eat chicken?

_____

3. Why didn't Helen eat beef?

_____

4. Who ate shrimp as a snack last night?

_____

5. Where does Helen buy her food at?

_____

Test

Write the answer next to the letter "A"

A: ___ **1.** Matthew ___ been looking very healthy recently.

a. have   b. having   c. has   d. was

A: ___ **2.** Helen didn't know he enjoyed ___ and ___.

a. sports, exercise   b. beef, salami   c. gym, chicken   d. ham, breakfast

A: ___ **3.** Matthew didn't eat ___ and ___ for lunch.

a. ham, bacon   b. lamb, fish   c. salami, sausage   d. beef, salad

A: ___ **4.** Helen has lots of ___ in her refrigerator.

a. salad   b. meat   c. pork   d. shrimp

A: ___ **5.** Helen didn't eat ___ because she wanted ___.

a. sausage, chicken   b. salami, chicken   c. lamb, fish   d. beef, cake

A: ___ **6.** When did Helen eat shrimp?

a. For breakfast.   b. For dinner.   c. Every day.   d. Last night.

A: ___ **7.** Helen said she likes ___.

a. eating   b. supermarkets   c. being healthy   d. playing sports

A: ___ **8.** Matthew ___ Helen really ___ a lot of food.

a. saying, ate   b. thinking, eating   c. think, eat   d. thinks, eats

Answers on page 372

Lesson 20: Vegetables

Sebzeler

What will you cook tonight?
I will cook pumpkin.

Learn the words

1. **pumpkin**
   Balkabağı
2. **potato**
   Patates
3. **carrot**
   Havuç
4. **asparagus**
   Kuşkonmaz
5. **broccoli**
   Brokoli
6. **corn**
   Mısır
7. **cabbage**
   Lahana
8. **spinach**
   Ispanak
9. **mushroom**
   Mantar
10. **onion**
    Soğan

Learn a verb

cook – cooking – cooked – cooked pişirmek

Mary: Yes, my sister is cooking a big meal tomorrow night.

Learn an idiom

Carrot on a stick

Meaning: A reward that is promised upon completion of a task.

"The coach gave his players a *carrot on a stick* and promised to take them all out for dinner if they win the game."

Conversation

Tom: Wow! You really like to go shopping. That's a lot of stuff.

Mary: Yes, my sister is cooking a big meal tomorrow night.

Tom: What will she cook tomorrow?

Mary: We all like vegetables, so she'll cook mushrooms.

Tom: Will she only cook mushrooms?

Mary: No, she will also cook pumpkin, broccoli, and corn.

Tom: I see you also bought asparagus and cabbage.

Mary: Yes, she is really good at cooking. Hey, you should come!

Tom: I'm not sure if I can. I have to study English.

Mary: Emily will be there, and I know you like her.

Tom: You're just using her as a carrot on a stick, so I'll go.

Mary: Well, there will also be lots of great food.

Tom: Will your sister cook spinach? I love spinach.

Mary: Of course. She will also cook potato and carrot.

Tom: That's a lot. What won't she cook tomorrow?

Mary: She won't cook onion because it makes her cry.

Tom: If I don't go, I think I'll also cry. It sounds really great.

Mary: If you want to, you can bring some drinks.

Tom: Okay. I'll bring some juice, tea, and soda. How's that?

Mary: Good. Maybe also bring some fruit, meat, and ice cream.

Tom: Alright. Do you need anything else for this dinner?

Mary: Also, we need a little music, so you should play piano.

Tom: Wow! It sounds more like I'm the one having the party.

Learn the English

Put the sentences in order

Tom: I'm not sure if I can. I have to study English. ___

Mary: No, she will also cook pumpkin, broccoli, and corn. ___

Mary: We all like vegetables, so she'll cook mushrooms. ___

Mary: Emily will be there, and I know you like her. ___

Tom: I see you also bought asparagus and cabbage. ___

Mary: Yes, she is really good at cooking. You should come! ___

Tom: What will she cook tomorrow? ___

Tom: Will she only cook mushrooms? ___

Answer the questions

1. Who will cook a big meal tomorrow night?

_____

2. Why won't she cook onion?

_____

3. What did Mary also buy?

_____

4. Why is Tom not sure if he can go?

_____

5. What vegetables will she cook?

_____

Test

Write the answer next to the letter "A"

A: ___ **1.** Mary really ___ to go ___.

a. like, cooking   b. likes, cook   c. likes, shopping   d. like, shopping

A: ___ **2.** Her sister is cooking a big meal ___.

a. tomorrow night   b. tonight   c. on Monday   d. today

A: ___ **3.** Will she only cook mushrooms?

a. Yes, she will.   b. No, they can't.   c. No, she won't.   d. Yes, they cook.

A: ___ **4.** Mary also ___ asparagus.

a. shopped   b. cooked   c. fought   d. bought

A: ___ **5.** Tom loves ___.

a. Emily   b. spinach   c. potato   d. English

A: ___ **6.** She won't cook ___ because it makes her ___.

a. carrot, sad   b. onion, cry   c. onion, study   d. carrot, stick

A: ___ **7.** Tom said he'll ___ some drinks.

a. need   b. drink   c. buy   d. bring

A: ___ **8.** Mary said Tom should ___ the ___.

a. play, piano   b. find, drinks   c. bring, piano   d. cook, meat

Answers on page 372

Lesson 21: At school

Okulda

> Where is the art room?
> The art room is next to the gym.

Learn the words

1. **classroom**
   Sınıf
2. **office**
   Ofis
3. **nurse's office**
   Revir
4. **gym**
   Spor salonu
5. **hall**
   Salon

6. **computer lab**
   Bilgisayar laboratuarı
7. **art room**
   Sanat odası
8. **music room**
   Müzik odası
9. **science lab**
   Bilim laboratuarı
10. **lunchroom**
    Yemek odası

Learn a verb

put – putting – put – put koymak

Peter: I thought I had put it in the classroom, but it's not there.

Learn an idiom

Old school

Meaning: To do something the old-fashioned way.

"We're going to do this *old school* and use a hammer."

Conversation

Peter: Hey, Mary. Have you seen my towel?

Mary: No, I haven't. Why do you need it?

Peter: I have a swimming class at the gym today.

Mary: When did you last see it?

Peter: I thought I had put it in the classroom, but it's not there.

Mary: I saw you in the lunchroom this morning. Maybe it's there.

Peter: No, I checked.

Mary: What color is the towel?

Peter: It's yellow and blue.

Mary: I remember seeing a yellow and blue towel in the art room.

Peter: That's strange. Where is the art room?

Mary: It's across from the nurse's office. Why is that strange?

Peter: I don't take any art classes, so I don't go to the art room.

Mary: That is strange. Maybe that towel I saw isn't yours.

Peter: I really hope I can find it. My class starts in ten minutes.

Mary: Usually, people put lost property in the office.

Peter: Which one? There are two offices at this school.

Mary: The one next to the science lab.

Peter: Is that the office where Mr. Miller works?

Mary: Yes, that's the one.

Peter: He's old school. You must knock on his door before entering.

Mary: Hey, Peter. What's that blue thing sticking out of your bag?

Peter: Ha! That's my towel. I'm so embarrassed.

Learn the English

Fill in the blanks

Mary: When _____ you _____ see it?

Peter: I _____ I had put it in the _____, but it's not there.

Mary: That is strange. _____ that towel I saw isn't _____.

Peter: _____ one? There are two _____ at this school.

Mary: Usually, people put lost _____ in the _____.

Peter: Is that the office _____ Mr. Miller _____?

Mary: Yes, _____ the _____.

Answer the questions

1. What is Peter looking for?

_____

2. Why does Peter need a towel?

_____

3. Where did Mary see Peter this morning?

_____

4. Where is the art room?

_____

5. When does Peter's swimming class start?

_____

Test

Write the answer next to the letter "A"

A: ___ **1.** Peter ___ a swimming class ___ the gym today.

a. has, at b. have, in c. has, on d. have, at

A: ___ **2.** Peter thought the towel was in the ___.

a. science lab b. nurse's office c. classroom d. art room

A: ___ **3.** Mary saw a blue and yellow towel in the ___.

a. science lab b. nurse's office c. classroom d. art room

A: ___ **4.** The art room is ___ the nurse's office.

a. across for b. across c. across of d. across from

A: ___ **5.** Does Peter take any art classes now?

a. Yes, he does. b. No, he doesn't. c. Yes, he did. d. No, he didn't.

A: ___ **6.** Did Peter look for his towel at Mr. Miller's office?

a. Yes, he does. b. No, he doesn't. c. Yes, he did. d. No, he didn't.

A: ___ **7.** Peter's class is ___ ten minutes.

a. at b. on c. in d. of

A: ___ **8.** There ___ two offices at the school.

a. was b. are c. were d. is

Answers on page 373

Lesson 22: School subjects

Okul dersleri

What class do you have after math?
I have an art class after math.

Learn the words

1. **science**
   Fen
2. **English**
   İngilizce
3. **P.E.**
   Beden eğitimi
4. **geography**
   Coğrafya
5. **social studies**
   Sosyal bilgiler
6. **math**
   Matematik
7. **art**
   Sanat
8. **music**
   Müzik
9. **history**
   Tarih
10. **computer**
    Bilgisayar

Learn a verb

do – doing – did – done yapmak

Kevin: That surprises me. You always do well on science tests.

Learn an idiom

Cut class

Meaning: To miss class on purpose.

"Jenny *cut class* after she realized she didn't do her math homework."

Conversation

Jessica: Hey, Kevin. Did you study for today's math test?

Kevin: Yes, but only a little. I studied more for the English test.

Jessica: Why? Your English is really good.

Kevin: I'm worried about the words. They are difficult to spell.

Jessica: I'm nervous about the science test tomorrow.

Kevin: That surprises me. You always do well on science tests.

Jessica: This semester, I cut a lot of classes.

Kevin: I'm so happy there is no history test this semester!

Jessica: Me, too. However, there was a lot of homework.

Kevin: I know. The teacher always gives a lot of history homework.

Jessica: I thought yesterday's geography test was easy.

Kevin: Really? I thought it was difficult.

Jessica: Why did you think the test was difficult?

Kevin: There were too many questions about countries in Asia.

Jessica: I traveled around Asia last year, so it was easy for me.

Kevin: You are lucky. I had no idea where half the cities were!

Jessica: Hey, what time is it now?

Kevin: It's a quarter to one.

Jessica: I better go. I have a social studies class at one o'clock.

Kevin: What class do you have after social studies?

Jessica: I have an art class after social studies.

Kevin: Me, too. I'll see you in class.

Jessica: Sure. Good luck on the English test today!

Learn the English

Unscramble the sentences

1. test / nervous / tomorrow / science / the / I'm / about

_____

2. yesterday's / was / I / geography / easy / thought / test

_____

3. social studies / class / an / after / have / art / I

_____

Answer the questions

1. Which test did Kevin study more for?

_____

2. Why is Jessica nervous about the science test this semester?

_____

3. Which test did they both have yesterday?

_____

4. When did Jessica travel around Asia?

_____

5. What time does the social studies class start?

_____

Test

Write the answer next to the letter "A"

A: ___ **1.** Kevin studied ___ the English test.

a. more of   b. less for   c. more for   d. more than

A: ___ **2.** Kevin is ___ about his English test.

a. sad   b. happy   c. excited   d. worried

A: ___ **3.** Jessica always does ___ science tests.

a. badly on   b. well on   c. good for   d. bad for

A: ___ **4.** Is there a history test this semester?

a. No, it isn't.   b. No, it doesn't.   c. No, there isn't.   d. No, there doesn't.

A: ___ **5.** Jessica thought the ___ test ___ easy.

a. art, is   b. English, will be   c. geography, was   d. history, was

A: ___ **6.** Jessica ___ around Asia last year.

a. traveled   b. travels   c. travel   d. traveling

A: ___ **7.** Jessica has a social studies class ___ one o'clock.

a. in   b. at   c. on   d. by

A: ___ **8.** Which class will Jessica and Kevin have together today?

a. Art class.   b. Social studies.   c. Science.   d. Geography.

Answers on page 373

Lesson 23: Chores

Ev işleri

> What do you need to do today?
> I need to feed the pets.

Learn the words

1. **wash the dishes**
   Bulaşık yıkamak
2. **feed the pets**
   Hayvanları beslemek
3. **vacuum the carpet**
   Halıyı süpürmek
4. **take out the trash**
   Çöpü atmak
5. **clean the bedroom**
   Yatak odasını temizlemek
6. **mop the floor**
   Yerleri silmek
7. **cook dinner**
   Yemek yapmak
8. **do the laundry**
   Çamaşır yıkamak
9. **iron the clothes**
   Kıyafetleri ütülemek
10. **make the beds**
    Yatakları toplamak

Learn a verb

know – knowing – knew – known bilmek

Matthew: I didn't know you can cook.

Learn an idiom

All in a day's work

Meaning: A normal day without a change in routine.

"Taking out the trash before school is *all in a day's work*."

Conversation

Matthew: Hi, Susan. How are you?

Susan: I'm a little tired. I've been doing chores all weekend.

Matthew: Is nobody helping you?

Susan: My mom is sick in bed and Dad's out working.

Matthew: What chores did you have to do?

Susan: I had to cook dinner and wash the dishes last night.

Matthew: I didn't know you can cook.

Susan: I'm not very good, but I know how to cook spaghetti.

Matthew: This morning, I fed the pets. That's an easy chore.

Susan: This morning, I vacuumed the carpet and made the beds.

Matthew: You really are busy! What do you need to do today?

Susan: I need to iron the clothes and mop the floor.

Matthew: You will be really tired later!

Susan: It's all in a day's work for my parents. I'm happy to help.

Matthew: That's very good of you.

Susan: My parents usually do all the chores every day.

Matthew: Mine, too. They're both really busy people.

Susan: I didn't realize how much there is to do around the house.

Matthew: Maybe we should both help out more.

Susan: Do you have any more chores to do this weekend?

Matthew: Yes, I do. I still have to take out the trash.

Susan: I better get back to it. I want to finish the chores and rest.

Matthew: Sounds good. Don't work too hard.

Learn the English

Find the mistakes and write the sentence correctly

Susan: My dad is sick in bed and Mom's out working.

_____

Susan: I need to do the laundry and make the beds.

_____

Matthew: I will be really happy later!

_____

Answer the questions

1. How is Susan feeling right now?

_____

2. Why does Susan have to do all the chores?

_____

3. Which chore did Matthew do this morning?

_____

4. What did Susan cook for dinner last night?

_____

5. Which chores does Susan still need to do today?

_____

Test

Write the answer next to the letter "A"

A: ___ **1.** Susan has been ___ chores all day.

a. do   b. doing   c. done   d. did

A: ___ **2.** "I ___ cook dinner and wash the dishes last night."

a. had   b. have to   c. had to   d. has to

A: ___ **3.** "I ___ know you can cook."

a. don't   b. didn't   c. doesn't   d. won't

A: ___ **4.** Susan ___ how to cook spaghetti.

a. knowing   b. know   c. knew   d. knows

A: ___ **5.** Which chore didn't Susan complete?

a. Mop the floor.   b. Cook dinner.   c. Make the beds.   d. Wash the dishes.

A: ___ **6.** Which chore does Susan still need to do?

a. Wash the dishes.   b. Make the beds.   c. Cook dinner.   d. Iron the clothes.

A: ___ **7.** "It's all in a day's ___ for my parents."

a. work   b. job   c. housework   d. chore

A: ___ **8.** "___ you have any more chores to ___ this weekend?"

a. Did, did   b. Do, do   c. Does, does   d. Does, do

Answers on page 373

Lesson 24: At the toy store

Oyuncak mağazasında

What are you playing with?
I'm playing with my ball.

Learn the words

1. **doll**
   Oyuncak bebek
2. **teddy bear**
   Ayıcık
3. **car**
   Araba
4. **airplane**
   Uçak
5. **dinosaur**
   Dinozor
6. **robot**
   Robot
7. **ball**
   Top
8. **jump rope**
   Atlama ipi
9. **board game**
   Masa oyunu
10. **blocks**
    Bloklar

Learn a verb

borrow – borrowing – borrowed – borrowed ödünç almak

Dad: She'd like that. She always borrows Matthew's jump rope.

Learn an idiom

Like a kid with a new toy

Meaning: To be really happy with something.

"He was *like a kid with a new toy* when he drove the car for the first time."

Conversation

Mom: We should get a gift for Susan.

Dad: That's a good idea. She really helped us a lot last week.

Mom: I know. Doing all those chores is not easy.

Dad: What do you think we should get her?

Mom: I'm not sure. What is she playing with now?

Dad: She is playing with her dolls.

Mom: We can't get her another doll. She has too many!

Dad: Susan really likes dinosaurs.

Mom: They are studying them in history class at school now.

Dad: Perhaps we can give her a book on dinosaurs.

Mom: That's an excellent idea. She'll be like a kid with a new toy.

Dad: But Susan's always inside. I'd like her to do more exercise.

Mom: I agree. Maybe we can get her a jump rope as well.

Dad: She'd like that. She always borrows Matthew's jump rope.

Mom: Let's go to the toy store and see if they have one.

Dad: Look! There is the robot from the movie we saw last week.

Mom: I don't think Susan would like a robot.

Dad: It would look great on my desk in the office.

Mom: You're like a little boy!

Dad: Can I get the robot?

Mom: Yes, but let's find a jump rope for Susan first.

Dad: Here's a green one. That's Susan's favorite color.

Mom: Since you're getting the robot, I'm getting this board game!

Learn the English

Put the sentences in order

Mom: I know. Doing all those chores is not easy. ___

Dad: What do you think we should get her? ___

Mom: I'm not sure. What is she playing with now? ___

Dad: That's a good idea. She really helped us a lot last week. ___

Mom: We should get a gift for Susan. ___

Dad: Susan really likes dinosaurs. ___

Mom: We can't get her another doll. She has too many! ___

Dad: She is playing with her dolls. ___

Answer the questions

1. What did Susan help her parents do last week?

_____

2. Why didn't Mom want to get Susan another doll?

_____

3. What is Susan learning about in history class?

_____

4. Where does Dad want to put the robot?

_____

5. What does Mom want to buy for herself?

_____

Test

Write the answer next to the letter "A"

A: ___ **1.** "We should get a gift ___ Susan."

a. give   b. to   c. of   d. for

A: ___ **2.** "___ all the chores ___ not easy."

a. Do, is   b. Doing, is   c. Done, are   d. Doing, are

A: ___ **3.** Will Susan's parents get her a doll?

a. Yes, they will.   b. No, they won't.   c. Yes, they did.   d. No, they don't.

A: ___ **4.** What did Susan's father suggest to get a book about?

a. Dinosaurs.   b. Dolls.   c. Jump ropes.   d. Robots.

A: ___ **5.** There ___ a robot at the toy store from the movie they had seen.

a. has   b. were   c. was   d. have

A: ___ **6.** Where ___ Susan's father ___ to go?

a. does, wants   b. do, want   c. did, wanted   d. does, want

A: ___ **7.** Susan's mother ___ Susan would like a robot.

a. isn't thinking   b. didn't thought   c. doesn't think   d. don't think

A: ___ **8.** Mom wanted to find a ___ before getting the ___.

a. jump rope, robot   b. robot, jump rope   c. doll, robot   d. board game, doll

Answers on page 373

Lesson 25: In the Kitchen

Mutfakta

What was he cleaning?
He was cleaning the stove.

Learn the words

1. **refrigerator**
   Buzdolabı
2. **coffee maker**
   Kahve makinesi
3. **microwave oven**
   Mikrodalga fırın
4. **stove**
   Ocak
5. **blender**
   Karıştırıcı
6. **cupboard**
   Dolap
7. **rice cooker**
   Pilav pişirme makinesi
8. **dish rack**
   Bulaşıklık
9. **pan**
   Tava
10. **toaster**
    Tost makinesi

Learn a verb

clean – cleaning – cleaned – cleaned temizlemek

Kevin: Mom asked me to clean the things in the kitchen.

Learn an idiom

Too many cooks in the kitchen

Meaning: When too many people try to take control.

"We couldn't find a solution because there were *too many cooks in the kitchen.*"

Conversation

Peter: We haven't spoken for a while, so I thought I'd phone you.

Kevin: Sorry, I've been really busy lately.

Peter: What have you been doing?

Kevin: Recently, I spoke to Susan about doing more chores.

Peter: Why do you want to do more chores?

Kevin: I think it's good to help Mom and Dad.

Peter: What chores have you been doing?

Kevin: Mom asked me to clean the things in the kitchen.

Peter: I see. What were you cleaning?

Kevin: I was cleaning the stove and cupboard yesterday.

Peter: What else were you cleaning?

Kevin: This morning, I was cleaning the refrigerator.

Peter: Cleaning the refrigerator is not easy.

Kevin: I know. You have to take everything out first.

Peter: Mom has been replacing a few old items in our kitchen.

Kevin: What did she replace?

Peter: She replaced the toaster and rice cooker. They're too old.

Kevin: I hope she didn't replace the blender. It's the best!

Peter: Of course not! I would be so upset.

Kevin: How about the coffee maker?

Peter: Yes, that's also gone, but Mom hasn't bought a new one yet.

Kevin: I bet your dad wasn't happy. Did he say anything to her?

Peter: Mom told him that there are too many cooks in the kitchen!

Learn the English

Fill in the blanks

Kevin: Recently, I _____ to Susan about doing _____ chores.

Peter: Mom has been _____ a few old items in our _____.

Peter: _____ the refrigerator is not _____.

Kevin: Mom _____ me to clean the _____ in the kitchen.

Kevin: I hope she _____ replace the _____. It's the _____!

Peter: Of _____ not! I _____ be so upset.

Kevin: I bet your dad _____ happy. Did he say _____ to her?

Answer the questions

1. Who did Kevin speak to about doing chores?

_____

2. Why does Kevin want to do more chores?

_____

3. What was Kevin cleaning yesterday?

_____

4. What has Peter's mother been doing in the kitchen?

_____

5. Why did Peter's mother want to replace the toaster?

_____

310

Test

Write the answer next to the letter "A"

A: ___ **1.** Were Kevin and Peter talking on the phone?

a. No, they weren't.   b. No, they wasn't.   c. Yes, they was.   d. Yes, they were.

A: ___ **2.** Kevin spoke to Susan about ___ more chores.

a. do   b. doing   c. did   d. done

A: ___ **3.** Kevin ___ it's good ___ help his parents.

a. thinks, to   b. think, of   c. thinks, for   d. think, to

A: ___ **4.** Kevin was ___ the stove and cupboard yesterday.

a. cleaned   b. cleaning   c. clean   d. cleans

A: ___ **5.** Peter thinks cleaning the ___ is not easy.

a. stove   b. toaster   c. blender   d. refrigerator

A: ___ **6.** What ___ Peter's mother been doing?

a. had   b. was   c. has   d. is

A: ___ **7.** Has Peter's mother bought a new coffee maker yet?

a. No, she didn't.   b. Yes, she did.   c. No, she hasn't.   d. Yes, she has.

A: ___ **8.** Peter's father really likes the ___.

a. coffee maker   b. toaster   c. blender   d. rice cooker

Answers on page 373

Lesson 26: In the toolbox

Alet çantası

> What were you using to fix the chair?
> I was using the electric drill.

Learn the words

1. **hammer**
   Çekiç
2. **electric drill**
   Elektrikli matkap
3. **screwdriver**
   Tornavida
4. **paintbrush**
   Boya fırçası
5. **shovel**
   Kürek
6. **tape measure**
   Mezür
7. **axe**
   Balta
8. **pliers**
   Pense
9. **ladder**
   Merdiven
10. **wrench**
    İngiliz anahtarı

Learn a verb

use – using – used – used kullanmak

Dad: You can check. Use the tape measure to measure the size.

Learn an idiom

Tools of the trade

Meaning: Things that are needed for a specific job.

"My cell phone, diary and calculator are all *tools of the trade*."

Conversation

Dad: Peter, Mom asked me to fix the cupboard in the kitchen.

Peter: What's wrong with the cupboard?

Dad: The cupboard door doesn't close properly.

Peter: Do you need my help?

Dad: Yes, please. Hand me the tools while I'm up on the ladder.

Peter: Sure. Which tool do you need?

Dad: We need to unscrew the door first. Hand me a screwdriver.

Peter: I can't find it. It's not in the toolbox.

Dad: It should be there. I was using it to fix the chair yesterday.

Peter: Oh, here it is. It was under the wrench.

Dad: Forget the screwdriver. I'll use the electric drill instead.

Peter: Why do you want to use an electric drill?

Dad: The screws are old and difficult to turn.

Peter: Maybe you should use a hammer!

Dad: Let's stick to the tools of the trade. The electric drill, please.

Peter: Good job! But you've scratched the cupboard.

Dad: That's okay. I'll paint over the scratch.

Peter: Here's the paintbrush. What color paint do you need?

Dad: We'll keep the color the same. Give me the white paint.

Peter: Do we need to replace the cupboard door?

Dad: You can check. Use the tape measure to measure the size.

Peter: The measurements are the right size.

Dad: That's good news. The problem must be the old screws then.

Learn the English

Unscramble the sentences

1. door / cupboard / The / close / properly / doesn't

_____

2. old / turn / are / The / and / to / screws / difficult

_____

3. right / The / size / the / are / measurements

_____

Answer the questions

1. What does Peter's mother want his father to fix?

_____

2. Who was standing up on the ladder?

_____

3. What was the first tool that Peter gave his father?

_____

4. Why did Dad want to use the electric drill?

_____

5. Which tool did Peter use to measure the cupboard door?

_____

Test

Write the answer next to the letter "A"

A: ___ **1.** "The cupboard door ___ close ___."

a. won't, good   b. didn't, proper   c. don't, proper   d. doesn't, properly

A: ___ **2.** "___ you need my help?"

a. Have   b. Does   c. Do   d. Are

A: ___ **3.** The screwdriver was ___ the ___.

a. by, paintbrush   b. under, wrench   c. on, hammer   d. under, ladder

A: ___ **4.** Did they change the color of the cupboard door?

a. Yes, they did.   b. No, they didn't.   c. No, they don't.   d. Yes, they do.

A: ___ **5.** What did Dad use to fix the chair? He used a ___.

a. pliers   b. screwdriver   c. hammer   d. shovel

A: ___ **6.** Which tool did they not use to fix the cupboard?

a. Screwdriver.   b. Ladder.   c. Pliers.   d. Tape measure.

A: ___ **7.** Did they replace the cupboard door?

a. No, they didn't.   b. Yes, they did.   c. No, they hadn't.   d. Yes, they had.

A: ___ **8.** Peter said the measurement of the cupboard door was ___.

a. wrong   b. right   c. bad   d. correctly

Answers on page 373

Lesson 27: Transportation

Ulaşım

> How will you be going to Rome?
> I will be taking a bus.

Learn the words

1. **catch a bus**
   Otobüsü yakalamak
2. **take a taxi**
   Taksiye binmek
3. **take a ferry**
   Vapura binmek
4. **ride a motorcycle**
   Motorsiklet binmek
5. **take the subway**
   Metroya binmek
6. **take a train**
   Trene binmek
7. **drive a car**
   Araba sürmek
8. **ride a scooter**
   Mobilet sürmek
9. **ride a bicycle**
   Bisiklet sürmek
10. **take an airplane**
    Uçağa binmek

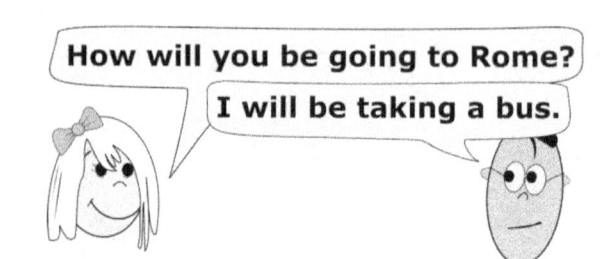

Learn a verb

take – taking – took – taken almak

Emily: After Sydney, I'll be taking a train to Melbourne.

Learn an idiom

Lose one's train of thought

Meaning: To forget what you were thinking about.

"I'm sorry, I *lost my train of thought*. What were we talking about?"

Conversation

Helen: Are you going anywhere this summer?

Emily: Yes, I am. I'm going to Sydney.

Helen: Great! How will you be going to Sydney?

Emily: I'll be taking an airplane.

Helen: That sounds great. Will you go anywhere else?

Emily: After Sydney, I'll be taking a train to Melbourne.

Helen: Why do you want to go to Melbourne?

Emily: I would like to see the penguins.

Helen: Will you be going to the zoo?

Emily: No, I won't be. You can see penguins on a nearby island.

Helen: I didn't know that you can see penguins in Australia.

Emily: Yes, you can. We'll be taking a ferry to the island.

Helen: Your summer sounds better than mine.

Emily: Why? What will you be doing?

Helen: I'll be staying at my grandparent's house on the farm.

Emily: That doesn't sound too bad.

Helen: True. At least I won't be taking the subway every day.

Emily: What will you do on the farm?

Helen: I'm sorry. I lost my train of thought. What did you ask?

Emily: What will you be doing while you're staying on the farm?

Helen: My brother and I love to ride motorcycles over the hills.

Emily: That sounds really fun! I've only ever ridden a bicycle.

Helen: Yes, you're right. We will both have a great summer!

Learn the English

Find the mistakes and write the sentence correctly

Emily: Before Sydney, I'll be taking a bus to Melbourne.

_____

Helen: My summer sounds better than yours.

_____

Helen: My sister and I love to ride bicycles over the hills.

_____

Answer the questions

1. Where is Emily going this summer?

_____

2. How will Emily be going to Melbourne?

_____

3. Why does Emily want to go to Melbourne?

_____

4. Where is Helen going this summer?

_____

5. What will Helen be doing with her brother?

_____

Test

Write the answer next to the letter "A"

A: ___ **1.** Emily will ___ to Sydney this summer.

a. going   b. be going   c. be go   d. have go

A: ___ **2.** Emily will be ___ an airplane to Sydney.

a. driving   b. catching   c. riding   d. taking

A: ___ **3.** Emily ___ to see the penguins.

a. would   b. like   c. want   d. would like

A: ___ **4.** Helen didn't know there ___ penguins in Australia.

a. have   b. are   c. is   d. was

A: ___ **5.** Emily will be taking a ___ to the island.

a. ferry   b. bus   c. train   d. subway

A: ___ **6.** Will Helen be going to Sydney with Emily?

a. No, she will.   b. No, she will not.   c. No, she won't be.   d. No, she won't.

A: ___ **7.** Helen lost her train ___ thought.

a. in   b. with   c. of   d. for

A: ___ **8.** Emily ___ only ever ___ a bicycle.

a. has, ridden   b. has, ride   c. have, rode   d. have, ridden

Answers on page 373

Lesson 28: Clothes

Giysiler

Whose jacket is that?
It's mine.

Learn the words

1. **T-shirt**
   Tişört
2. **blouse**
   Bluz
3. **scarf**
   Atkı
4. **coat**
   Palto
5. **dress**
   Elbise
6. **hat**
   Şapka
7. **sweater**
   Süveter
8. **jacket**
   Ceket
9. **skirt**
   Etek
10. **necktie**
    Kravat

Learn a verb

wear – wearing – wore – worn giymek

Susan: Right now, I'm wearing a skirt. I think I should change.

Learn an idiom

Wear somebody out

Meaning: To make someone tired.

"My boss completely *wore me out* today."

Conversation

Jessica: Are you ready to go?

Susan: Not yet. I don't know what to wear.

Jessica: We're going hiking, so you don't need a pretty dress!

Susan: Are you sure we can go hiking today? It's pretty cold.

Jessica: I checked the weather. It's not going to rain.

Susan: Right now, I'm wearing a skirt. I think I should change.

Jessica: Yes, you should. I suggest you wear a pair of pants.

Susan: I like the jacket you're wearing. Whose jacket is that?

Jessica: It's my sister's jacket. She's lending it to me for a day.

Susan: I only have this purple coat.

Jessica: Perhaps you should also wear a sweater underneath.

Susan: That's a good idea. I have a sweater in my bag.

Jessica: I'm only wearing a T-shirt, but this jacket is really warm.

Susan: Okay, I think I'm ready to go.

Jessica: I've prepared two water bottles and some fruit.

Susan: Thanks. I heard the mountain we're hiking is really high.

Jessica: It is. We are definitely going to be worn out.

Susan: I agree. We can take a rest at the top of the mountain.

Jessica: The view from the top should be really beautiful.

Susan: I'm worried that it will be too cloudy.

Jessica: I think you're right. I'm not going to bring my hat.

Susan: Me, neither. It's not a sunny day today.

Jessica: I think we've got everything we need. Let's go hiking!

Learn the English

Put the sentences in order

Susan: Not yet. I don't know what to wear. ____

Jessica: I checked the weather. It's not going to rain. ____

Susan: I like the jacket you're wearing. Whose jacket is that? ____

Jessica: We're going hiking, so you don't need a pretty dress! ____

Susan: Are you sure we can go hiking today? It's pretty cold. ____

Jessica: Are you ready to go? ____

Susan: Right now, I'm wearing a skirt. I think I should change. ____

Jessica: Yes, you should. I suggest you wear a pair of pants. ____

Answer the questions

1. Who doesn't know what to wear?

_____

2. What did Jessica suggest to wear?

_____

3. What does Susan have in her bag?

_____

4. How many bottles did Jessica prepare?

_____

5. Why aren't they bringing a hat?

_____

Test

Write the answer next to the letter "A"

A: ___ **1.** Susan ___ know what to wear.

a. not   b. isn't   c. doesn't   d. don't

A: ___ **2.** Susan is concerned about the weather ___ too cold to go hiking.

a. be   b. being   c. is   d. was

A: ___ **3.** Susan is ___ a skirt.

a. wear   b. wore   c. wearing   d. wears

A: ___ **4.** "I suggest you wear ___ pants."

a. pair of   b. pairs of   c. a pair   d. a pair of

A: ___ **5.** "I've prepared two water ___ and ___ fruit."

a. bottle, some   b. bottles, any   c. bottle, a lot of   d. bottles, some

A: ___ **6.** "I heard the mountain we're hiking ___ high."

a. really   b. real   c. is really   d. is real

A: ___ **7.** ___ Susan have a sweater in her bag? Yes, she ___.

a. Does, does   b. Does, did   c. Do, does   d. Do, do

A: ___ **8.** Susan ___ that the weather will be too cloudy.

a. is worry   b. is worried   c. worry   d. worried

Answers on page 373

Lesson 29: More clothes

Daha fazla giysi

Learn the words

1. **pants**
   Pantolon
2. **shorts**
   Şort
3. **shoes**
   Ayakkabı
4. **dresses**
   Elbise
5. **shirts**
   Gömlek
6. **jeans**
   Kot
7. **socks**
   Çorap
8. **gloves**
   Eldiven
9. **pajamas**
   Pijama
10. **boots**
    Bot

Learn a verb

lend – lending – lent – lent ödünç vermek

John: These shoes are my brother's. He lent them to me.

Learn an idiom

Fits like a glove

Meaning: Something is the right size.

"The new shirt you bought me *fits like a glove*."

Conversation

Matthew: Thanks for coming with me to the clothes store.

John: You're welcome. I'm happy to help.

Matthew: Mom said I need to buy some clothes for summer.

John: I need to buy some shoes. My shoes are getting old.

Matthew: Your shoes don't look old. Whose shoes are those?

John: These shoes are my brother's. He lent them to me.

Matthew: Maybe we can go to the shoe shop later.

John: That would be great. So, what do you need for summer?

Matthew: I think it's too hot to wear jeans, so I'd like some shorts.

John: I read that this year will be the hottest summer.

Matthew: I better get some shirts, too.

John: There are summer pants you can also buy.

Matthew: What are summer pants?

John: They are lightweight pants made of cotton.

Matthew: I can wear them when I work. They fit like a glove, too.

John: Do you have a job now?

Matthew: Yes, I'm working at the Thai restaurant as a waiter.

John: That's great! How long have you been working there?

Matthew: I've been working there since last Monday.

John: I think the clothes you chose look great.

Matthew: Me, too. Let's go to the shoe shop now.

John: The shoe shop sells sports socks as well.

Matthew: All my socks have holes in them, so get me ten pairs!

Learn the English

Fill in the blanks

Matthew: Mom said I need to buy some _____ for _____.

John: These shoes are my _____. He _____ them to me.

Matthew: _____ we can go to the shoe shop _____.

John: They are _____ pants made of _____.

Matthew: Yes, I'm _____ at the Thai _____ as a waiter.

Matthew: I've _____ working there _____ last Monday.

John: The shoe shop _____ sports socks as _____.

Answer the questions

1. Where are the boys?

_____

2. Is John wearing his brother's shoes?

_____

3. Where is Matthew working now?

_____

4. When did Matthew start working at the Thai restaurant?

_____

5. What does John need to buy?

_____

Test

Write the answer next to the letter "A"

A: ___ **1.** "Thanks ___ coming ___ me to the clothes store."

a. for, to   b. of, with   c. to, for   d. for, with

A: ___ **2.** John ___ some new shoes because his ___ getting old.

a. need, is   b. needs, are   c. needed, was   d. wants, is

A: ___ **3.** John's brother ___ a pair of shoes to him.

a. lend   b. lent   c. borrowed   d. lending

A: ___ **4.** Matthew thinks it's too hot to wear ___, so he wants to buy ___.

a. jeans, shorts   b. shorts, jeans   c. pants, shorts   d. shorts, pants

A: ___ **5.** John read that this year will be ___ summer.

a. the hotter   b. the hot   c. the hottest   d. hottest

A: ___ **6.** The lightweight pants ___ cotton.

a. made from   b. are made of   c. are made for   d. is made of

A: ___ **7.** Matthew is working at a Thai restaurant ___ a waiter.

a. as   b. be   c. to be   d. is

A: ___ **8.** Which clothes did the two boys not talk about?

a. Shorts.   b. Pajamas.   c. Jeans.   d. Pants.

Answers on page 373

Lesson 30: In the living room

Oturma odasında

Where is the coffee table?
It's in front of the sofa.

Learn the words

1. **bookcase**
   Kitaplık
2. **television**
   Televizyon
3. **clock**
   Saat
4. **coffee table**
   Sehpa
5. **armchair**
   Koltuk
6. **painting**
   Tablo
7. **TV stand**
   Televizyon büfesi
8. **rug**
   Kilim
9. **sofa**
   Kanepe
10. **vase**
    Vazo

Learn a verb

move – moving – moved – moved hareket etmek

Eric: The sofa is the biggest thing, so let's move that first.

Learn an idiom

A race against the clock

Meaning: To not have too much time left to complete a task.

"It's *a race against the clock* to finish this project."

Conversation

Betty: Thanks for helping me move into my new apartment.

Eric: It's no problem. However, I only have one hour to help.

Betty: Let's start with the living room furniture then.

Eric: Good idea. The furniture is the most difficult to move.

Betty: I have a lot of stuff, so it's a race against the clock!

Eric: The sofa is the biggest thing, so let's move that first.

Betty: Put the sofa against the wall.

Eric: This sofa is too heavy for me. You need to take one end.

Betty: Sure. It'll be easier to move with two people.

Eric: Okay, so what's the next thing to move?

Betty: Please put the big vase on the left of the sofa.

Eric: That looks good, but you need a nice plant to put in the vase.

Betty: My aunt said she'd give me one as a housewarming gift.

Eric: Do you want the coffee table in the middle of the living room?

Betty: Yes, but first put a rug on the floor.

Eric: Should the rug go underneath the coffee table?

Betty: Yes, it should. I don't want the table to scratch the floor.

Eric: I guess the TV stand should be across from the sofa?

Betty: That's right. And move the bookcase next to the TV stand.

Eric: I've plugged the television in, so it's ready to use.

Betty: The clock can go in my bedroom. Just leave it on the sofa.

Eric: This painting is beautiful. I love it!

Betty: Eric, you've been such a great help today. You can have it.

Learn the English

Unscramble the sentences

1. left / put / sofa / the / vase / the / of / Please / the / on / big

___

2. the / to / don't / floor / scratch / table / I / the / want

___

3. to / furniture / the / is / move / difficult / The / most

___

Answer the questions

1. How long can Eric help Betty?

___

2. What will they move to the living room first?

___

3. Could Eric move the sofa by himself?

___

4. What was put next to the TV stand?

___

5. What did Betty give Eric for helping her?

___

Test

Write the answer next to the letter "A"

A: ___ **1.** "Thanks ___ helping me ___ into my new apartment."

a. for, moves   b. to, move   c. to, moving   d. for, move

A: ___ **2.** Eric only ___ one hour to help Betty.

a. got   b. has   c. have   d. is

A: ___ **3.** The furniture is ___ difficult to move.

a. the more   b. more   c. the most   d. most

A: ___ **4.** "I have a lot of stuff, ___ it's a race ___ the clock!"

a. so, against   b. but, for   c. so, on   d. but, to

A: ___ **5.** Will Betty's uncle give her a plant? No, her aunt ___.

a. does   b. will be   c. did   d. will

A: ___ **6.** The ___ is next to the TV stand.

a. sofa   b. bookcase   c. television   d. coffee table

A: ___ **7.** Which item did Eric not help Betty move?

a. Sofa.   b. Armchair.   c. Coffee table.   d. Bookcase.

A: ___ **8.** Betty put the rug ___ the coffee table.

a. on   b. by   c. underneath   d. below

Answers on page 373

Lesson 31: In the bathroom

Banyoda

> What is above the sink?
>
> There is a mirror above the sink.

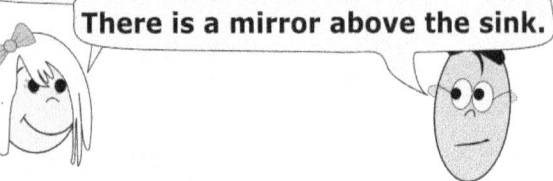

Learn the words

1. **mirror**
   Ayna
2. **bath towel**
   Banyo havlusu
3. **shower**
   Duş
4. **toilet paper**
   Tuvalet kağıdı
5. **bath mat**
   Banyo paspası
6. **shelf**
   Raf
7. **sink**
   Lavabo
8. **toilet**
   Klozet
9. **bathtub**
   Küvet
10. **soap**
    Sabun

Learn a verb

wash – washing – washed – washed yıkamak

Emily: No, there isn't. We still haven't washed everything.

Learn an idiom

Throw in the towel

Meaning: To give up or quit.

"After trying three times, he decided to *throw in the towel*."

Conversation

Bob: Hey, I heard you were fixing your bathroom.

Emily: Yes, we decided to change some things and improve it.

Bob: When did you do all this work?

Emily: I had some time last month, so I worked on weekends.

Bob: Did you do the work all by yourself?

Emily: My aunt helped me. I borrowed some tools from my uncle.

Bob: What kinds of things did you change?

Emily: Well, we bought a new toilet, bathtub, and bath mat.

Bob: Wow! That really sounds like a lot of hard work!

Emily: Yeah, a few times I wanted to throw in the towel.

Bob: You did a lot. So, what is beside the sink now?

Emily: There is a shelf beside the sink. I use it to put the soap on.

Bob: Is there a mirror above the sink?

Emily: No, there isn't. There is a large mirror next to the shower.

Bob: What is beside the bathtub?

Emily: There is a new bath mat beside the bathtub.

Bob: Where do you put your bath towels?

Emily: After we wash them, there is a shelf beside the shower.

Bob: So there are towels on the shelf now?

Emily: No, there aren't any bath towels in the bathroom.

Bob: It isn't finished yet? Is there toilet paper beside the toilet?

Emily: No, there isn't. We still haven't washed everything.

Bob: I have to go home then. I need to use a bathroom!

> **Learn the English**

Find the mistakes and write the sentence correctly

Emily: I had some time last week, so she worked on Mondays.

_____

Emily: No, it isn't. There is a small mirror next to the toilet.

_____

Emily: There is an old bath mat across from the shower.

_____

Answer the questions

1. When did Emily do all the work?

_____

2. Who did Emily borrow some tools from?

_____

3. Where does Emily put the soap?

_____

4. What is beside the bathtub?

_____

5. Why does Bob need to go home?

_____

Test

Write the answer next to the letter "A"

A: ___ **1.** Emily ___ her bathroom last ___.

a. fixed, month   b. washed, month   c. changed, week   d. fix, weekend

A: ___ **2.** Emily's uncle ___ her some tools.

a. borrowed   b. bought   c. sold   d. lent

A: ___ **3.** Sometimes she felt like she wanted to throw in the ___.

a. toilet   b. bathtub   c. soap   d. towel

A: ___ **4.** Is there a shelf below the sink?

a. Yes, there is.   b. No, there isn't.   c. Yes, it is.   d. No, there hasn't.

A: ___ **5.** There is a ___ next to the shower.

a. soap   b. sink   c. mirror   d. bath mat

A: ___ **6.** Emily bought a new ___ and ___.

a. bathtub, shelf   b. toilet, soap   c. bathtub, toilet   d. bath mat, sink

A: ___ **7.** Emily still hasn't ___ everything.

a. fixed   b. washed   c. bought   d. borrowed

A: ___ **8.** Are there any bath towels in the bathroom?

a. Yes, there are.   b. Yes, they have.   c. No, there aren't.   d. No, they haven't.

Answers on page 373

Lesson 32: In the bedroom

Yatak odasında

What is on the left of the bed?
There is a lamp on the left of the bed.

Learn the words

1. **bed**
   Yatak
2. **pillow**
   Yastık
3. **mattress**
   Döşek
4. **blanket**
   Battaniye
5. **drawers**
   Çekmece
6. **lamp**
   Lamba
7. **alarm clock**
   Çalar saat
8. **wardrobe**
   Gardırop
9. **bed sheets**
   Yatak çarşafı
10. **nightstand**
    Komodin

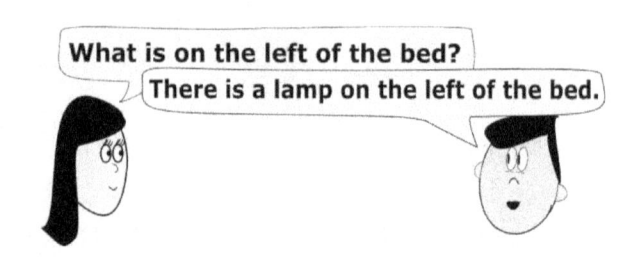

Learn a verb

change – changing – changed – changed değiştirmek

Jack: Yes, I want to change my mattress and pillow, too.

Learn an idiom

Get up on the wrong side of the bed

Meaning: To describe somebody who is in a bad mood.

"Mom's in a really bad mood. I think she *got up on the wrong side of the bed*."

Conversation

Amy: I heard you moved into a new house.

Jack: That's right, but I still have to get a few more things.

Amy: What do you need to get?

Jack: For example, there aren't any drawers on the left of the bed.

Amy: Is there a nightstand on the left of the bed?

Jack: Yes, there is. I put my alarm clock and lamp on it.

Amy: I see. What is on the right of the bed?

Jack: There is a wardrobe on the right of the bed.

Amy: Do you need to get anything else for your new room?

Jack: Yes, I want to change my mattress and pillow, too.

Amy: You really need to get a lot for your bedroom.

Jack: Yes. It's a nice room, but it's a bit empty right now.

Amy: That's great! We should go to the mall together.

Jack: Do you want to go shopping for your bedroom, too?

Amy: Yes, I need to buy some new bed sheets and a blanket.

Jack: Yeah, now that it's December it's really cold at night.

Amy: Let's ask Kevin to go with us, I think he needs a new lamp.

Jack: I talked to him this morning, but he wasn't in a good mood.

Amy: Why was he so unhappy?

Jack: I guess he just got up on the wrong side of the bed.

Amy: Well, I'm sure that buying new stuff would change his mood.

Jack: Why do you think that?

Amy: Every time I have a bad mood, shopping makes me happy.

Learn the English

Put the sentences in order

Jack: Yes. It's a nice room but it's a bit empty right now. ___

Amy: Yes, I need to buy some new bed sheets and a blanket. ___

Amy: Do you need to get anything else for your new room? ___

Amy: That's great! We should go to the mall together. ___

Jack: Yeah, now that it's December it's really cold at night. ___

Jack: Yes, I want to change my mattress and pillow, too. ___

Jack: Do you want to go shopping for your bedroom, too? ___

Amy: You really need to get a lot for your bedroom. ___

Answer the questions

1. Where is Jack's nightstand?

___

2. What is on the right of the bed?

___

3. Where does Amy want to go?

___

4. Who needs a new lamp?

___

5. When did Jack talk to Kevin?

___

Test

Write the answer next to the letter "A"

A: ___ **1.** Jack still ___ to get a few more things.

a. have   b. must   c. need   d. has

A: ___ **2.** Are there any drawers on the left of the bed?

a. No, there aren't.   b. Yes, there is.   c. No, there isn't.   d. Yes, there are.

A: ___ **3.** Jack ___ his lamp on the nightstand.

a. keep   b. puts   c. wants   d. putting

A: ___ **4.** There is a wardrobe on the ___ of the ___.

a. left, lamp   b. left, room   c. right, bed   d. right, drawers

A: ___ **5.** Jack wants to ___ his pillow.

a. changing   b. changed   c. change   d. changes

A: ___ **6.** ___ needs to buy new bed sheets.

a. Jack   b. Amy   c. Kevin   d. December

A: ___ **7.** Their friend woke up on the ___ side of the ___.

a. wrong, bed   b. right, blanket   c. left, bed   d. left, pillow

A: ___ **8.** Shopping ___ Amy ___.

a. make, happy   b. has, unhappy   c. mall, likes   d. makes, happy

Answers on page 373

Lesson 33: Around the house

Evin etrafında

> What will he be doing this weekend?
> He will be fixing the gate.

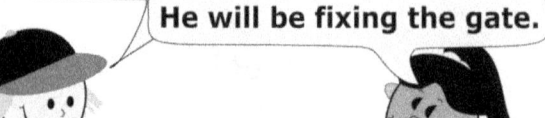

Learn the words

1. **work in the garage**
   Garajda çalışmak
2. **fix the mailbox**
   Posta kutusunu tamir etmek
3. **fix the gate**
   Kapıyı tamir etmek
4. **work in the garden**
   Bahçede çalışmak
5. **clean the pool**
   Havuzu temizlemek
6. **work in the yard**
   Avluda çalışmak
7. **fix the fence**
   Çitleri tamir etmek
8. **clean the balcony**
   Balkonu temizlemek
9. **clean the outdoor furniture**
   Dış mekan mobilyalarını temizlemek
10. **clean the barbecue**
    Izgarayı temizlemek

Learn a verb

fix – fixing – fixed – fixed tamir etmek

Max: Ted can't come because he'll be fixing the gate.

Learn an idiom

On the house

Meaning: To get something for free.

"The waiter apologized and gave him the meal *on the house*."

Conversation

Max: This weekend the weather will be good. Let's go to the park.

Julie: That's a good idea, we can play soccer. Can Ted come?

Max: He can't come because he'll be fixing the gate. Let's ask Bob.

Julie: Bob will be cleaning the outdoor furniture this weekend.

Max: What will Susan be doing on Saturday?

Julie: She'll be working in the yard. She'll also be fixing the fence.

Max: What will Emily be doing this weekend?

Julie: She won't be working in the garden. She hurt her foot.

Max: That means she can't play soccer, too. No one can play.

Julie: Well, there are many things to do around the house, too.

Max: What do you mean? It's Friday today. I want to relax.

Julie: Mom will be cleaning the pool. Dad will be fixing the mailbox.

Max: Right. I also heard Dad will be working in the garage.

Julie: It seems like we're the only people who won't be working.

Max: Will Mom be cleaning the balcony, too? It's really dirty.

Julie: Yes, she will be. We should probably help her.

Max: I think you're right, but first we should eat something.

Julie: Yes, we can eat the hot dogs that I got for free.

Max: Why did the supermarket give you hot dogs on the house?

Julie: They were a gift because I bought so many things.

Max: We can barbecue them. Now, I'll be busy this weekend, too.

Julie: Why? What will you be doing this weekend?

Max: I'll be cleaning the barbecue tomorrow.

Learn the English

Fill in the blanks

Max: What _____ Susan be _____ on Saturday?

Julie: She'll be _____ in the yard. She'll be _____ the fence.

Max: _____ will Emily be doing this _____?

Julie: She _____ be _____ in the garden. She hurt her foot.

Max: That _____ she can't _____ soccer, too.

Julie: Well, _____ are many things to do _____ the house.

Max: What do you _____? It's Friday _____. I want to relax.

Answer the questions

1. Why can't Ted play soccer this weekend?

_____

2. When will Susan be working in the yard?

_____

3. Who will be cleaning the pool?

_____

4. Where did Julie get the hot dogs?

_____

5. What will Max be doing tomorrow?

_____

Test

Write the answer next to the letter "A"

A: ___ **1.** Julie ___ to ___ soccer at the park.

a. want, plays   b. like, do   c. wants, play   d. likes, doing

A: ___ **2.** Susan will be ___ the ___.

a. fixing, gate   b. cleaning, pool   c. cleaning, balcony   d. fixing, fence

A: ___ **3.** Will Susan be working in the yard on Sunday?

a. No, she can't.   b. Yes, she can.   c. No, she won't be.   d. Yes, she will be.

A: ___ **4.** There are many things to do ___ the house.

a. on   b. around   c. through   d. working

A: ___ **5.** Mom will be ___ the pool.

a. swimming   b. cleaning   c. fixing   d. working

A: ___ **6.** The ___ is really ___.

a. balcony, dirty   b. gate, fixing   c. yard, working   d. pool, broken

A: ___ **7.** The hot dogs were ___ the house.

a. around   b. in   c. through   d. on

A: ___ **8.** Max will be cleaning the ___ this weekend.

a. barbecue   b. mailbox   c. hot dogs   d. garage

Answers on page 373

Lesson 34: Hobbies

Hobiler

What do you enjoy doing on the weekend?
I enjoy going hiking.

Learn the words

1. **do gardening**
   Bahçecilik yapmak
2. **go hiking**
   Dağ yürüyüşüne çıkmak
3. **take photographs**
   Fotoğraf çekmek
4. **play video games**
   Video oyunları oynamak
5. **listen to music**
   Müzik dinlemek
6. **go camping**
   Kampa gitmek
7. **play chess**
   Satranç oynamak
8. **watch movies**
   Film izlemek
9. **go fishing**
   Balık tutmak
10. **sing karaoke**
    Karaoke yapmak

Learn a verb

enjoy – enjoying – enjoyed – enjoyed zevk almak

Kate: I think it's a really good idea to enjoy many hobbies.

Learn an idiom

Face the music

Meaning: To face the consequences of one's actions.

"You need to own up to your mistake and *face the music*."

Conversation

Kate: I just watched a really good movie at the cinema.

Peter: That sounds fun. Who did you go with?

Kate: Matthew. He enjoys watching movies every day.

Peter: Yes. He has many other hobbies, too.

Kate: Oh? What else does he enjoy doing?

Peter: He also enjoys listening to music and going hiking.

Kate: I think it's a really good idea to enjoy many hobbies.

Peter: I agree. What do you enjoy doing on the weekend?

Kate: I enjoy taking photographs and playing chess.

Peter: Do you like playing video games?

Kate: No, I enjoy doing gardening. I like to be outside.

Peter: That's probably a good idea.

Kate: I remember you like playing video games a lot.

Peter: Yeah, but now I have to face the music.

Kate: I heard your grades at school weren't very good.

Peter: Yes, so now I have to fix the problem.

Kate: You could try a new outdoor hobby.

Peter: My brother enjoys going camping and going fishing.

Kate: You and your brother could do the same hobbies together.

Peter: Thanks for the idea. I think we'll go next Saturday.

Kate: Also, do you enjoy singing karaoke?

Peter: Yes, I do. Why do you ask?

Kate: On Sunday, we'll sing karaoke. You two can come along.

Learn the English

Unscramble the sentences

1. has / other / too / Yes / many / he / hobbies

___

2. playing / taking / and / enjoy / I / chess / photographs

___

3. like / games / you / video / Do / playing

___

Answer the questions

1. Who enjoys watching movies every day?

___

2. What does Kate think is a good idea to enjoy?

___

3. Does Kate like playing video games?

___

4. Why does Peter have to face the music?

___

5. When will Peter go camping?

___

Test

Write the answer next to the letter "A"

A: ___ **1.** Kate just ___ a really good movie.

a. watching   b. watched   c. watch   d. watches

A: ___ **2.** ___ has many other hobbies.

a. Kate   b. Peter   c. Kate's brother   d. Matthew

A: ___ **3.** Kate ___ enjoy ___ video games.

a. don't, play   b. doesn't, playing   c. really, playing   d. don't, playing

A: ___ **4.** Does Kate enjoy playing chess on the weekend?

a. Yes, she do.   b. Yes, she enjoy.   c. No, she doesn't.   d. Yes, she does.

A: ___ **5.** Peter has bad grades, so he has to ___ the ___.

a. play, music   b. sing, karaoke   c. face, music   d. taste, problem

A: ___ **6.** Peter's brother ___ going ___.

a. enjoy, camp   b. enjoys, fish   c. enjoys, camping   d. enjoy, fishing

A: ___ **7.** Who enjoys taking photographs on the weekend?

a. Kate.   b. Matthew.   c. Peter.   d. Peter's brother.

A: ___ **8.** They will ___ karaoke on ___.

a. sing, Sunday   b. singing, Sunday   c. face, Sunday   d. singing, Saturday

Answers on page 373

Lesson 35: Countries

Ülkeler

> Which countries have you been to?
> I have been to Brazil and Mexico.

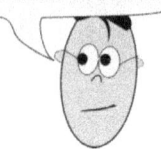

Learn the words

1. **Japan**
   Japonya
2. **Canada**
   Kanada
3. **Brazil**
   Brezilya
4. **Australia**
   Avustralya
5. **South Africa**
   Güney Afrika
6. **China**
   Çin
7. **Mexico**
   Meksika
8. **Argentina**
   Arjantin
9. **New Zealand**
   Yeni Zelanda
10. **Kenya**
    Kenya

Learn a verb

write – writing – wrote – written yazmak

John: Yes, he wrote a book about traveling there.

Learn an idiom

Second to none

Meaning: To describe something that is the best.

"The mountains in Canada are *second to none* for skiing."

Conversation

John: You look pretty tired. Didn't you sleep well?

Helen: Actually, I just got back from traveling, so I'm very sleepy.

John: Oh right! I heard you went on a trip with your sister.

Helen: Yes, we traveled to Mexico. Have you been to Mexico?

John: Yes, I have. The beaches there are second to none.

Helen: Yes, they were great. We went swimming every day.

John: I remember the food was delicious, too. You're so lucky!

Helen: We also went to Brazil. It was a really fun country.

John: I haven't been there. Have you been to Argentina?

Helen: No, we haven't. We didn't have time on this trip.

John: It's a nice place. Which other countries have you been to?

Helen: I've been to Japan and China. I want to go to Australia.

John: My brother went to Australia. He loves to travel.

Helen: Which countries has he been to?

John: He has been to South Africa and Kenya.

Helen: I've heard that those are both amazing places.

John: Yes, he wrote a book about traveling there last year.

Helen: They must have been good countries if he wrote a book.

John: That's true. He has also been to Canada and New Zealand.

Helen: Wow! He has really traveled all over the world.

John: Yeah, I think he spends a lot of his time at airports.

Helen: I'm not sure how your brother does it. That seems tiring.

John: I'll ask him next time he wakes up. He's usually sleeping!

Learn the English

Find the mistakes and write the sentence correctly

Helen: Yes, they were bad. We went walking every hour.

_____

Helen: He also went to Canada. It was a really small country.

_____

John: My father went to New Zealand. He hates to travel.

_____

Answer the questions

1. Why is Helen so sleepy?

_____

2. Who did Helen travel with to Mexico?

_____

3. What did Helen do every day on her trip?

_____

4. Where does Helen want to go to?

_____

5. When did John's brother write a book?

_____

Test

Write the answer next to the letter "A"

A: ___ **1.** Helen and her ___ just got back from ___.

a. brother, Australia   b. sister, Japan   c. sister, Mexico   d. aunt, Kenya

A: ___ **2.** The beaches in Mexico were really ___.

a. none   b. great   c. second   d. sleepy

A: ___ **3.** Helen ___ swimming every day.

a. went   b. go   c. been   d. be

A: ___ **4.** Did John like the food in Mexico?

a. Yes, he did.   b. No, he didn't.   c. Yes, he remembers.   d. Yes, he can.

A: ___ **5.** Where else did Helen travel to?

a. Canada.   b. Australia.   c. South Africa.   d. Brazil.

A: ___ **6.** Helen ___ heard that ___ is amazing.

a. have, Canada   b. is, China   c. has, Japan   d. has, Kenya

A: ___ **7.** John's brother ___ a book last ___.

a. read, month   b. wrote, year   c. bought, week   d. written, year

A: ___ **8.** John's brother spends a lot of time at ___.

a. New Zealand   b. airports   c. Canada   d. home

Answers on page 373

Lesson 36: Landscapes

Manzaralar

What had you prepared for yesterday's math class?
I had prepared a video about lakes.

Learn the words

1. **river**
   Nehir
2. **beach (es)**
   Kumsal
3. **mountain**
   Dağ
4. **volcano (es)**
   Yanardağ
5. **forest**
   Orman
6. **lake**
   Göl
7. **waterfall**
   Şelale
8. **island**
   Ada
9. **ocean**
   Okyanus
10. **jungle**
    Orman

Learn a verb

prepare – preparing – prepared – prepared hazırlamak

Mary: Had you prepared anything for yesterday's geography class?

Learn an idiom

A drop in the ocean

Meaning: To only make a tiny impact.

"We donated money to the victims of the tsunami, but I'm afraid it is just *a drop in the ocean*."

Conversation

Tom: Last week in science class, we were talking about pollution.

Mary: Do you mean pollution in the oceans and lakes?

Tom: Yeah, and it's also polluted in the forests.

Mary: Well, we started a group to help clean up the beaches.

Tom: It's a good start, but it's just a drop in the ocean.

Mary: It sounds like you really want to change things.

Tom: I do, but then I forgot to do my other homework.

Mary: Had you prepared anything for yesterday's geography class?

Tom: No, I hadn't. What had you prepared for yesterday's class?

Mary: I had prepared a video about volcanoes and waterfalls.

Tom: Had you prepared anything for yesterday's history class?

Mary: Yes, I had written a speech and article about a mountain.

Tom: What had our classmates prepared for yesterday's class?

Mary: They had made a poster about jungles and islands.

Tom: I think I'm the only one that hadn't prepared anything.

Mary: Yes, but you were thinking about cleaning our landscapes.

Tom: I could have made a presentation on pollution.

Mary: It's an important subject. Some rivers are really dirty.

Tom: The teacher was angry I hadn't done my homework.

Mary: Maybe she'll be happy if you prepare a video about pollution.

Tom: That's true. I can also prepare a quiz to give the class.

Mary: I'm pretty sure the other students don't like quizzes.

Tom: That's a good point, but I think the teacher likes them.

Learn the English

Put the sentences in order

Mary: Had you prepared anything for yesterday's class? ____

Mary: Well, we started a group to help clean up the beaches. ____

Tom: I do, but then I forgot to do my other homework. ____

Mary: Do you mean pollution in the oceans and lakes? ____

Tom: No, I hadn't. What had you prepared for class? ____

Tom: Yeah, and it's also polluted in the forests. ____

Mary: It sounds like you really want to change things. ____

Tom: It's a good start, but it's just a drop in the ocean. ____

Answer the questions

1. In which class were they talking about pollution?

_____

2. What kind of group did Mary start?

_____

3. What had Mary prepared for geography class?

_____

4. Why hadn't Tom prepared anything?

_____

5. Who doesn't like quizzes?

_____

Test

Write the answer next to the letter "A"

A: ___ **1.** Tom talked about pollution last ___ in ___ class.

a. week, geography   b. week, science   c. year, history   d. month, science

A: ___ **2.** Tom feels that cleaning the beaches is just a drop in the ___.

a. lake   b. forest   c. ocean   d. waterfall

A: ___ **3.** Mary had ___ a ___ for history class.

a. prepared, video   b. make, article   c. prepared, speech   d. made, poster

A: ___ **4.** Had Tom prepared anything for geography class?

a. No, he hadn't.   b. Yes, he had.   c. No, I hadn't.   d. No, he doesn't.

A: ___ **5.** ___ was the only one that ___ prepared anything.

a. Classmates, had   b. Teacher, really   c. Students, didn't   d. Tom, hadn't

A: ___ **6.** The teacher was angry he hadn't ___ his homework.

a. preparing   b. done   c. present   d. give

A: ___ **7.** Their classmates had prepared a ___ about ___.

a. video, lakes   b. speech, volcanoes   c. article, mountains   d. poster, islands

A: ___ **8.** Who does Tom think likes quizzes?

a. Other students.   b. Classmates.   c. The teacher.   d. Mary.

Answers on page 373

Lesson 37: Everyday life

Günlük yaşam

> When will you have woken up by?
> I will have woken up by six o'clock.

Learn the words

1. **woken up**
   Uyandım
2. **brushed my teeth**
   Dişimi fırçaladım
3. **done homework**
   Ödevimi yaptım
4. **cooked dinner**
   Yemek yaptım
5. **taken out the trash**
   Çöpü attım
6. **eaten breakfast**
   Kahvaltı ettim
7. **gone to school**
   Okula gittim
8. **taken a shower**
   Duş aldım
9. **gone to sleep**
   Uyudum
10. **gone shopping**
    Alışverişe gittim

Learn a verb

wake – waking – woke – woken uyanmak

Ted: I will have woken up by a quarter past five.

Learn an idiom

Hit the nail on the head

Meaning: To say something that is correct.

"I agree with what you said. You really *hit the nail on the head*."

Conversation

Kevin: I just saw a TV show about planning everyday life.

Ted: Did it say that people should organize their time well?

Kevin: Yes! You hit the nail on the head!

Ted: It's a really good idea. Let's plan what we'll do this week.

Kevin: Okay. Tomorrow morning, when will you have woken up by?

Ted: I will have woken up by a quarter past five.

Kevin: That's early. Will you have taken a shower by six o'clock?

Ted: Yes, I will have, and I'll have eaten breakfast by half past six.

Kevin: That seems like a really good start to the day.

Ted: That's right, and I will have taken out the trash, too.

Kevin: Are you sure? I've never seen you wake up so early.

Ted: You're right. Actually, I'll probably have gone to school late.

Kevin: Yeah, it's not so easy to be as organized as I am.

Ted: Are you saying that you're better at planning things?

Kevin: Yes. I think I'm much more organized than you are.

Ted: That's not true! I think I always get things done!

Kevin: Really? What time will you have gone to sleep tonight?

Ted: I'll have brushed my teeth and gone to sleep by ten o'clock.

Kevin: Maybe that's true, but will you have done your homework?

Ted: Probably not, but that's because I like video games so much.

Kevin: I think you really need to plan your time better.

Ted: No, I just think the days are too short. I never have time.

Kevin: Here's a secret: the days are longer if you wake up earlier.

Learn the English

Fill in the blanks

Kevin: _____ morning, when will you have _____ up by?

Ted: I will _____ woken up by a _____ past five.

Kevin: Will you have _____ a shower by six _____?

Ted: Yes, and I'll have _____ breakfast by _____ past six.

Kevin: That _____ like a really good _____ to the day.

Ted: _____ right, and I will have taken out the _____, too.

Kevin: Are you _____? I've never _____ you wake up early.

Answer the questions

1. When will Ted have woken up by tomorrow morning?

_____

2. What will Ted have done by six o'clock?

_____

3. Why won't Ted have done his homework?

_____

4. Who has never woken up early?

_____

5. When will Ted have eaten breakfast by?

_____

Test

Write the answer next to the letter "A"

A: ___ **1.** Kevin's TV show was about ___ everyday life.

a. planning   b. hitting nails in   c. eating breakfast in   d. waking up for

A: ___ **2.** Ted will have ___ breakfast by a ___ past six.

a. ate, half   b. eaten, half   c. eat, quarter   d. eating, ten

A: ___ **3.** Will Ted have taken a shower by six o'clock?

a. Yes, he has.   b. No, he hasn't.   c. No, he didn't.   d. Yes, he will have.

A: ___ **4.** Kevin has never ___ Ted ___ up so early.

a. saw, wakes   b. seeing, woke   c. seen, wake   d. see, waking

A: ___ **5.** Kevin ___ he is ___ more organized than Ted is.

a. thinks, much   b. think, much   c. thought, better   d. think, way

A: ___ **6.** Will Ted have gone to sleep by nine o'clock tonight?

a. Yes, he will have.   b. Yes, he does.   c. No, he can't.   d. No, he won't have.

A: ___ **7.** Ted ___ he never ___ enough time.

a. feels, have   b. feels, has   c. thinks, does   d. says, having

A: ___ **8.** When will Ted have brushed his teeth by?

a. Half past six.   b. A quarter past five.   c. Ten o'clock.   d. Six o'clock.

Answers on page 373

Lesson 38: Languages

Diller

How long have you been learning German?
I have been learning German for one year.

Learn the words

1. **English**
   İngilizce
2. **German**
   Almanca
3. **Portuguese**
   Portekizce
4. **Japanese**
   Japonca
5. **Vietnamese**
   Vietnamca
6. **Spanish**
   İspanyolca
7. **French**
   Fransızca
8. **Chinese**
   Çince
9. **Hindi**
   Hintçe
10. **Arabic**
    Arapça

Learn a verb

speak – speaking – spoke – spoken konuşmak

Helen: He has been speaking it for six months. He loves it.

Learn an idiom

Speak the same language

Meaning: To share the same understanding and be in agreement.

"I agree with everything you are saying. I think we're *speaking the same language.*"

Conversation

Jessica: I just came from the library. Your brother was there.

Helen: Yeah, he has a language class. He's learning German.

Jessica: How long has he been studying German?

Helen: He has been speaking it for six months. He loves it.

Jessica: I heard there are many language classes at the library.

Helen: Yes, I know they have Hindi, Portuguese and French, too.

Jessica: My aunt and uncle started learning Japanese.

Helen: Have they been studying Japanese for a long time?

Jessica: No, they haven't been. I think they started last spring.

Helen: They must like languages. They also speak Vietnamese.

Jessica: It's a fun hobby. In school we had to study languages.

Helen: Did you learn Arabic, Chinese, or Spanish?

Jessica: I learned some Arabic and some Spanish, actually.

Helen: How long have you been studying Spanish?

Jessica: I have been learning Spanish for four years.

Helen: That's great! It's very useful to speak other languages.

Jessica: Yes, I like to watch Spanish movies in my free time.

Helen: Speaking of movies, do you want to go to the cinema?

Jessica: Great idea! We can also get some food and drinks.

Helen: Nice! I think we're speaking the same language now.

Jessica: So, which film do you want to watch?

Helen: I know you like Spanish movies, but I don't speak it.

Jessica: No problem! We'll watch an English movie.

Learn the English

Unscramble the sentences

1. been / German / he / studying / long / has / How

_____

2. studying / they / time / been / a / Have / for / Japanese / long

_____

3. have / Spanish / years / for / I / learning / been / four

_____

Answer the questions

1. Where did Jessica see Helen's brother?

_____

2. When did Jessica's aunt and uncle start learning Japanese?

_____

3. How long has Jessica been learning Spanish?

_____

4. Who likes to watch Spanish movies?

_____

5. What did Helen say was very useful?

_____

Test

Write the answer next to the letter "A"

A: ___ **1.** There are many language classes at the ___.

a. cinema   b. spring   c. school   d. library

A: ___ **2.** Jessica's aunt is learning ___.

a. Spanish   b. German   c. Japanese   d. French

A: ___ **3.** Helen's brother has been learning German ___.

a. since spring   b. for four years   c. for six months   d. a long time

A: ___ **4.** Jessica's aunt and uncle ___ been learning for a long time.

a. hasn't   b. have   c. has   d. haven't

A: ___ **5.** Jessica learned some ___ in ___.

a. Hindi, library   b. Arabic, school   c. Spanish, cinema   d. German, spring

A: ___ **6.** She has been ___ Spanish for four years.

a. learning   b. spoken   c. learned   d. studies

A: ___ **7.** Helen ___ it's ___ to speak other languages.

a. saying, great   b. studies, fun   c. learned, love   d. thinks, useful

A: ___ **8.** Helen ___ speak Spanish.

a. don't   b. do   c. doesn't   d. does

Answers on page 373

Lesson 39: Pets

Evcil hayvanlar

> What is faster than a mouse?
> A rabbit is faster than a mouse.

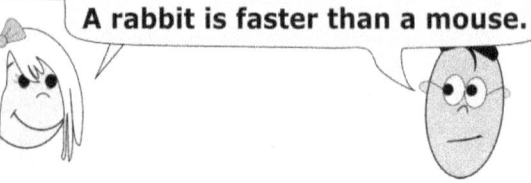

Learn the words

1. **dog**
   Köpek
2. **fish**
   Balık
3. **bird**
   Kuş
4. **rabbit**
   Tavşan
5. **guinea pig**
   Kobay faresi

6. **cat**
   Kedi
7. **turtle**
   Kaplumbağa
8. **mouse**
   Fare
9. **hamster**
   Hamster
10. **snake**
    Yılan

Learn a verb

feed – feeding – fed – fed beslemek

Jason: Yes, it is. And I have to feed it a lot of food every day.

Learn an idiom

The teacher's pet

Meaning: A student whom the teacher favors.

"Her classmates are jealous of her because she is *the teacher's pet*."

Conversation

Emily: Do you know a lot about animals?

Jason: I love animals! I even have a pet hamster.

Emily: Is a hamster more expensive than a mouse?

Jason: Yes, it is. And I have to feed it a lot of food every day.

Emily: Yesterday at school, we were learning about animals.

Jason: You're the teacher's pet! I guess you knew all the answers.

Emily: I just like to study more than other students do.

Jason: Did you talk about dogs and cats?

Emily: Yes, and we also learned about birds and guinea pigs.

Jason: I like all animals, but I like smaller ones better.

Emily: Yes, they're easier and cheaper to have as a pet.

Jason: So as a pet, what is better than a hamster?

Emily: A fish is more colorful than a hamster. I like fish better.

Jason: Is a snake is worse than a turtle?

Emily: Yes, it is. I don't like snakes at all! I saw a scary one on TV.

Jason: A turtle is slower than a snake. I think that's boring.

Emily: I don't like pets that are bigger than a rabbit.

Jason: What is bigger than a rabbit?

Emily: A dog is bigger than a rabbit, and it's faster, too.

Jason: I like dogs. My grandfather walks his dogs at the park.

Emily: People really have personalities just like their pets.

Jason: Do you mean how my grandfather and dogs like exercise?

Emily: Yes, and how you and your hamster like to eat a lot.

Learn the English

Find the mistakes and write the sentence correctly

Emily: Last week at the park we were learning about pets.

_____

Jason: I hate all animals, but she likes bigger ones better.

_____

Jason: Is a fish is cheaper than a bird?

_____

Answer the questions

1. When was Emily learning about animals?

_____

2. What does Emily like better than a hamster?

_____

3. Who thinks turtles are boring?

_____

4. Where does Jason's grandfather go walking?

_____

5. Why doesn't Emily like snakes?

_____

Test

Write the answer next to the letter "A"

A: ___ **1.** Jason ___ to ___ his hamster every day.

a. have, fed   b. is, feeding   c. does, feed   d. has, feed

A: ___ **2.** Where was Emily talking about dogs and cats?

a. The park.   b. At school.   c. On TV.   d. At the pet store.

A: ___ **3.** Who has dogs as pets?

a. Emily.   b. The teacher.   c. Jason's grandfather.   d. Jason.

A: ___ **4.** Is a fish more colorful than a hamster?

a. Yes, it is.   b. No, it's not.   c. Yes, it does.   d. No, it can't.

A: ___ **5.** Emily ___ a snake is ___ than a turtle.

a. saw, scary   b. thinks, worse   c. thinks, better   d. likes, smaller

A: ___ **6.** Jason thinks a turtle is ___ because it's ___ than a snake.

a. better, smaller   b. great, bigger   c. boring, slower   d. scary, faster

A: ___ **7.** Emily ___ like ___ pets.

a. don't, dog   b. doesn't, expensive   c. can't, faster   d. doesn't, bigger

A: ___ **8.** Jason thinks a ___ is more expensive than a ___.

a. mouse, hamster   b. turtle, snake   c. rabbit, dog   d. hamster, mouse

Answers on page 373

Lesson 40: Fast food

Hazır yemek

> What is the sweetest food?
> The sweetest food is the pancake.

Section A — Words

1. **doughnut**
   Tatlı çörek
2. **cheeseburger**
   Çizburger
3. **chicken nuggets**
   Tavuk nugget
4. **pancake**
   Krep
5. **taco**
   Tako
6. **french fries**
   Patates kızartması
7. **onion rings**
   Soğan halkası
8. **hot dog**
   Sosisli sandviç
9. **fried chicken**
   Kızarmış tavuk
10. **burrito**
    Burrito

Learn a verb

try – trying – tried – tried denemek

Ted: Did he say to try the cheeseburger or the hot dog?

Learn an idiom

You are what you eat

Meaning: The food that you eat affects your health.

"Careful not to eat too much fast food. *You are what you eat.*"

Conversation

Ted: I'm glad we're finally going to eat. I'm really hungry.

Matthew: Kevin told me this fast food restaurant is pretty good.

Ted: Did he say to try the cheeseburger or the hot dog?

Matthew: He said the burrito is the best thing on the menu.

Ted: The burrito is the most expensive! What's the cheapest food?

Matthew: The cheapest food is the taco, but it's also the saltiest.

Ted: Are the onion rings the worst thing? They look unhealthy.

Matthew: Yes, they are. Remember that you are what you eat.

Ted: That's true. I was feeling really tired in gym class last week.

Matthew: We're having fast food today, so it won't be too healthy.

Ted: Okay, so what is the most delicious food?

Matthew: I think the most delicious food is the fried chicken.

Ted: That's harder to eat. I think I'll try the chicken nuggets.

Matthew: Also, let's share some french fries.

Ted: Good idea. Are the pancakes the sweetest?

Matthew: No, they aren't. The doughnuts are the sweetest.

Ted: When I eat fast food, I like to get dessert, too.

Matthew: I want the burrito. Susan ate it on Tuesday and loved it.

Ted: I'll try the hot dog because it looks bigger. I also want a taco.

Matthew: That's a lot of food to eat at once. You're really hungry!

Ted: Well, I didn't eat breakfast this morning because I was late.

Matthew: That's why you should plan your time better.

Ted: I also forgot to bring money, so can I borrow some?

Learn the English

Put the sentences in order

Ted: That's true. I was feeling really tired in gym class. ___

Ted: Are the onion rings the worst thing? They look unhealthy. ___

Matthew: He said the burrito is the best thing on the menu. ___

Matthew: Yes, they are. Remember that you are what you eat. ___

Matthew: The cheapest food is the taco. It's also the saltiest. ___

Ted: The burrito is the most expensive! What's the cheapest? ___

Ted: Did he say to try the cheeseburger or the hot dog? ___

Matthew: We're having fast food so it won't be too healthy. ___

Answer the questions

1. Who wants to eat a burrito?

_____

2. What is the cheapest food?

_____

3. Why is Ted so hungry?

_____

4. When did Susan eat fast food?

_____

5. Which food is the sweetest?

_____

Test

Write the answer next to the letter "A"

A: ___ **1.** Kevin said to ___ the ___.

a. eat, cheeseburger   b. taste, taco   c. try, burrito   d. try, hot dog

A: ___ **2.** Is the taco the saltiest food?

a. Yes, it is.   b. Yes, it has.   c. Yes, it can.   d. No, it's not.

A: ___ **3.** The burrito is the ___ fast food on the menu.

a. cheapest   b. most expensive   c. saltiest   d. sweetest

A: ___ **4.** Ted was feeling ___ last ___.

a. happy, Tuesday   b. late, night   c. hungry, Tuesday   d. tired, week

A: ___ **5.** They are having fast food ___.

a. last week   b. today   c. on Tuesday   d. for breakfast

A: ___ **6.** The most ___ food is the fried chicken.

a. expensive   b. best   c. cheapest   d. delicious

A: ___ **7.** Who loved the burrito?

a. Kevin.   b. Matthew.   c. Susan.   d. Ted.

A: ___ **8.** Matthew and Ted are going to share the ___.

a. french fries   b. fried chicken   c. onion rings   d. chicken nuggets

Answers on page 373

Answers

Lesson 1 test	1. c 2. a 3. b 4. b 5. d 6. b 7. c 8. b
Lesson 2 test	1. b 2. b 3. d 4. b 5. d 6. c 7. a 8. d
Lesson 3 test	1. b 2. c 3. a 4. d 5. d 6. b 7. a 8. d
Lesson 4 test	1. b 2. a 3. b 4. d 5. c 6. c 7. d 8. d
Lesson 5 test	1. b 2. d 3. c 4. b 5. b 6. a 7. d 8. a
Lesson 6 test	1. b 2. a 3. a 4. c 5. d 6. c 7. b 8. a
Lesson 7 test	1. b 2. d 3. a 4. a 5. c 6. c 7. d 8. a
Lesson 8 test	1. b 2. d 3. b 4. c 5. c 6. a 7. c 8. b
Lesson 9 test	1. d 2. a 3. b 4. d 5. c 6. d 7. a 8. c
Lesson 10 test	1. b 2. a 3. c 4. a 5. b 6. c 7. a 8. d
Lesson 11 test	1. b 2. c 3. b 4. a 5. d 6. d 7. a 8. c
Lesson 12 test	1. d 2. a 3. b 4. c 5. c 6. b 7. a 8. d
Lesson 13 test	1. d 2. d 3. b 4. b 5. c 6. d 7. a 8. c
Lesson 14 test	1. b 2. b 3. c 4. d 5. a 6. a 7. c 8. d
Lesson 15 test	1. d 2. b 3. d 4. a 5. c 6. c 7. a 8. b
Lesson 16 test	1. b 2. d 3. a 4. a 5. b 6. c 7. d 8. c
Lesson 17 test	1. a 2. d 3. a 4. c 5. c 6. b 7. b 8. c
Lesson 18 test	1. a 2. c 3. d 4. c 5. d 6. b 7. b 8. a
Lesson 19 test	1. c 2. a 3. c 4. b 5. d 6. d 7. a 8. d
Lesson 20 test	1. c 2. a 3. c 4. d 5. b 6. b 7. d 8. a

Lesson 21 test	1. a 2. c 3. d 4. d 5. b 6. d 7. c 8. b
Lesson 22 test	1. c 2. d 3. b 4. c 5. c 6. a 7. b 8. a
Lesson 23 test	1. b 2. c 3. b 4. d 5. a 6. d 7. a 8. b
Lesson 24 test	1. d 2. b 3. b 4. a 5. c 6. d 7. c 8. a
Lesson 25 test	1. d 2. b 3. a 4. b 5. d 6. c 7. c 8. a
Lesson 26 test	1. d 2. c 3. b 4. b 5. b 6. c 7. a 8. b
Lesson 27 test	1. b 2. d 3. d 4. b 5. a 6. c 7. c 8. a
Lesson 28 test	1. c 2. b 3. c 4. d 5. d 6. c 7. a 8. b
Lesson 29 test	1. d 2. b 3. b 4. a 5. c 6. b 7. a 8. b
Lesson 30 test	1. d 2. b 3. c 4. a 5. d 6. b 7. b 8. c
Lesson 31 test	1. a 2. d 3. d 4. b 5. c 6. c 7. b 8. c
Lesson 32 test	1. d 2. a 3. b 4. c 5. c 6. b 7. a 8. d
Lesson 33 test	1. c 2. d 3. c 4. b 5. b 6. a 7. d 8. a
Lesson 34 test	1. b 2. d 3. b 4. d 5. c 6. c 7. a 8. a
Lesson 35 test	1. c 2. b 3. a 4. a 5. d 6. d 7. b 8. b
Lesson 36 test	1. b 2. c 3. c 4. a 5. d 6. b 7. d 8. c
Lesson 37 test	1. a 2. b 3. d 4. c 5. a 6. d 7. b 8. c
Lesson 38 test	1. d 2. c 3. c 4. d 5. b 6. a 7. d 8. c
Lesson 39 test	1. d 2. b 3. c 4. a 5. b 6. c 7. d 8. d
Lesson 40 test	1. c 2. a 3. b 4. d 5. b 6. d 7. c 8. a

Preston Lee's
Read & Write ENGLISH

Lesson 1 - 40

For Turkish Speakers

CONTENTS

Lesson 1: My family Ailem — Page 378

Lesson 2: My pencil case Kalem kutum — Page 382

Lesson 3: In the classroom Sınıfta — Page 386

Lesson 4: The weather Hava durumu — Page 390

Lesson 5: Places Yerler — Page 394

Lesson 6: Sports Spor — Page 398

Lesson 7: At the zoo Hayvanat bahçesinde — Page 402

Lesson 8: Colors Renkler — Page 406

Lesson 9: Activities Aktiviteler — Page 410

Lesson 10: Food & Drinks Yiyecek ve içecekler — Page 414

Lesson 11: At the fruit market Manavda — Page 418

Lesson 12: Shapes Şekiller — Page 422

Lesson 13: At the supermarket Süpermarket — Page 426

Lesson 14: At the ice cream shop Dondurma dükkanında — Page 430

Lesson 15: In the refrigerator Buzdolabında — Page 434

Lesson 16: Jobs Meslekler — Page 438

Lesson 17: Names İsimler — Page 442

Lesson 18: More places Daha çok yer — Page 446

Lesson 19: Meats Etler — Page 450

Lesson 20: Vegetables Sebzeler — Page 454

Lesson 21: At school Okulda — Page 458

Lesson 22: School subjects Okul dersleri — Page 462

Lesson 23: Chores Ev işleri — Page 466

Lesson 24: At the toy store Oyuncak mağazasında — Page 470

Lesson 25: In the kitchen Mutfakta — Page 474

Lesson 26: In the toolbox Alet çantası — Page 478

Lesson 27: Transportation Ulaşım — Page 482

Lesson 28: Clothes Giysiler — Page 486

Lesson 29: More clothes Daha fazla giysi — Page 490

Lesson 30: In the living room Oturma odasında — Page 494

Lesson 31: In the bathroom Banyoda — Page 498

Lesson 32: In the bedroom Yatak odasında — Page 502

Lesson 33: Around the house Evin etrafında — Page 506

Lesson 34: Hobbies Hobiler — Page 510

Lesson 35: Countries Ülkeler — Page 514

Lesson 36: Landscapes Manzaralar — Page 518

Lesson 37: Everyday life Günlük yaşam — Page 522

Lesson 38: Languages Diller — Page 526

Lesson 39: Pets Evcil hayvanlar — Page 530

Lesson 40: Fast food Hazır yemek — Page 534

Answers — Page 538

Lesson 1: My family

Ailem

Learn the words

1. **mother**
   Anne
2. **grandmother**
   Büyükanne
3. **sister**
   Kız kardeş
4. **baby sister**
   Bebek kız kardeş
5. **aunt**
   Yenge
6. **father**
   Baba
7. **grandfather**
   Büyükbaba
8. **brother**
   Erkek kardeş
9. **baby brother**
   Bebek erkek kardeş
10. **uncle**
    Amca

Learn a verb

see – seeing – saw – seen görmek

He hasn't <u>seen</u> Peter for a long time.

Learn an idiom

Like one of the family

Meaning: To be like a person in one's family.

"A few years ago, they were *like one of the family*, so Mary agrees it would be a good idea to invite them all."

Grammar tenses	Past	Present	Future
Simple	✓	✓	✓
Continuous		✓	✓
Perfect	✓	✓	
Perfect Continuous		✓	

Reading

The birthday party!

Mary is a little worried. It's her **aunt's** birthday this weekend and she still hasn't gotten a gift for her. She has been discussing with her **brother**, Roger, about what to get her, but they still haven't agreed on anything.

Roger thinks they should get their **aunt** a Thai cookbook because her **aunt's** dream is to travel to Thailand one day. However, Mary thinks this gift is too cheap for their beloved **aunt**. She suggested buying her a ticket to Thailand instead.

A ticket to Thailand is too expensive for both of them to afford, but Mary is thinking about asking her **mother** and **father** to help pay. Perhaps their **uncle** can also offer some money to pay for part of the ticket.

The birthday party is on Saturday, and the whole family will be attending except Mary's **grandfather**. Unfortunately, her **grandfather** is in the hospital. Mary's **grandmother** said he is feeling a lot better, but will not be out of the hospital before the party. Mary said she would take a lot of photos for him to look at.

Roger is thinking about inviting an old classmate, Peter, to the party. He hasn't seen Peter for a long time. However, Mary spoke to Peter a few days ago, and he had asked about Roger. Mary also saw Peter's **mother** and **baby sister** at the park. A few years ago, they *were like one of the family*, so Mary agrees it would be a good idea to invite them all.

One thing is for sure. This is going to be a fun party!

| Learn the English |

Find nine different verbs from the Reading

1._____   4._____   7._____

2._____   5._____   8._____

3._____   6._____   9._____

Fill in the blanks

A _____ to Thailand is too _____ for both of them to _____, but Mary is thinking _____ asking her mother and father to help pay. Perhaps their _____ can also offer some _____ to pay for part of the _____.

Answer the questions

1. Whose birthday is it this weekend?

_____

2. Why can't they buy a ticket to Thailand for their aunt?

_____

3. Who won't be going to the birthday party?

_____

4. How does Roger know Peter?

_____

Test

Write the answer next to the letter "A"

True, False or Not given?

A: ___ **1.** Mary and Roger agreed to buy a Thai cookbook for their aunt.

a. True   b. False   c. Not given

A: ___ **2.** Mary is thinking about asking her parents to help pay for the ticket.

a. True   b. False   c. Not given

A: ___ **3.** The whole family will be attending the party on Saturday.

a. True   b. False   c. Not given

A: ___ **4.** Mary's grandfather is getting out of the hospital on Sunday.

a. True   b. False   c. Not given

Multiple choice questions

A: ___ **5.** Mary ___ a cookbook is too cheap for her beloved aunt.

a. thinking about   b. thinks   c. think

A: ___ **6.** Roger ___ Peter for a long time.

a. didn't saw   b. won't see   c. hasn't seen

A: ___ **7.** Had Mary spoken to Peter a few days ago?

a. Yes, she has.   b. No, she hadn't.   c. Yes, she had.

A: ___ **8.** What is Roger thinking about doing?

a. Inviting his friend.   b. Paying for the ticket.   c. Going to the park.

Answers on page 538

Lesson 2: My pencil case

Kalem kutum

Learn the words

1. **a pencil**
   Kalem
2. **an eraser**
   Silgi
3. **glue**
   Tutkal
4. **a pencil sharpener**
   Kalemtıraş
5. **whiteout**
   Daksil
6. **a pen**
   Dolma kalem
7. **a ruler**
   Cetvel
8. **tape**
   Bant
9. **a marker**
   Keçeli kalem
10. **a crayon**
    Pastel boya

Learn a verb

buy – buying – bought – bought satın almak

While they were out, they also <u>bought</u> some food and drinks.

Learn an idiom

Cross your fingers

Meaning: To wish for luck.

"She *crossed her fingers* and hoped that she could borrow a pencil from her classmate, Kevin."

Grammar tenses	Past	Present	Future
Simple	✓	✓	
Continuous	✓		
Perfect	✓		
Perfect Continuous			

Reading

Jessica's pencil case!

Last Friday, Jessica went to Mary's house. The two friends were making a birthday card for Mary's aunt whose birthday party was the next day. Rather than <u>buying</u> a card, Mary wanted to create something special. Jessica loves drawing, so she brought her pencil case to help make it.

The girls were very careful, and used a **pen** and a **ruler** to make sure the drawing was perfect. However, as they were using **crayons** and **markers** to add some color, Mary's pet cat jumped onto the table and ripped the picture in half!

An **eraser** or **whiteout** couldn't fix that kind of mistake! Jessica didn't have any **tape** in her pencil case, nor did she have any **glue**. Therefore, the two of them decided to go and <u>buy</u> some **tape** at the nearby store.

While they were out, they also <u>bought</u> some food and drinks. They hadn't eaten much all day, so they were both really hungry. They sat at the park for a long time, eating and talking about many things. After a while, Jessica realized it was late and decided it was time to go home. However, she had forgotten to take her pencil case with her from Mary's house.

Jessica didn't notice her missing pencil case until Monday morning when she went to school. Just as she got to art class, she remembered that she didn't have it.

She *crossed her fingers* and hoped that she could borrow a **pencil** from her classmate, Kevin.

Learn the English

Unscramble the sentences

1. create / special / wanted / something / Mary / to

_____

2. some / buy / to / decided / the / at / They / store / tape

_____

3. sat / park / at / for / long / the / a / They / time

_____

4. her / case / pencil / forgot / take / Jessica / to

_____

Answer the questions

1. Who were the girls making a birthday card for?

_____

2. How did the picture get ripped in half?

_____

3. Why were they both really hungry?

_____

4. When did Jessica notice that her pencil case was missing?

_____

Test

Write the answer next to the letter "A"

True, False or Not given?

A: ___ **1.** There is a birthday party for Mary's aunt on Saturday.

a. True   b. False   c. Not given

A: ___ **2.** Mary's pet cat, which jumped on the table, is black.

a. True   b. False   c. Not given

A: ___ **3.** The girls had eaten a lot for breakfast that day.

a. True   b. False   c. Not given

A: ___ **4.** Jessica had forgotten her pencil case at school.

a. True   b. False   c. Not given

Multiple choice questions

A: ___ **5.** The two friends were ___ a birthday card for Mary's aunt.

a. made   b. makes   c. making

A: ___ **6.** They ___ crayons and markers to add some color.

a. have used   b. were using   c. use

A: ___ **7.** Did they sit and eat at the park?

a. Yes, they did.   b. Yes, they were.   c. Yes, they had.

A: ___ **8.** Who did she hope to borrow a pencil from?

a. Jessica.   b. Mary.   c. Kevin.

Answers on page 538

Lesson 3: In the Classroom

Sınıfta

Learn the words

1. **chair**
   Sandalye
2. **blackboard**
   Karatahta
3. **poster**
   Afiş
4. **globe**
   Küre
5. **clock**
   Saat
6. **desk**
   Sıra
7. **whiteboard**
   Beyaz tahta
8. **bookshelf**
   Kitaplık
9. **computer**
   Bilgisayar
10. **book**
    Kitap

Learn a verb

look – looking – looked – looked bakmak

Matthew found himself <u>looking</u> at the clock a lot.

Learn an idiom

Class clown

Meaning: A student who often makes everyone laugh in the classroom.

"John, who is the *class clown*, was dancing like a robot and knocked it off the teacher's desk."

Grammar tenses	Past	Present	Future
Simple	✓	✓	
Continuous	✓		
Perfect	✓	✓	
Perfect Continuous		✓	

Reading

Susan's classroom!

Matthew is happy to be back at school because his holidays were boring. Both his parents had to work, and he had to live with his grandparents. Matthew loves his grandparents very much, but living at their house means he cannot play video games, nor can he play with his friends much. Matthew found himself <u>looking</u> at the **clock** a lot.

When Matthew saw his new classroom, he was excited to see that there were new **desks** and **chairs**. The **bookshelf** also had many new **books**. He likes to read novels, and his favorite **books** were all included.

Matthew's classmate, Susan, was feeling very different. She had a fantastic time on the school holidays. This is because her family traveled to Canada and she learned how to ski for the first time. Susan's father had promised to take her and her friend, Helen, to Canada for over five years, and she really loved it there.

While Susan enjoyed her holidays, she is not happy about her new classroom. Unlike Matthew's classroom, too many things in the classroom are too old. For example, the computer had not been updated, and it is the same one they have been using for two years. There is also a **blackboard** instead of a **whiteboard**. The dust from the chalk makes Susan sneeze.

There is one thing Susan is pleased about, though. The teacher has replaced the **globe** that was broken last year. John, who is the *class clown*, was dancing like a robot and knocked it off the teacher's **desk**. It was funny nonetheless, and even the teacher laughed.

Learn the English

Find the two mistakes and write the sentence correctly

Two parents had to work, and he have to live with his grandparents.

_____

He like to read novels, and his favorite books weren't all included.

_____

The teacher has replaced the globe that were broken last month.

_____

There is too a blackboard instead for a whiteboard.

_____

Answer the questions

1. Why did Matthew stay with his grandparents on the holidays?

_____

2. What did Susan learn how to do while visiting Canada?

_____

3. Why doesn't Susan like blackboards?

_____

4. How did the globe in the classroom break?

_____

Test

Write the answer next to the letter "A"

True, False or Not given?

A: ___ **1.** Matthew's grandparents love him very much.

a. True	b. False	c. Not given

A: ___ **2.** Both Susan and Matthew are happy about their classrooms.

a. True	b. False	c. Not given

A: ___ **3.** Susan's family went to Canada five years ago.

a. True	b. False	c. Not given

A: ___ **4.** John had to pay for a new globe for the classroom.

a. True	b. False	c. Not given

Multiple choice questions

A: ___ **5.** Matthew was ___ to see new desks and chairs in the classroom.

a. exciting	b. excited	c. boring

A: ___ **6.** In Susan's classroom, the computer ___ updated.

a. had not been	b. is not	c. will not be

A: ___ **7.** Did Susan learn how to ski while she was in Canada?

a. Yes, she was.	b. Yes, she had.	c. Yes, she did.

A: ___ **8.** How are the things in Susan's classroom unlike Matthew's?

a. They're updated.	b. They're old.	c. They're new.

Answers on page 538

Lesson 4: The weather

Hava durumu

Learn the words

1. **snowy**
   Karlı
2. **sunny**
   Güneşli
3. **rainy**
   Yağmurlu
4. **windy**
   Rüzgarlı
5. **cloudy**
   Bulutlu
6. **hot**
   Sıcak
7. **cold**
   Soğuk
8. **warm**
   Ilık
9. **cool**
   Serin
10. **freezing**
    Çok Soğuk

Learn a verb

feel – feeling – felt – felt hissetmek

It looked like they were <u>feeling</u> really unhappy.

Learn an idiom

It's raining cats and dogs

Meaning: It's raining heavily.

"*It was raining cats and dogs*, and they were totally wet."

Grammar tenses	Past	Present	Future
Simple	✓	✓	
Continuous	✓		
Perfect	✓		
Perfect Continuous			

Reading

A rainy day!

Almost every weekend, Jada enjoys going swimming at the swimming pool that is next to the big park. She <u>feels</u> the best time to go is early in the morning. There are fewer people at that time, and the weather is usually good.

Two weeks ago, on Saturday, she left her house around seven o'clock and rode her bike to the park. At that time, it was **cloudy** and **cool**, but it wasn't really bad weather at all. Jada prefers **cold** weather to **hot**, especially on days when she does exercise. There were only three other people in the pool that day, so it wasn't too crowded.

Jada swam twenty laps of the pool. She finished her swim at around quarter to eight, and she <u>felt</u> fantastic. Jada always <u>feels</u> great after her swim. She grabbed her towel and walked to the change rooms to change into dry clothes.

When she went outside, the weather had suddenly changed a lot! It was cold and **rainy**, and it had become really **windy**, too. Luckily, she was wearing enough clothes for the poor weather and she had an umbrella. If not, she would probably <u>feel</u> **freezing**.

To get home, she passed by the park and the basketball courts. As she was riding past basketball court 2, she noticed her two friends, Tom and John, standing under a tree. It *was raining cats and dogs*, and they were totally wet. It looked like they were <u>feeling</u> really unhappy. She stopped to say hello, and told them that it's best to check the weather report before going to play in the park.

Sadly, when the boys had checked the weather, it said, "no rain"!

Learn the English

Write the opposite with the word "not"

Jada enjoys going swimming at the swimming pool.
<u>Jada does not enjoy going swimming at the swimming pool.</u>

It was cloudy and cool.

_____

Jada swam twenty laps of the pool.

_____

Jada feels great after her swim.

_____

She had an umbrella.

_____

Answer the questions

1. Why does Jada like to go swimming early in the morning?

_____

2. What was the weather like at seven o'clock?

_____

3. Who did Jada see at the basketball courts?

_____

4. Why were the two boys standing under a tree?

_____

Test

Write the answer next to the letter "A"

True, False or Not given?

A: ___ **1.** Jada prefers exercising in hot weather.

a. True	b. False	c. Not given

A: ___ **2.** Every time Jada goes swimming, she goes alone.

a. True	b. False	c. Not given

A: ___ **3.** Her friends, Tom and John, don't know how to swim.

a. True	b. False	c. Not given

A: ___ **4.** The big park is next to the swimming pool.

a. True	b. False	c. Not given

Multiple choice questions

A: ___ **5.** Jada always ___ great after her swim.

a. feels	b. feeling	c. feel

A: ___ **6.** Jada ___ her house around seven o'clock and ___ her bike to the park.

a. leaves, rides	b. left, ridden	c. left, rode

A: ___ **7.** Was the weather bad before she went swimming?

a. Yes, it had been.	b. No, it didn't.	c. No, it wasn't.

A: ___ **8.** What were her friends doing at the park?

a. Playing basketball.	b. Standing.	c. Swimming.

Answers on page 538

Lesson 5: Places

Yerler

Learn the words

1. **park**
   Park
2. **beach**
   Plaj
3. **night market**
   Akşam pazarı
4. **store**
   Mağaza
5. **supermarket**
   Süpermarket
6. **restaurant**
   Restoran
7. **swimming pool**
   Yüzme havuzu
8. **department store**
   Alışveriş merkezi
9. **cinema**
   Sinema
10. **gym**
    Spor salonu

Learn a verb

walk – walking – walked – walked yürümek

It is also convenient because Kevin can <u>walk</u> there from the gym.

Learn an idiom

Have a change of heart

Meaning: To change your mind about something.

"However, Kevin has recently had a *change of heart* about his chances."

Grammar tenses	Past	Present	Future
Simple	✓	✓	✓
Continuous		✓	
Perfect	✓	✓	
Perfect Continuous		✓	

Reading

Let's go swimming!

Kevin loves swimming. His favorite place to go swimming is at the **beach**. He loves swimming there because you can enjoy different activities while staying healthy. For example, whenever Kevin goes to the **beach**, he likes to bring a ball so that he can play fun games.

Last weekend, Kevin's father had planned to take him to the ocean because Kevin wanted to practice for the upcoming swimming race in two weeks. Besides swimming, Kevin has been going to the **gym** three times a week to get stronger. However, the weather was too cold, so they decided to go to the **swimming pool** instead.

Near the big **park**, there is a very nice **swimming pool** where Kevin likes to go. He likes this one because it has warm water, so if the weather is too cold for the **beach**, then he can still practice there. It is also convenient because Kevin can walk there from the **gym**.

On the way to the **swimming pool**, Kevin's father decided to stop at the **store** to pick up some new swimming goggles for him. Kevin's father is proud of how much he is preparing for the race. Kevin's father promised that when the competition is over, he will take him to his favorite **restaurant** and see the latest movie at the **cinema**.

At first, Kevin didn't think he could win the swimming race because a lot of his classmates are strong swimmers. However, Kevin has recently had a *change of heart* about his chances. Since he has been exercising at the **gym**, swimming laps at the **swimming pool**, and having fun in the water at the **beach**, he is feeling confident that he can be number one!

Learn the English

Find nine different adjectives from the Reading

1. _____   4. _____   7. _____

2. _____   5. _____   8. _____

3. _____   6. _____   9. _____

Complete the sentence using 3 or 4 words

Kevin's favorite place to go swimming _____

Kevin wanted to practice for _____

Kevin's father will take him to _____

Kevin is confident that he can _____

Answer the questions

1. What does Kevin take to the beach?

_____

2. How many times a week has Kevin been going to the gym?

_____

3. What did Kevin's father buy on the way to the swimming pool?

_____

4. Why didn't Kevin think he could win the race at first?

_____

Test

Write the answer next to the letter "A"

True, False or Not given?

A: ___ **1.** Last weekend, Kevin's father took him to the beach.

a. True   b. False   c. Not given

A: ___ **2.** It's too far for Kevin to walk to the swimming pool.

a. True   b. False   c. Not given

A: ___ **3.** Exercising at the gym has helped Kevin's confidence.

a. True   b. False   c. Not given

A: ___ **4.** Kevin's father also really enjoys swimming at the beach.

a. True   b. False   c. Not given

Multiple choice questions

A: ___ **5.** Besides ___, Kevin has been going to the gym to get stronger.

a. has been swimming   b. swimming   c. swim

A: ___ **6.** Kevin's father ___ to stop at the store to pick up some goggles.

a. is deciding   b. decides   c. decided

A: ___ **7.** Are Kevin's classmates also good at swimming?

a. Yes, they are.   b. Yes, they can.   c. Yes, they strong.

A: ___ **8.** When is Kevin going to have a swimming competition?

a. In two weeks.   b. Upcoming.   c. Last weekend.

Answers on page 538

Lesson 6: Sports

Spor

Learn the words

1. **basketball**
   Basketbol
2. **soccer**
   Futbol
3. **badminton**
   Badminton
4. **golf**
   Golf
5. **hockey**
   Hokey
6. **cricket**
   Kriket
7. **tennis**
   Tenis
8. **baseball**
   Beyzbol
9. **volleyball**
   Voleybol
10. **football**
    Amerikan futbolu

Learn a verb

play – playing – played – played oynamak

When Mary was younger, she seldom <u>played</u> any sports at all.

Learn an idiom

A good sport

Meaning: Someone who can accept losing or be made fun of.

"She lost the game, but she was *a good sport* about it."

Grammar tenses	Past	Present	Future
Simple	✓		
Continuous	✓		
Perfect	✓		
Perfect Continuous			

Reading

Loving sports!

When Mary was younger, she seldom <u>played</u> any sports at all. One time when she was four years old, Mary and her family went to the beach together. Her older brother started <u>playing</u> a **soccer** game with her, and he was much better than she was.

She lost the game, but she was *a good sport* about it. However, this made her realize that she wanted to improve. Mary also had a lot of fun being active and running around. She decided to practice every day until she became a good **soccer** player. Soon, she not only could beat her brother, but she also became a more confident person. In the end, losing to her brother that day at the beach was good for her.

As she got older, she worked really hard and tried many different sports. While she wasn't always the best, she certainly enjoyed it. In her free time, she would go to the park to <u>play</u> **baseball** with her friends. Sometimes, she went to the **basketball** court to practice alone. It didn't matter if it was a team sport or not, Mary liked them all.

One of her favorite people to spend time together with was her best friend, Susan. Almost every Sunday, the two friends would go to <u>play</u> **badminton** at the gym near Susan's house. On sunny days, they enjoyed going outside to <u>play</u> **volleyball**, or even to <u>play</u> **cricket**. Susan had learned **cricket** when she lived in England for a summer.

The only sport that Mary didn't like as much was **tennis**. She thought it was difficult to <u>play</u>. A few years before, while she was <u>playing</u> with her uncle, she got hit really hard in the face with a ball. After that, **tennis** wasn't a sport she enjoyed <u>playing</u> very much.

Learn the English

Complete the questions to the answers

How _____?

Mary was four years old when her brother first played soccer with her.

Where _____?

Mary would go to the park in her free time.

Who _____?

Susan is Mary's best friend.

Why _____?

Mary doesn't enjoy tennis because she got hit in the face with a ball.

Answer the questions

1. What did Mary decide to do after she lost the soccer game?

_____

2. Why was losing the game good for Mary?

_____

3. Where would Susan and Mary play badminton?

_____

4. Where did Susan learn how to play cricket?

_____

Test

Write the answer next to the letter "A"

True, False or Not given?

A: ___ **1.** Mary's older brother is a good sport when he loses.

a. True　　　　　　　　b. False　　　　　　　　c. Not given

A: ___ **2.** As a result of losing, Mary ended up being more confident.

a. True　　　　　　　　b. False　　　　　　　　c. Not given

A: ___ **3.** When she was four years old, Mary ran slower than her brother.

a. True　　　　　　　　b. False　　　　　　　　c. Not given

A: ___ **4.** Mary often played sports when she was younger.

a. True　　　　　　　　b. False　　　　　　　　c. Not given

Multiple choice questions

A: ___ **5.** Sometimes, she ___ to the basketball court to practice alone.

a. going　　　　　　　　b. went　　　　　　　　c. had gone

A: ___ **6.** While she was ___ with her uncle, she got ___ really hard in the face.

a. played, hits　　　　　b. playing, hit　　　　　c. play, hit

A: ___ **7.** Do the friends play badminton almost every Sunday at the gym?

a. Yes, they play.　　　b. Yes, they go.　　　　c. Yes, they do.

A: ___ **8.** On what kind of days would they go outside to play volleyball?

a. Sunny days.　　　　b. Summer days.　　　　c. Beach days.

Answers on page 538

Lesson 7: At the zoo

Hayvanat bahçesinde

Learn the words

1. **monkey**
   Maymun
2. **lion**
   Aslan
3. **tiger**
   Kaplan
4. **rhino**
   Gergedan
5. **bear**
   Ayı
6. **penguin**
   Penguen
7. **giraffe**
   Zürafa
8. **elephant**
   Fil
9. **kangaroo**
   Kanguru
10. **crocodile**
    Timsah

Learn a verb

like – liking – liked – liked beğenmek

The zookeepers hope everyone will <u>like</u> the name.

Learn an idiom

Let the cat out of the bag

Meaning: To let someone know a secret.

"Emily kept it a secret to surprise Helen, but she finally *let the cat out of the bag* this morning."

Grammar tenses	Past	Present	Future
Simple	✓	✓	✓
Continuous		✓	
Perfect		✓	
Perfect Continuous			

Reading

New animals!

Helen and Emily just arrived at the zoo. Both girls are animal lovers, so they are very pleased to be there. They are especially happy today because the zoo has new animals that Helen and Emily have never seen before. Last week, Helen invited Emily to come with her to the zoo after hearing about all the new animals the zoo now has. Helen hasn't visited the zoo for over two years, and is looking forward to seeing the **monkeys** and **elephants** again.

The zookeepers recently brought in a family of four **giraffes**. One of the four is a baby that is now famous around the city. It's the first time the zoo has ever had a baby **giraffe** and they held a competition this month to name it. The winning name will be announced next week. Everyone is excited to find out what the adorable baby will be called. The zookeepers hope everyone will <u>like</u> the name.

While everyone is talking about how cute the baby **giraffe** is, Emily is more interested in the **penguins**. **Lions** are Emily's favorite animal, but she thinks **penguins** are the cutest animals. She can watch the them for hours as they dive in the water and play with each other.

However, today Emily came to the zoo for another animal. She knows Helen's favorite animal is a **kangaroo,** and the zoo has two new baby **kangaroos** that just arrived three days ago. Emily kept it a secret to surprise Helen, but she finally *let the cat out of the bag* this morning. Helen has never felt so excited before. She has wanted to see joeys since she first saw one on the nature channel on TV when she was five years old!

Learn the English

Past, Present or Future?

The two girls just arrived at the zoo. _____

The winning name will be announced next week. _____

It's the first time the zoo has ever had a baby giraffe. _____

She finally let the cat out of the bag. _____

Emily is more interested in the penguins. _____

Answer the questions

1. How long hasn't Helen visited the zoo for?
_____

2. Why is the baby giraffe famous around the city?
_____

3. Which animal is Emily's favorite?
_____

4. What was Helen feeling so excited about?
_____

Test

Write the answer next to the letter "A"

True, False or Not given?

A: ___ **1.** As an animal lover, Helen has gone to the zoo more than ten times.

a. True b. False c. Not given

A: ___ **2.** Helen hasn't been to the zoo for over two years.

a. True b. False c. Not given

A: ___ **3.** The zoo has three new baby kangaroos.

a. True b. False c. Not given

A: ___ **4.** The winning name for the giraffe will be announced next month.

a. True b. False c. Not given

Multiple choice questions

A: ___ **5.** Emily is more ___ the penguins than the baby giraffe.

a. interested in b. interesting than c. interesting in

A: ___ **6.** The zookeepers ___ everyone ___ like the name.

a. hope, will b. had hoped, can c. have, will

A: ___ **7.** Is it the first time the zoo has had a baby giraffe?

a. Yes, it has. b. Yes, it is. c. No, it hasn't.

A: ___ **8.** When did Helen first see a baby kangaroo?

a. Three days ago. b. This morning. c. When she was five.

Answers on page 538

Lesson 8: Colors

Renkler

Learn the words

1. **red**
   Kırmızı
2. **blue**
   Mavi
3. **orange**
   Turuncu
4. **pink**
   Pembe
5. **black**
   Siyah
6. **yellow**
   Sarı
7. **green**
   Yeşil
8. **purple**
   Mor
9. **brown**
   Kahverengi
10. **white**
    Beyaz

Learn a verb

draw – drawing – drew – drawn çizmek

Last year, she <u>drew</u> a picture of her family on pink paper.

Learn an idiom

Feeling blue

Meaning: Feeling unhappy.

"Her grandmother loves getting her yearly cards, especially if she's *feeling blue* because it always cheers her up."

Grammar tenses	Past	Present	Future
Simple	✓	✓	
Continuous	✓		
Perfect	✓	✓	
Perfect Continuous			

Reading

A colorful season

Starting from when she was a young girl, Jessica had always enjoyed <u>drawing</u>, painting, and making art. One of Jessica's fondest memories is when her grandmother took her to the bookstore to buy paper and colored pencils. The two of them would sit and <u>draw</u> pictures together for hours, and Jessica's grandmother taught her many things about art and color.

Jessica's favorite season is autumn, because she prefers the cooler weather. She also likes seeing the leaves change to many different colors. During the summer, all the leaves on the trees were bright **green**, but now they have changed to **red**, **yellow**, and **orange**. She enjoys wearing her warm, **blue** jacket and walking around the neighborhood at this time of year, looking at the pretty scenery.

Another reason she likes this time of year is because it's Thanksgiving. Every year, she always takes the time to make a thank-you card for her grandmother. Last year, she <u>drew</u> a picture of her family on **pink** paper. This time, she wants to use her favorite color, **purple**. Her grandmother loves getting her yearly cards, especially if she's *feeling blue* because it always cheers her up.

This year, everyone needed cheering up, because the weather had gotten cold sooner than usual. One day, when Jessica was walking to Susan's new house, it even started to snow! By the time she arrived, everything was **white**! Even the bright **yellow** flowers in Susan's front yard were covered in snow. Although it was Thanksgiving, many people weren't thankful for the snowy weather!

Learn the English

Put the sentences in order

She enjoys walking around the neighborhood. ___

Jessica prefers the cooler weather in autumn. **1**

The weather was colder than usual this year. ___

Everything was covered in snow. ___

The thank-you cards always cheer her up. ___

Jessica likes seeing the leaves change color. ___

Many people weren't happy about the snowy weather. ___

She makes a thank-you card for her grandmother every year. ___

Answer the questions

1. What did Jessica's grandmother teach her about?

_____

2. What color are the leaves on the trees in summer?

_____

3. What color paper does Jessica want to use this year?

_____

4. What happened when Jessica was walking to Susan's house?

_____

Test

Write the answer next to the letter "A"

True, False or Not given?

A: ___ **1.** Jessica prefers purple to pink.

a. True   b. False   c. Not given

A: ___ **2.** In Jessica's opinion, the best time of year is autumn.

a. True   b. False   c. Not given

A: ___ **3.** Jessica's grandmother likes the color yellow more than orange.

a. True   b. False   c. Not given

A: ___ **4.** It was in the morning when Jessica walked to Susan's house.

a. True   b. False   c. Not given

Multiple choice questions

A: ___ **5.** Her grandmother ___ her many things about art and color.

a. teaching   b. teaches   c. taught

A: ___ **6.** She enjoys ___ her warm, blue jacket and ___ around.

a. wearing, walking   b. wear, to walk   c. taking, seeing

A: ___ **7.** Where did her grandmother buy the colored pencils from?

a. The supermarket.   b. The bookstore.   c. Susan.

A: ___ **8.** Were many people happy about the snowy weather?

a. Yes, they're thankful.   b. No, they weren't.   c. No, they didn't.

Answers on page 538

Lesson 9: Activities

Aktiviteler

Learn the words

1. **play piano**
   Piyano çalmak
2. **read books**
   Kitap okumak
3. **play video games**
   Video oyunu oynamak
4. **surf the internet**
   İnternette gezinmek
5. **take photos**
   Fotoğraf çekmek
6. **watch TV**
   Televizyon izlemek
7. **sing songs**
   Şarkı söylemek
8. **study English**
   İngilizce çalışmak
9. **play cards**
   Kart oynamak
10. **go shopping**
    Alışverişe gitmek

Learn a verb

read – reading – read – read okumak

He had an English test to study for, but was <u>reading</u> about a video game and decided that he would like to buy it.

Learn an idiom

Shop around

Meaning: To shop at different stores to find the best price.

"John suggested *shopping around* online to find a cheaper price."

Grammar tenses	Past	Present	Future
Simple	✓	✓	
Continuous	✓		
Perfect	✓		
Perfect Continuous	✓		

Reading

The new video game!

Matthew really likes to **play video games** to help him relax. He had an English test to study for, but was reading about a video game and decided that he would like to buy it. It was the new hockey game that his friends and him have been talking about all year. He went to the department store where he usually **goes shopping** to see if they were selling it. He was excited to discover that they were. However, to his disappointment, the game cost ninety-nine dollars.

Matthew had never paid ninety-nine dollars for a video game before. He thought this was very expensive and made a decision not to buy it. He left the store thinking that he would have to spend his week **reading the book** that his aunt had given to him instead. This made Matthew feel better and he went home.

When Matthew got home, he decided to take a rest and **watch TV** for a while. The first thing that came on the TV was an advertisement for the hockey game that Matthew wanted. It looked like an awesome game and this made Matthew feel disappointed again.

Suddenly, Matthew's best friend, John, called. John contacted Matthew to tell him about the new video game that he had been playing. It was the same hockey game that Matthew wanted to buy. John suggested *shopping around* online to find a cheaper price.

Later that evening, Matthew **surfed the internet** and found it selling for eighty dollars with a one-day delivery time. Matthew thought this was acceptable, even if he would have to wait one day. In the meantime, he could **study English** for next week's test.

Learn the English

Put a check next to the correct answer

1. Matthew didn't buy the hockey game because

- his friend, John, already had the game. ____

- the game was too expensive. ____

2. John called Matthew to talk about

- the TV advertisement that Matthew was watching. ____

- the new video game that he was playing. ____

3. Matthew surfed the internet that evening to

- find the cheapest price for the video game. ____

- study for his English test next week. ____

Answer the questions

1. What was Matthew reading about?

_____

2. What was the first thing Matthew saw on TV?

_____

3. What was John's suggestion for Matthew to try?

_____

4. How much did Matthew find the video game selling for online?

_____

Test

Write the answer next to the letter "A"

True, False or Not given?

A: ___ **1.** In his free time, Matthew's favorite sport is hockey.

a. True   b. False   c. Not given

A: ___ **2.** At school, Matthew has low grades in English class.

a. True   b. False   c. Not given

A: ___ **3.** Matthew's friend told him that he might find a cheaper price online.

a. True   b. False   c. Not given

A: ___ **4.** Matthew's uncle had given him a book to read.

a. True   b. False   c. Not given

Multiple choice questions

A: ___ **5.** After he got home, Matthew decided ___ TV for a while.

a. watching   b. to watch   c. watch

A: ___ **6.** He saw an advertisement for the video game that he ___.

a. want   b. wanting   c. wanted

A: ___ **7.** Had his friend John been playing the hockey game before he called?

a. Yes, he had been.   b. No, he hadn't been.   c. Yes, was playing.

A: ___ **8.** What was Matthew going to do while he waited for his delivery?

a. One-day.   b. Study English.   c. Surf the internet.

Answers on page 538

Lesson 10: Food & Drinks

Yiyecek ve içecekler

Learn the words

1. **cake**
   Pasta
2. **cheese**
   Peynir
3. **milk**
   Süt
4. **tea**
   Çay
5. **soda**
   Soda
6. **pizza**
   Pizza
7. **water**
   Su
8. **juice**
   Meyve suyu
9. **coffee**
   Kahve
10. **pie**
    Turta

Learn a verb

want – wanting – wanted – wanted istemek

Of course, many of them <u>want</u> a lot of soda, too.

Learn an idiom

Put food on the table

Meaning: To make money for the household expenses.

"Although she's often very busy, her job is a good way to *put food on the table*."

Grammar tenses	Past	Present	Future
Simple	✓	✓	✓
Continuous			
Perfect		✓	
Perfect Continuous		✓	

Reading

Mom's cooking!

It was near the end of the work day, and Helen's mother remembered that she needed to go shopping. She loves her job as a teacher, and she always works hard. Although she's often very busy, her job is a good way to *put food on the table*. Her daughter, Helen, doesn't play a lot of sports, but she certainly loves eating a lot of food. For this reason, Helen's mother often has to go to the supermarket.

Helen has many friends, and they often come over to their house to visit. Whenever there are guests, it's always good to have a lot of food and drinks to share. While the kids don't drink a lot of **coffee**, they always have a lot of **juice** and **milk**. Of course, many of them want a lot of **soda**, too.

Recently, Helen has been spending a lot of time with her friend, Kevin. Kevin is very active and he enjoys playing many different sports. Helen's mother hopes that this will make Helen more interested in being healthy and being active, too.

Just yesterday, Kevin came over to see Helen. However, instead of playing some sports, the two of them just ate a lot of food from the refrigerator. Not only did they have **cheese pizza** and apple **pie**, they also drank some lemon **soda** and milk **tea**. Instead of Kevin helping Helen to play more sports, Helen has helped Kevin to want more food!

One of the problems is that Helen's mother is a really great cook. For example, she always bakes delicious chocolate **cake** that everyone loves to eat. If she really wants Helen to change, she will have to stop making such tasty food!

Learn the English

Write the names: Helen, Kevin or Mom?

_____ teaches at a school to put food on the table.

_____ loves eating a lot of food, but doesn't play many sports.

_____ is a really great cook.

_____ is very active and enjoys playing sports.

_____ has many friends.

_____ wants to eat more food now.

_____ bakes delicious chocolate cake.

Answer the questions

1. Which drink don't the children drink a lot of?

_____

2. Who has Helen recently been spending time with?

_____

3. What did Helen and Kevin do instead of playing sports?

_____

4. Why is it a problem that Helen's mother is such a good cook?

_____

Test

Write the answer next to the letter "A"

True, False or Not given?

A: ___ **1.** Kevin doesn't enjoy playing many kinds of sports.

a. True   b. False   c. Not given

A: ___ **2.** The chocolate cake that Helen's mother makes is really good.

a. True   b. False   c. Not given

A: ___ **3.** Helen's mother has worked as a teacher for many years.

a. True   b. False   c. Not given

A: ___ **4.** Yesterday, they drank milk tea and ate apple pie.

a. True   b. False   c. Not given

Multiple choice questions

A: ___ **5.** Helen's mother often ___ to go to the supermarket.

a. having   b. has   c. have

A: ___ **6.** Her mother wants Helen more interested in ___ healthy and active.

a. been   b. become   c. being

A: ___ **7.** Did Kevin come over to Helen's house yesterday?

a. Yes, he did.   b. Yes, he come.   c. Yes, he had.

A: ___ **8.** How does Helen's mom feel about her job?

a. She's a great cook.   b. She works hard.   c. She loves it.

Answers on page 538

Lesson 11: At the fruit market

Manavda

Learn the words

1. **orange**
   Portakal
2. **pear**
   Armut
3. **watermelon**
   Karpuz
4. **strawberry**
   Çilek
5. **cherry**
   Vişne
6. **lemon**
   Limon
7. **banana**
   Muz
8. **grape**
   Üzüm
9. **pineapple**
   Ananas
10. **apple**
    Elma

Learn a verb

need – needing – needed – needed gerekmek

Helen will <u>need</u> to replace the cherries with another fruit for her salad.

Learn an idiom

A bad apple

Meaning: The one bad person in a good group.

"These days, none of the girls spend much time with Mary because she turned out to be a *bad apple*."

Grammar tenses	Past	Present	Future
Simple	✓	✓	✓
Continuous		✓	✓
Perfect	✓	✓	
Perfect Continuous			

Reading

Helen's fruit salad!

Helen is at the fruit market looking for some fresh fruit for tonight's dinner. She has invited three of her closest friends over. Two of them, Emily and Susan, were her classmates in elementary school and they have remained friends ever since. They used to play together every weekend along with another girl, Mary.

These days, none of the girls spend much time with Mary because she turned out to be a *bad apple*. Ever since Mary had started working at a top company in New York, she likes to brag about herself. She constantly reminds everyone that she is living in the Big **Apple**. This makes the girls feel uncomfortable. Therefore, Helen decided not to invite her to the dinner tonight.

John, Helen's new friend from work, is also coming for dinner. He is a very good cook, and can bake delicious cakes that he sometimes shares with his coworkers in the office. His **lemon** cake is Helen's favorite. This evening, Helen won't be having cake for dessert. She has decided to make fruit salad instead.

Helen has already found some **oranges**, but is now looking for **pears**, which are next to the **strawberries**. She can't seem to find the **cherries**, so she decides to ask the salesclerk. Unfortunately, the **cherries** had sold out ten minutes before she arrived.

Helen will need to replace the **cherries** with another fruit for her salad. She discovers the **grapes** are on sale and should taste fine. She also gets some **lemons** for John. Perhaps he can make his yummy cake for her!

Learn the English

Find nine different verbs from the Reading

1. _____   4. _____   7. _____

4. _____   5. _____   8. _____

5. _____   6. _____   9. _____

Fill in the blanks

She has _____ found some _____, but is now _____ for pears, which are next to the _____. She can't seem to find the cherries, so she decides to ask the _____. Unfortunately, the _____ had sold out ten _____ before she arrived.

Answer the questions

1. Why is Helen at the fruit market?

_____

2. How does Helen know Emily?

_____

3. What will she be making for dessert?

_____

4. Which fruit did Helen replace the cherries with?

_____

Test

Write the answer next to the letter "A"

True, False or Not given?

A: ___ **1.** Emily and Susan have been friends since they were children.

a. True   b. False   c. Not given

A: ___ **2.** John never shares his cakes with his co-workers.

a. True   b. False   c. Not given

A: ___ **3.** Mary won't go to the dinner at Helen's house tonight.

a. True   b. False   c. Not given

A: ___ **4.** Mary used to play basketball with her classmates in elementary school.

a. True   b. False   c. Not given

Multiple choice questions

A: ___ **5.** Mary's new friend from work ___ also coming for dinner.

a. will   b. is   c. can

A: ___ **6.** She ___ to make fruit salad tonight.

a. 's deciding   b. has decided   c. had decides

A: ___ **7.** Had the cherries sold out before Marry arrived?

a. Yes, it had.   b. Yes, it did.   c. Yes, they had.

A: ___ **8.** What will Helen need to replace for her fruit salad?

a. The cherries.   b. The grapes.   c. The lemons.

Answers on page 538

Lesson 12: Shapes

Şekiller

Learn the words

1. **square**
   Kare
2. **circle**
   Çember
3. **star**
   Yıldız
4. **heart**
   Kalp
5. **octagon**
   Sekizgen
6. **triangle**
   Üçgen
7. **rectangle**
   dikdörtgen
8. **oval**
   Oval
9. **diamond**
   Elmas
10. **pentagon**
    Beşgen

Learn a verb

find – finding – found – found bulmak

Basically, he needs to <u>find</u> different shapes that are different colors.

Learn an idiom

Be out of shape

Meaning: To be unfit or overweight.

"He used to really enjoy playing sports, but after he discovered games on his phone, he started to really *be out of shape*."

Grammar tenses	Past	Present	Future
Simple	✓	✓	
Continuous	✓	✓	
Perfect		✓	
Perfect Continuous		✓	

Reading

Fun and games!

It's a sunny Saturday afternoon, and Jason is spending it playing a new video game he recently <u>found</u>. He used to really enjoy playing sports, but after he discovered games on his phone, he started to really *be out of shape*. Now, instead of spending time with his friend, Susan, at the park, he spends his time looking at his phone or computer.

The latest game Jason has been playing is simple, but it keeps his attention for hours. Basically, he needs to <u>find</u> different shapes that are different colors. To play, he needs to <u>find</u> a blue **square**, or a green **pentagon** in a very short time. Sometimes, he chooses incorrectly. For example, the game asks him to choose a red **oval**, but he chooses an **octagon** instead. The game is very fast and has many different shapes and colors. Like many of these games, it's hard for Jason to stop. Not only that, but he's now always behind with his homework.

Susan is worried about her friend, so she went to Jason's house to see if he would go for a walk with her. When she arrived, she showed him a new exercise app she has on her phone. It has many shapes that show you how much activity you've gotten each day. There's a **heart** shape to show your **heart** rate, and a small **circle** at the top that shows how many steps you've taken. If you achieve your goals for the day, it even gives you a big yellow **star** as a reward.

She was planning to walk to the baseball **diamond**, so Susan asked Jason to go along. When he saw how excited Susan was about the new app, he agreed to go with her. He was also excited because all of the shapes and colors reminded him of his video games.

Learn the English

Unscramble the sentences

1. playing / enjoy / sports / used / Jason / to

_____

2. find / needs / shapes / Jason / different / to

_____

3. behind / is / homework / Jason / his / with / always

_____

4. her / is / friend / about / Susan / worried

_____

Answer the questions

1. How is Jason spending his Saturday afternoon?

_____

2. Why is Jason behind with his homework?

_____

3. What did Susan show Jason on her phone?

_____

4. What does the heart shape represent on the exercise app?

_____

Test

Write the answer next to the letter "A"

True, False or Not given?

A: ___ **1.** Jason plays video games every Saturday afternoon.

a. True   b. False   c. Not given

A: ___ **2.** Jason has been playing the shape game for many hours.

a. True   b. False   c. Not given

A: ___ **3.** A square at the top of Susan's app shows how many steps you take.

a. True   b. False   c. Not given

A: ___ **4.** Susan was planning to walk to the basketball diamond.

a. True   b. False   c. Not given

Multiple choice questions

A: ___ **5.** To ___, he needs to ___ a blue square or a green pentagon.

a. playing, finding   b. play, finding   c. play, find

A: ___ **6.** When she ___, she ___ him a new app on her phone.

a. walked, gave   b. arrived, showed   c. went, found

A: ___ **7.** To play the game, does Jason need to find different shapes?

a. Yes, he does.   b. No, he doesn't.   c. Yes, he can.

A: ___ **8.** What does the app give you for achieving your goals each day?

a. A red oval.   b. A heart shape.   c. A yellow star.

Answers on page 538

Lesson 13: At the supermarket

Süpermarket

Learn the words

1. **milk**
   Süt
2. **juice**
   Meyve suyu
3. **meat**
   Et
4. **drinks**
   İçecek
5. **vegetables**
   Sebze
6. **ice cream**
   Dondurma
7. **fruit**
   Meyve
8. **bread**
   Ekmek
9. **fish**
   Balık
10. **pizza**
    Pizza

Learn a verb

get – getting – got – gotten almak

In the end, they only <u>got</u> fish and meat from there.

Learn an idiom

A rip off

Meaning: Something is too expensive.

"Max thought it was *a* huge *rip off.*"

Grammar tenses	Present	Past	Future
Simple	✓	✓	
Continuous		✓	
Perfect			
Perfect Continuous			

Reading

A crazy shopper!

Max's favorite pastime is shopping. He loves finding the best prices for everyday items, and often shops around at many different places before making a purchase.

His friend, Julie, thinks he is a little crazy. For example, once Max had to buy some **bread** and **milk**. Max went to four different stores, which took the whole morning. While Julie thought this was quite boring, Max seemed to enjoy himself a lot. Max explained to Julie that **bread** and **milk** are both things that almost everyone buys regularly. If people started checking where these items are the cheapest to buy in their local area, they would save a lot of money over the year.

Once Julie wanted to buy some **fruit** from the local supermarket near her home and Max stopped her. He couldn't believe that she would spend so much money on **fruit**. Max thought it was *a huge rip off*. In the end, they only got **fish** and **meat** from there. Julie also wanted some **drinks**, but decided against it in case Max would give her a hard time about the price of them.

One of the more interesting places Max once went shopping was in Japan. Max couldn't believe his eyes. It was a supermarket full of vending machines. There were no employees and it was open 24 hours. Each vending machine had a different item, and there was so much to choose from. There was even a frozen food section where you could buy **vegetables**, frozen **pizza** and **ice cream**.

Max spent hours in there and felt like he was in heaven. He can't stop talking about the **juice** that he bought from that supermarket.

Learn the English

Find the two mistakes and write the sentence correctly

Julie loves finding the best drinks for everyday items.

_____

For example, once Max has to buy some fruit and milk.

_____

There were no vegetables and it was open 24 hour.

_____

Max spent days in there and felt like he was in supermarket.

_____

Answer the questions

1. Why does Max often shop around at different stores?

_____

2. What did Max think about the fruit at Julie's local supermarket?

_____

3. Why was the supermarket in Japan interesting?

_____

4. What did Max buy from the supermarket in Japan?

_____

Test

Write the answer next to the letter "A"

True, False or Not given?

A: ___ **1.** One of the interesting places Max once went shopping was in China.

a. True   b. False   c. Not given

A: ___ **2.** Julie's favorite pastime is shopping.

a. True   b. False   c. Not given

A: ___ **3.** Once, Max stopped Julie from buying some fruit at the supermarket.

a. True   b. False   c. Not given

A: ___ **4.** Max went to four different stores while shopping for milk and bread.

a. True   b. False   c. Not given

Multiple choice questions

A: ___ **5.** Max ___ people should start ___ where items are the cheapest to buy.

a. feeling, checking   b. felt, checked   c. feels, checking

A: ___ **6.** His friend, Julie, ___ Max is a little crazy because of ___ shopping habits.

a. thinks, his   b. thinking, those   c. think, her

A: ___ **7.** Did Julie buy some fish from the local supermarket near her home?

a. No, she didn't.   b. Yes, she did.   c. Yes, she had.

A: ___ **8.** What did Julie decide against buying?

a. Frozen pizza.   b. Some drinks.   c. Some ice cream.

Answers on page 538

Lesson 14: At the ice cream shop

Dondurma dükkanında

Learn the words

1. **chocolate**
   Çikolata
2. **strawberry**
   Çilek
3. **mint**
   Nane
4. **raspberry**
   Ahududu
5. **cherry**
   Vişne
6. **vanilla**
   Vanilya
7. **coffee**
   Kahve
8. **almond**
   Badem
9. **caramel**
   Karame
10. **coconut**
    Hindistan cevizi

Learn a verb

have/has – having – had – had sahip olmak

He had always wanted to <u>have</u> his own small ice cream shop.

Learn an idiom

Flavor of the month

Meaning: Something is suddenly popular for a short time.

"For her, playing volleyball could be just the *flavor of the month*."

Grammar tenses	Past	Present	Future
Simple	✓	✓	
Continuous			
Perfect	✓		
Perfect Continuous			

Reading

Favorite flavors!

A few months ago, Jerry quit his job to follow his dream. He had always wanted to have his own small ice cream shop. He also really enjoyed spending time near the ocean, so he opened his shop next to the beach.

Not only did he have classic flavors like **chocolate**, **strawberry**, and **vanilla**, Jerry also sold **caramel**, **coconut**, and **mint**. His shop was very popular, especially in the summer.

Last Tuesday, Bob and some of his friends took a trip to the beach to play volleyball. Bob's brother, sister, and two friends all played on the sand for a few hours. Actually, Bob's sister only joined the game for a short time because she wasn't very interested. She always tries new things and then quickly loses interest. For her, playing volleyball could be just the *flavor of the month*.

After finishing their game, the group decided to get some ice cream from Jerry's ice cream shop. It was difficult for them to choose what to order, as the shop had so many amazing flavors. Bob's brother doesn't like **cherry** flavor, so he had the **raspberry** ice cream instead. His sister tried the **coffee** flavor and loved it. Bob couldn't decide what to get, so he ended up ordering a little bit of every flavor!

When the friends finished eating, they left the ice cream shop and went outside. Just then, Bob noticed a gym next door, and it made him think about his diet. Although he enjoyed sports like volleyball on the beach, he realized that he likes ice cream a little too much. At that moment, he decided to try eating more vegetables in the future.

Learn the English

Write the opposite with the word "not"

He also enjoyed spending time near the ocean.
He also didn't enjoy spending time near the ocean.

His shop was very popular.

_____

Bob took a trip to the beach to play volleyball.

_____

Bob's brother doesn't like cherry flavor.

_____

He decided to try to eat more vegetables in the future.

_____

Answer the questions

1. Where did Jerry open his ice cream shop?

_____

2. When did most people go to his shop?

_____

3. Why was it difficult for Bob and his friends to choose a flavor?

_____

4. What did Bob notice next to the ice cream shop?

_____

Test

Write the answer next to the letter "A"

True, False or Not given?

A: ___ **1.** Bob's brother doesn't like cherry flavored ice cream.

a. True					b. False					c. Not given

A: ___ **2.** Jerry's ice cream shop wasn't very popular.

a. True					b. False					c. Not given

A: ___ **3.** The ice cream shop's most popular flavor is almond.

a. True					b. False					c. Not given

A: ___ **4.** The friends played volleyball before they got ice cream.

a. True					b. False					c. Not given

Multiple choice questions

A: ___ **5.** Bob's sister ___ the coffee flavor and ___ it.

a. tried, loved				b. ate, loving				c. getting, loves

A: ___ **6.** Jerry ___ the ocean, so he ___ his shop near the beach.

a. enjoyed, opened			b. dreamed, sold			c. near, opening

A: ___ **7.** Did the friends eat their ice cream outside?

a. Yes, they did.			b. No, she hadn't.			c. No, they didn't.

A: ___ **8.** Where did the friends play for a few hours?

a. In the ocean.			b. On the sand.				c. At the gym.

Answers on page 538

Lesson 15: In the refrigerator

Buzdolabında

Learn the words

1. **rice**
   Pirinç
2. **salad**
   Salata
3. **toast**
   Tost
4. **soup**
   Çorba
5. **dumplings**
   Hamur köftesi
6. **tea**
   Çay
7. **cola**
   Kola
8. **eggs**
   Yumurta
9. **water**
   Su
10. **ice**
    Buz

Learn a verb

sell – selling – sold – sold satmak

A man was <u>selling</u> dumplings, and she also bought some farm eggs there.

Learn an idiom

Be as cold as ice

Meaning: To describe someone who is very unfriendly.

"Mary tried to talk to Emily, but she *was as cold as ice*."

Grammar tenses	Past	Present	Future
Simple	✓	✓	
Continuous	✓		
Perfect			
Perfect Continuous	✓		

Reading

A fridge with no drinks!

Mary just got home from a fun game of soccer. Her team won and Mary scored three goals. She'd been practicing her kicking every day and she was feeling happy with her performance. She felt a little uncomfortable after the game because her friend, Emily, plays for the opposing team. Mary tried to talk to Emily, but she *was as cold as ice*.

After the game, Mary didn't have a chance to eat anything except a small **salad**, which wasn't very filling. It was now one o'clock in the afternoon and she was really hungry. Mary opened her refrigerator to see what she could find to eat.

There was some food that she bought the night before at the night market. A man was selling **dumplings**, and she also bought some farm **eggs** there. However, Mary didn't have much energy to cook anything, so she decided to have some **toast** instead.

As she put the bread back in the refrigerator, she noticed there weren't any drinks besides **milk**. Therefore, she drank a glass of **water**. Then, she remembered that Peter and his brother would be coming over shortly, and she would need to prepare some drinks for them.

She ate her **toast** quickly and raced to the convenience store to pick up some drinks. She didn't know what Peter and his brother like to drink, so she decided to choose a few different beverages. She quickly grabbed some lemon **soda** and **cola**. She also got some tea just in case the boys didn't like sweet drinks. For herself, she bought some tomato **juice**. The store didn't sell any **ice**, so she couldn't get any.

Just as she put the drinks in the refrigerator, the doorbell rang.

Learn the English

Find nine different adjectives from the Reading

1. _____   4. _____   7. _____

2. _____   5. _____   8. _____

3. _____   6. _____   9. _____

Complete the sentence using 3 or 4 words

Mary was feeling happy _____

Emily plays for _____

Mary didn't have much energy _____

She quickly grabbed some _____

Answer the questions

1. Which sport did Mary play today?

_____

2. What did Mary eat after the soccer game?

_____

3. Where was the man selling dumplings?

_____

4. Why does Mary need to buy different beverages?

_____

_____

Test

Write the answer next to the letter "A"

True, False or Not given?

A: ___ **1.** Mary added carrots to the small salad she ate after the game.

a. True   b. False   c. Not given

A: ___ **2.** Mary didn't have much energy, so she decided to have some rice.

a. True   b. False   c. Not given

A: ___ **3.** Peter and his brother were coming over, so Mary bought some drinks.

a. True   b. False   c. Not given

A: ___ **4.** Mary bought some lemon juice for herself.

a. True   b. False   c. Not given

Multiple choice questions

A: ___ **5.** ___ the night market, a man was ___ dumplings.

a. In, sells   b. After, sold   c. At, selling

A: ___ **6.** ___ the soccer game, Mary ___ feeling happy with her performance.

a. During, wasn't   b. Before, was   c. After, was

A: ___ **7.** Did Mary buy the drinks for her friends at the supermarket?

a. No, she didn't.   b. Yes, she did.   c. Yes, she bought.

A: ___ **8.** What had Mary been practicing every day?

a. Her kicking.   b. Choosing beverages.   c. Getting ice.

Answers on page 538

Lesson 16: Jobs

Meslekler

Learn the words

1. **doctor**
   Doktor
2. **cook**
   Aşçı
3. **nurse**
   Hemşire
4. **police officer**
   Polis memuru
5. **taxi driver**
   Taksi şoförü
6. **teacher**
   Öğretmen
7. **farmer**
   Çiftçi
8. **salesclerk**
   Satıcı
9. **firefighter**
   İtfaiyeci
10. **builder**
    İnşaatçı

Learn a verb

work – working – worked – worked çalışmak

John is a good student, and he <u>works</u> really hard.

Learn an idiom

Keep up the good work

Meaning: To encourage someone to keep doing well.

"John thought the meal was fantastic, so he told his friend to *keep up the good work*."

Grammar tenses	Past	Present	Future
Simple	✓	✓	✓
Continuous	✓		
Perfect	✓		
Perfect Continuous		✓	

Reading

Interesting jobs!

Lately, John has been spending a lot of time thinking about what kind of **job** he wants in the future. Everywhere he has been going, he he's been asking people about their work. He asked his **teacher** for advice, who told him to continue studying hard. John is a good student, and he works really hard. Now, he's sure he'll achieve his goals.

Yesterday, John took a taxi into the city to buy some groceries. The **taxi driver** got lost while looking for the supermarket, which made John realize he probably couldn't do that job. John often gets lost, so it wouldn't be suitable for him.

After he bought some food from the **salesclerk**, John went walking around downtown. He saw his friend's father driving a police car. He remembered that friend's father used to be a **firefighter**, but then he changed jobs. John thought that he wouldn't want to be a **police officer** himself because it could be dangerous. However, it did make him realize that he wanted to work at a job that helps people, like being a **doctor** or a **nurse**.

The next day when John met with his friend, Sam, the two of them talked about jobs. Sam told him about his dream of working with food. While Sam didn't want to be a **farmer**, he thought being a **cook** would be ideal. Sam then used the groceries that John had bought the day before to prepare lunch. John thought the meal was fantastic, so he told his friend to *keep up the good work*.

The best part is that Sam thinks cooking is interesting, so he'll never be bored when he works!

Learn the English

Complete the questions to the answers

What _____?

His teacher told him to continue studying hard.

How _____?

John took a taxi into the city.

Who _____?

John saw his friend's father downtown.

Which _____?

A cook would be the ideal job for Sam.

Answer the questions

1. What has John been thinking about lately?

_____

2. Why did John want to go downtown?

_____

3. What were Sam and John talking about?

_____

4. What does Sam want to work with?

_____

Test

Write the answer next to the letter "A"

True, False or Not given?

A: ___ **1.** John's friend's father is working as a firefighter in the city.

a. True	b. False	c. Not given

A: ___ **2.** When John met Sam, the weather was perfect.

a. True	b. False	c. Not given

A: ___ **3.** John didn't want to work at a dangerous job.

a. True	b. False	c. Not given

A: ___ **4.** Sam prepared many different types of food for their lunch.

a. True	b. False	c. Not given

Multiple choice questions

A: ___ **5.** Sam told John about his dream of ___ with food.

a. planning	b. working	c. cooking

A: ___ **6.** Sam used the groceries that John had ___ to prepare lunch.

a. bought	b. buying	c. buys

A: ___ **7.** Did John ask his teacher for advice about jobs?

a. Yes, he asks.	b. No, he didn't.	c. Yes, he did.

A: ___ **8.** What is something that John often does?

a. He achieves his goals.	b. He walks downtown.	c. He gets lost.

Answers on page 538

Lesson 17: Names

İsimler

Learn the words

1. John
2. Matthew
3. Jason
4. Helen
5. Mary
6. Kevin
7. Tom
8. Emily
9. Jessica
10. Susan

Learn a verb

call – calling – called – called aramak

He learned to make dumplings from a beautiful woman <u>called</u> Susan Chang.

Learn an idiom

A household name

Meaning: To describe someone famous who everyone knows.

"He very quickly became a *household name*."

Grammar tenses	Past	Present	Future
Simple	✓	✓	
Continuous			
Perfect			
Perfect Continuous			

Reading

Ted's family!

Ted has an interesting family tree. There are family members from almost every part of the world. How Ted ended up being born in the USA is a fascinating story that his father, **Tom**, likes to tell every year on his birthday.

About thirty-five years ago, Aunt **Emily** decided to travel to Australia with her friend, **John**. On the way, she had a stopover in Hong Kong. Unfortunately, at the time there was a terrible typhoon that destroyed a lot of the island, including the airport. As a result, they were stuck in Hong Kong for over a week.

During their time in Hong Kong, both of them decided to take classes on how to cook traditional Chinese food. They learned to make dumplings from a beautiful woman <u>called</u> **Susan** Chang. Aunt **Emily** and **John** enjoyed the class so much that they decided to stay in Hong Kong longer.

A week later, Ted's father came to Hong Kong to visit his sister. Aunt Emily introduced him to **Susan** Chang and it was love at first sight for both of them! A year later, they got married and moved back to the USA where Ted's father opened up a Chinese restaurant with **John**. Soon after, Ted was born.

John's dumplings were so delicious that soon everyone knew about the restaurant, and he was offered his own TV show. He very quickly became a *household name*. **John** became a very rich man, but was lonely. **Susan** introduced **John** to her sister, **Jessica**. They got married and **John** became Ted's famous uncle.

Learn the English

Write the names: Jessica, Ted, Emily, John, Susan or Tom?

_____ came to Hong Kong to visit his sister.

_____ opened a restaurant and became a famous chef.

_____ taught people how to cook traditional Chinese food.

_____ married John.

_____ wanted to travel to Australia, but there was a typhoon.

_____ was born in the USA.

_____ introduced Tom to Susan Chang.

Answer the questions

1. Why were Aunt Emily and John stuck in Hong Kong?

_____

2. Why did they decide to stay in Hong Kong longer?

_____

3. Who opened a Chinese restaurant in the USA?

_____

4. Which food did everyone love at the Chinese restaurant?

_____

Test

Write the answer next to the letter "A"

True, False or Not given?

A: ___ **1.** About a year after they met, Tom and Susan got married.

a. True   b. False   c. Not given

A: ___ **2.** John became famous because of his delicious Chinese food.

a. True   b. False   c. Not given

A: ___ **3.** In Hong Kong, there was an earthquake that destroyed a lot of the island.

a. True   b. False   c. Not given

A: ___ **4.** Aunt Emily had a really great time when she traveled to Australia.

a. True   b. False   c. Not given

Multiple choice questions

A: ___ **5.** Every year, Ted's father ___ to tell a story on his birthday.

a. had liked   b. is liking   c. likes

A: ___ **6.** They learned to make dumplings from a woman ___ Susan Chang.

a. was called   b. called   c. has called

A: ___ **7.** Did Tom go to Hong Kong to take cooking classes?

a. No, he hadn't.   b. No, he didn't.   c. Yes, he did.

A: ___ **8.** How did John feel after he became famous?

a. He was lonely.   b. He was married.   c. He was a household.

Answers on page 538

Lesson 18: More places

Daha çok yer

Learn the words

1. **the library**
   Kütüphane
2. **school**
   Okul
3. **the hospital**
   Hastane
4. **the train station**
   Tren istasyonu
5. **the police station**
   Karakol
6. **the office**
   Ofis
7. **the factory**
   Fabrika
8. **the clinic**
   Klinik
9. **the bus stop**
   Otobüs durağı
10. **the fire station**
    İtfaiye merkezi

Learn a verb

go – going – went – gone gitmek

This past week, Kevin has <u>gone</u> to almost every place in the city.

Learn an idiom

Heart is in the right place

Meaning: To mean well and try to do the right thing.

"His *heart was in the right place*, but now he had to catch up with his classmates at school."

Grammar tenses	Past	Present	Future
Simple	✓	✓	
Continuous	✓		
Perfect	✓	✓	
Perfect Continuous			

Reading

Too many places!

This past week, Kevin has <u>gone</u> to almost every place in the city. He hadn't intended to have such a busy week, but after his sister got sick, his plans changed. Earlier in the week, Kevin's sister decided to <u>go</u> to **the clinic** to see a doctor. While she was waiting at **the bus stop**, the cold wind caused her to cough a lot. By the time she got home, she was actually feeling worse, so Kevin took her to **the hospital**.

Because he had to take care of his sister, Kevin didn't get his homework done on time. His *heart was in the right place*, but now he had to catch up with his classmates at **school**. To help him focus, he <u>went</u> to **the library** on Monday afternoon. It seemed that many people were also sick because **the library** was empty.

While studying, he remembered that he was supposed to meet his aunt at **the train station**. Kevin rushed over there and arrived just as her train did. His aunt has a stressful job working at **the police station**, so she planned a vacation to relax. She intended to visit some friends and see some sites with her family. The first friend she wanted to see works at **the factory**, so Kevin walked there with her.

On the way to **the factory**, Kevin and his aunt saw a house that was on fire! Smoke was coming out of the door, and there were flames in the windows.

Luckily, **the fire station** was just a block away, so Kevin ran over there to report the fire. The firefighters arrived at the house a few minutes later, and were able to put out the fire in time.

It was a tiring week for Kevin, but exciting all the same!

Learn the English

Put the sentences in order

Kevin didn't get his homework done on time. ___

His sister was feeling worse, so Kevin took her to the hospital. ___

On the way, Kevin and his aunt saw a house on fire. ___

Kevin went to the library to catch up to his classmates. ___

The firefighters came to the house and put out the fire. ___

Kevin rushed to the train station to meet his aunt. ___

Kevin's plans changed after his sister got sick. __1__

His aunt wanted to see her friend who works at the factory. ___

Answer the questions

1. What caused Kevin's sister to start coughing?

_____

2. Why couldn't Kevin get his homework done on time?

_____

3. Where does Kevin's aunt work?

_____

4. What did Kevin do when he saw the house on fire?

_____

Test

Write the answer next to the letter "A"

True, False or Not given?

A: ___ **1.** Kevin's aunt has a stressful job working at the fire station.

a. True   b. False   c. Not given

A: ___ **2.** Kevin's sister was waiting at the bus stop to go to the hospital.

a. True   b. False   c. Not given

A: ___ **3.** Kevin's aunt and uncle work together at the same place.

a. True   b. False   c. Not given

A: ___ **4.** Not many people were at the library when Kevin went on Monday.

a. True   b. False   c. Not given

Multiple choice questions

A: ___ **5.** The firefighters ___ there in a few minutes.

a. got   b. had got   c. gets

A: ___ **6.** This past week, Kevin ___ to more places than he had planned to.

a. had going   b. has gone   c. was gone

A: ___ **7.** Where does one of Kevin's aunt's friends work?

a. At the factory.   b. At the library.   c. At the police station.

A: ___ **8.** What did Kevin and his aunt see while walking together?

a. The office.   b. A house on fire.   c. The fire station.

Answers on page 538

Lesson 19: Meats

Etler

Learn the words

1. **beef**
   Sığır eti
2. **pork**
   Domuz
3. **bacon**
   Pastırma
4. **fish**
   Balık
5. **salami**
   Salam
6. **chicken**
   Tavuk
7. **lamb**
   Kuzu
8. **ham**
   Jambon
9. **sausage**
   Sosis
10. **shrimp**
    Karides

Learn a verb

eat – eating – ate – eaten yemek

One meat that Matthew cannot stop <u>eating</u> is salami.

Learn an idiom

Beef up

Meaning: To strengthen something or somebody.

"He wants to *beef up* so that his body can be stronger."

Grammar tenses	Past	Present	Future
Simple	✓	✓	
Continuous		✓	
Perfect		✓	
Perfect Continuous		✓	

Reading

Let's get healthy!

Matthew is trying to live healthier. He recently joined a gym and has been going there almost four times a week. He wants to *beef up* so that his body can be stronger. He feels it is helping him a lot, and he has also made some new friends there.

Besides going to the gym, he has also joined some sports teams. One of them is a basketball team that plays competitions every Tuesday night. They call themselves, the "Funky **Chickens**". Matthew isn't particularly good at basketball. In fact, he has never played before. Luckily, this is just is just a fun team where anyone is welcome to join.

Matthew has also cut down on eating so much meat. He wants to reduce his risk of getting a disease. He used to eat a lot of meat, especially **beef**. He no longer eats **bacon** in the morning and he stays away from **sausages**. This is quite difficult for Matthew because he enjoys eating a hot dog at the ball game.

He hasn't completely cancelled all meat in his diet. His gym instructor recommended him to eat some seafood. Matthew has continued to eat **fish** and started eating **shrimp** on the weekends. A little **pork** can be healthy, too.

One meat that Matthew cannot stop eating is **salami**. This is his favorite kind of meat, and he loves to put slices of **salami** in his sandwiches. Matthew knows this is not so healthy, therefore, he only eats **salami** once a week.

With his new diet and regular exercise, Matthew is feeling better already.

Learn the English

Put a check next to the correct answer

1. Matthew has started going to the gym to

- get healthier and stronger. ___

- make more friends. ___

2. Matthew stopped eating so much meat because

- he thinks it tastes bad. ___

- he doesn't want to get seriously sick. ___

3. Matthew won't stop eating salami as

- it is a healthier kind of meat. ___

- it is his favorite kind of meat. ___

Answer the questions

1. What is Matthew doing to get healthier?

_____

2. Which sports team did he join?

_____

3. Where does Matthew enjoy eating a hot dog?

_____

4. How often does he eat shrimp?

_____

Test

Write the answer next to the letter "A"

True, False or Not given?

A: ___ **1.** Matthew used to go to baseball games every Tuesday night.

a. True   b. False   c. Not given

A: ___ **2.** Having a gym instructor is helping Matthew to live healthier.

a. True   b. False   c. Not given

A: ___ **3.** Matthew lifts weights and goes running at the gym four times a week.

a. True   b. False   c. Not given

A: ___ **4.** Because it's his favorite, Matthew loves putting ham on his sandwiches.

a. True   b. False   c. Not given

Multiple choice questions

A: ___ **5.** He ___ going to the gym several times per week.

a. has being   b. has been   c. is been

A: ___ **6.** He ___ played basketball before.

a. is never   b. has ever   c. has never

A: ___ **7.** Did Matthew totally stop eating meat?

a. No, he didn't.   b. Yes, he did.   c. Yes, on the weekends.

A: ___ **8.** What did Matthew start to eat on the weekends?

a. Fish.   b. Salami.   c. Shrimp.

Answers on page 538

Lesson 20: Vegetables

Sebzeler

Learn the words

1. **pumpkin**
   Balkabağı
2. **potato**
   Patates
3. **carrot**
   Havuç
4. **asparagus**
   Kuşkonmaz
5. **broccoli**
   Brokoli
6. **corn**
   Mısır
7. **cabbage**
   Lahana
8. **spinach**
   Ispanak
9. **mushroom**
   Mantar
10. **onion**
    Soğan

Learn a verb

cook – cooking – cooked – cooked pişirmek

Her grandmother said if Jane helped her while <u>cooking</u> the cabbage, she could spend more time with her friend, Onion.

Learn an idiom

Carrot on a stick

Meaning: A reward that is promised upon completion of a task.

"Anytime her grandmother wanted Jane to help with the chores, she would use the cow as a *carrot on a stick*."

Grammar tenses	Past	Present	Future
Simple	✓	✓	
Continuous	✓		
Perfect	✓		
Perfect Continuous	✓		

Reading

Vegetables for dinner!

Last summer, Mary's sister, Jane, took a trip to her grandparents' beef farm. While she was there, she spent a lot of time with all of the animals, many of whom she really liked. There was one baby cow there that loved to eat **onions**. She loved the cow because it was very playful and always made her laugh. For fun, Jane named the cow, "**Onion**".

Anytime her grandmother wanted Jane to help with the chores, she would use the cow as a *carrot on a stick*. For example, her grandmother said if Jane helped her while cooking the **cabbage**, she could spend more time with her friend, **Onion**. For most of the summer, Jane was happy when she was spending time with the cow.

However, after a few weeks, **Onion** was sold to another farm and had to go away. Of course, Jane was really sad, and she missed her friend very much. After that, Jane decided she didn't want to eat meat anymore, so she became a vegetarian.

Upon returning to the city after her trip, Mary and her friend, Emily, planned to have a big meal to celebrate Jane's return. Jane's grandmother had taught her how to cook many delicious vegetables, such as **broccoli**, **pumpkin**, and **corn**. Mary had gone shopping and bought many of their favorites, such as **asparagus** and **mushroom**.

There was too much food for just the three of them, so Mary decided to ask Tom to come over and join them. Tom loves **spinach**, so Jane cooked some for him. It was convenient because Tom agreed to bring some drinks and fruit. Tom can also play the piano, so they had some dinner music as well!

| Learn the English |

Find nine different verbs from the Reading

1._____   4. _____   7. _____

6. _____   5. _____   8. _____

7. _____   6. _____   9. _____

Fill in the blanks

Upon _____ to the city _____ her trip, Mary and Emily planned to have a big _____ to celebrate Jane's return. Jane's _____ had taught her how to _____ many delicious _____, such as broccoli, _____, and corn.

Answer the questions

1. What kind of farm was it?

_____

2. Why was Jane really sad?

_____

3. What had Jane's grandmother taught her to do?

_____

4. Why did Mary decide to invite Tom?

_____

456

Test

Write the answer next to the letter "A"

True, False or Not given?

A: ___ **1.** Jane named the baby cow "Onion" because it looked like one.

a. True   b. False   c. Not given

A: ___ **2.** While on the farm, Jane also played with the chickens.

a. True   b. False   c. Not given

A: ___ **3.** For most of the spring, Jane was happy when she was with the cow.

a. True   b. False   c. Not given

A: ___ **4.** Jane's grandmother had taught her how to cook delicious vegetables.

a. True   b. False   c. Not given

Multiple choice questions

A: ___ **5.** Jane ___ she didn't want to eat meat anymore.

a. decides   b. decided   c. deciding

A: ___ **6.** Tom ___ spinach, so Jane ___ some for him.

a. cooked, eats   b. loves, cooked   c. is loving, cooked

A: ___ **7.** What had Jane's grandmother used as a carrot on a stick?

a. Carrot.   b. Asparagus.   c. Onion.

A: ___ **8.** Who planned to have a big meal to celebrate Jane's return?

a. Jane's sister and Emily.   b. Mary and Jane.   c. Tom and Emily.

Answers on page 538

Lesson 21: At school

Okulda

Learn the words

1. **classroom**
   Sınıf
2. **office**
   Ofis
3. **nurse's office**
   Revir
4. **gym**
   Spor salonu
5. **hall**
   Salon
6. **computer lab**
   Bilgisayar laboratuarı
7. **art room**
   Sanat odası
8. **music room**
   Müzik odası
9. **science lab**
   Bilim laboratuarı
10. **lunchroom**
    Yemek odası

Learn a verb

put – putting – put – put koymak

Peter was sure he put the towel on his desk in the classroom.

Learn an idiom

Old school

Meaning: To do something the old-fashioned way.

"The swim teacher's *old school* and is unhappy when students aren't on time."

Grammar tenses	Past	Present	Future
Simple	✓	✓	✓
Continuous	✓	✓	
Perfect			
Perfect Continuous			

Reading

Peter's towel!

Peter will have a swimming class at the **gym** today. He is worried he's going to be late because he cannot find his towel anywhere. The swim teacher's *old school* and is unhappy when students aren't on time. He makes them swim a lap of the pool for every minute they are late.

Peter was sure he put the towel on his desk in the **classroom**. He checked and it wasn't there. He tries to remember all the places he went to at school that day. At first, he went to the **lunchroom** where he was talking with his friends about the new computers that are in the **computer lab** now. Maybe the towel is in the **lunchroom**.

He decides to go to the **lunchroom** to check. Unfortunately, it's not there, and now he's concerned that he's going to be late for his music class, which is on the other side of the school.

As Peter is walking to the **music room**, he passes the **science lab**. He had a science class this morning. Perhaps his towel is there, he thinks to himself. He quickly runs to the **science lab** to check, but there is still no towel.

He looks at the time and only has ten minutes left before music class. There's no running allowed in the **hall**, so he walks as quickly as he can. On the way, he sees his friend, Mary, standing outside the teacher's **office**. He tells her he can't find his towel. Mary remembers seeing a towel in the **art room**, but Peter doesn't take art class, so it's impossible that it is his.

Suddenly, Mary sees a towel sticking out of Peter's school bag. Peter is so embarrassed!

Learn the English

Past, Present or Future?

Peter will have a swimming class at the gym today. _____

Peter was sure he put the towel on his desk. _____

He decides to go to the lunchroom to check. _____

He had a science class this morning. _____

Mary sees a towel sticking out of Peter's bag. _____

Answer the questions

1. What happens if the students are late for swimming class?
_____

2. Where was the first place Peter went to today?
_____

3. Who was standing outside the teacher's office?
_____

4. Where was Peter's towel?
_____

Test

Write the answer next to the letter "A"

True, False or Not given?

A: ___ **1.** While walking to the music room, Peter passed the science lab.

a. True	b. False	c. Not given

A: ___ **2.** Peter has swimming classes every day at the gym.

a. True	b. False	c. Not given

A: ___ **3.** In the lunchroom, Peter was talking to his friends about computers.

a. True	b. False	c. Not given

A: ___ **4.** Mary is at the teacher's office to talk about her art class.

a. True	b. False	c. Not given

Multiple choice questions

A: ___ **5.** Peter was sure he ___ something on his desk in the classroom.

a. was putting	b. puts	c. put

A: ___ **6.** At school, there's no running ___ in the hall.

a. allowed	b. is allowed	c. has allowed

A: ___ **7.** Did Peter check the science lab for his missing item?

a. Yes, he has.	b. Yes, he did.	c. Yes, he was.

A: ___ **8.** What did Mary remember seeing in the art room?

a. An art class.	b. A towel.	c. Peter's school bag.

Answers on page 539

Lesson 22: School subjects

Okul dersleri

Learn the words

1. **science**
   Fen
2. **English**
   İngilizce
3. **P.E.**
   Beden eğitimi
4. **geography**
   Coğrafya
5. **social studies**
   Sosyal bilgiler
6. **math**
   Matematik
7. **art**
   Sanat
8. **music**
   Müzik
9. **history**
   Tarih
10. **computer**
    Bilgisayar

Learn a verb

do – doing – did – done yapmak

Her parents think it's not only a great way to <u>do</u> new things, but it's also educational.

Learn an idiom

Cut class

Meaning: To miss class on purpose.

"Although traveling is a wonderful experience, Jessica has had to *cut class* many times this year."

Grammar tenses	Past	Present	Future
Simple	✓	✓	✓
Continuous			
Perfect		✓	
Perfect Continuous			

Reading

A better education!

Beginning when she was a young child, Jessica's mother and father tried to teach her in many different ways. They believe that travel is a great kind of education. The entire family often takes long trips to different parts of the world. Her parents think it's not only a great way to <u>do</u> new things, but it's also educational. In fact, Jessica always gets a high grade in her **history** class for this reason.

Just last year, her family traveled around Asia and visited many different cities. They <u>did</u> many fun things. When Jessica recently had a test in her **geography** class, many of the questions were about Asian countries. She thought it was really easy and she got a high score.

Jessica also <u>does</u> well in her **art** class because she has been to many museums in Europe. It is very lucky that she has seen the work of many great artists. She also has heard various kinds of music from around the world, so Jessica thinks **music** class is really interesting.

She looks forward to her world trips, and organizes them while she is in **computer** class. She uses her computer to make a schedule, and even plans the costs of things. Jessica has always <u>done</u> well in **math** class, so she's good at adding numbers, too.

Although traveling is a wonderful experience, Jessica has had to *cut class* many times this year. Because of this, she is a little behind in her **science** class. After **social studies** and before her **P.E.** class she has some free time, so she will study for her **science** test then. Her friend Kevin is good at science, so she is going to ask him for help. In exchange, she will help him with his **English**.

Learn the English

Find the two mistakes and write the sentence correctly

The entire family often takes short trips to different parts of the city.

_____

Jessica always getting a high grades in her history class for this reason.

_____

He uses her calendar to make a schedule.

_____

She is a little ahead in her math class.

_____

Answer the questions

1. What do Jessica's parents believe about traveling?

_____

2. Where did the family travel to last year?

_____

3. What does Jessica use to organize her schedule?

_____

4. Which subject is Jessica behind in?

_____

| Test |

Write the answer next to the letter "A"

True, False or Not given?

A: ___ **1.** Along with her family, Jessica has gone to Europe many times.

a. True	b. False	c. Not given

A: ___ **2.** One subject that Jessica finds boring is music class.

a. True	b. False	c. Not given

A: ___ **3.** Jessica's parents took her to Asia because she failed a geography test.

a. True	b. False	c. Not given

A: ___ **4.** Because of traveling, Jessica is a bit behind in her science class.

a. True	b. False	c. Not given

Multiple choice questions

A: ___ **5.** Jessica ___ always ___ well in math class.

a. is, do	b. has, done	c. can, doing

A: ___ **6.** Jessica ___ to ask her friend, Kevin, for help with science class.

a. will be	b. will going	c. is going

A: ___ **7.** Does Jessica always get a high grade in history class?

a. Yes, she gets.	b. Yes, she does.	c. No, she doesn't.

A: ___ **8.** When does Jessica organize schedules for her trips?

a. In computer class.	b. In math class.	c. After social studies.

Answers on page 539

Lesson 23: Chores

Ev işleri

Learn the words

1. **wash the dishes**
   Bulaşık yıkamak
2. **feed the pets**
   Hayvanları beslemek
3. **vacuum the carpet**
   Halıyı süpürmek
4. **take out the trash**
   Çöpü atmak
5. **clean the bedroom**
   Yatak odasını temizlemek
6. **mop the floor**
   Yerleri silmek
7. **cook dinner**
   Yemek yapmak
8. **do the laundry**
   Çamaşır yıkamak
9. **iron the clothes**
   Kıyafetleri ütülemek
10. **make the beds**
    Yatakları toplamak

Learn a verb

know – knowing – knew – known bilmek

She didn't <u>know</u> that her mother worked so hard every day.

Learn an idiom

All in a day's work

Meaning: A normal day without a change in routine.

"Her mother always says that it's *all in a day's work*."

Grammar tenses	Past	Present	Future
Simple	✓	✓	✓
Continuous		✓	
Perfect		✓	
Perfect Continuous			

Reading

So many chores!

Susan's mother is sick in bed and her father is away on a business trip in China. This means Susan has to do all the chores. She just finished **washing the dishes** and she is feeling very tired.

While Susan doesn't mind helping to do the chores around the house, she is not used to it. Her parents do the housework and Susan only has to **clean her bedroom**. Susan doesn't have much time to help because she is often studying.

Susan's father works a lot and only **takes out the trash** and **feeds the pets** when he gets home from work. On the weekends, he **vacuums the carpet**. He also doesn't have time to do much more.

As a result, her mother does most of the housework. She has a daily system she always follows. She begins by **doing the laundry** in the morning. While she waits for the washing machine to be done, she **mops the floor**. Once the laundry is dry, she **irons the clothes** and puts them away. In the evening, she **cooks dinner**. She enjoys cooking and her meals are delicious. She does the rest when she has time.

After doing all the chores for two days, Susan couldn't believe how much work it was. She didn't <u>know</u> that her mother worked so hard every day. Furthermore, Susan has never heard her complain. Her mother always says that it's *all in a day's work.*

Susan decided that from now on, she will find the time to help her mother out more. Susan's mother was very appreciative of her help.

With the extra time she now has, she can have more fun!

Learn the English

Unscramble the sentences

1. do / chores / Susan / the / to / This / all / has / means

___

2. of / housework / does / the / Her / most / mother

___

3. in / laundry / morning / doing / the / begins / She / the / by

___

4. couldn't / Susan / work / was / much / it / believe / how

___

Answer the questions

1. Why does Susan have to do all the chores?

___

2. Which chores does Susan's father do?

___

3. Who usually does most of the housework?

___

4. What does Susan want to do from now on?

___

Test

Write the answer next to the letter "A"

True, False or Not given?

A: ___ **1.** The first chore Susan's mother usually does is mop the floors.

a. True   b. False   c. Not given

A: ___ **2.** Susan's father often travels to China for business trips.

a. True   b. False   c. Not given

A: ___ **3.** Both Susan's mother and father are sick in bed.

a. True   b. False   c. Not given

A: ___ **4.** Because of Susan's help, her mother can now have more fun.

a. True   b. False   c. Not given

Multiple choice questions

A: ___ **5.** Susan didn't ___ how much work her mother usually does.

a. know   b. believe   c. complain

A: ___ **6.** She ___ the other chores when she has time.

a. works   b. do   c. does

A: ___ **7.** Did Susan's mother put the clothes away after she ironed them?

a. Yes, she did.   b. No, she didn't.   c. Yes, she had.

A: ___ **8.** When does Susan's father take out the trash?

a. In the morning.   b. When he gets home.   c. On weekends.

Answers on page 539

Lesson 24: At the toy store

Oyuncak mağazasında

Learn the words

1. **doll**
   Oyuncak bebek
2. **teddy bear**
   Ayıcık
3. **car**
   Araba
4. **airplane**
   Uçak
5. **dinosaur**
   Dinozor
6. **robot**
   Robot
7. **ball**
   Top
8. **jump rope**
   Atlama ipi
9. **board game**
   Masa oyunu
10. **blocks**
    Bloklar

Learn a verb

borrow – borrowing – borrowed – borrowed ödünç almak

Their vacuum cleaner is broken, so Susan even <u>borrowed</u> one from the neighbors.

Learn an idiom

Like a kid with a new toy

Meaning: To be really happy with something.

"She thought vacuuming was fun, so she was *like a kid with a new toy*."

Grammar tenses	Past	Present	Future
Simple	✓	✓	
Continuous	✓	✓	
Perfect	✓		
Perfect Continuous			

Reading

Some new toys!

After being unwell last week, Mom is feeling much better now. Looking around the house, she sees that everything is nice and clean and the chores have been done. Susan was really busy helping out when Mom was sick. Their vacuum cleaner is broken, so Susan even borrowed one from the neighbors. She actually thought vacuuming was fun, so she was *like a kid with a new toy*.

As a reward for Susan's hard work, Mom and Dad decided to get her a gift. At the toy store, there are so many choices. They didn't want to get her another **doll** or **teddy bear** because she already has so many. She isn't interested in **airplanes** or **cars**, so those aren't good choices, either. Of course, Susan is too old for **blocks**, even though they look fun.

Then, Mom remembered that Susan's history class is learning about **dinosaurs**, so they thought a **dinosaur** book would be perfect. The only problem is that they also want Susan to do more exercise, and reading isn't very active. Mom's idea was to get a **jump rope** for her as well. The store even had one in Susan's favorite color, green.

Naturally, the toy store has something for everyone, so Dad fell in love with a toy **robot** he saw in a movie the week before. Seeing that Dad was having fun, Mom also decided to get herself something. Between a **ball** and a **board game**, she chose the **board game**. It was the one that her friend had recommended.

At the cashier, Dad discovered that he'd forgotten to bring money, so he had to borrow some from Mom. Luckily, she had her purse!

Learn the English

Write the opposite with the word "not"

Dad fell love with a toy robot.
Dad didn't fall in love with a toy robot.

The vacuum cleaner is broken.
_____

Mom and Dad decided to get her a gift.
_____

The store has something for everyone.
_____

It was the one that her friend had recommended.
_____

Answer the questions

1. Who did Susan borrow a vacuum cleaner from?
_____

2. Why did they decide to not get Susan a dinosaur book?
_____

3. What did Mom choose for herself?
_____

4. What had Dad forgotten to bring to the toy store?
_____

Test

Write the answer next to the letter "A"

True, False or Not given?

A: ___ **1.** When Mom was sick, Susan enjoyed vacuuming the floor.

a. True b. False c. Not given

A: ___ **2.** Her parents thought it was a good idea to get Susan a doll.

a. True b. False c. Not given

A: ___ **3.** The book about dinosaurs was really expensive.

a. True b. False c. Not given

A: ___ **4.** They decided to buy a blue jump rope for Susan's gift.

a. True b. False c. Not given

Multiple choice questions

A: ___ **5.** Her parents ___ Susan to do more ___.

a. wanting, chores b. wants, vacuuming c. want, exercise

A: ___ **6.** Because hers was broken, Susan ___ a vacuum cleaner.

a. has borrowed b. borrowed c. borrowing

A: ___ **7.** Is Susan too old for some of the toys at the toy store?

a. Yes, she old. b. Yes, she does. c. Yes, she is.

A: ___ **8.** Where did Dad see the robot that he really likes?

a. In a board game. b. In a book. c. In a movie.

Answers on page 539

Lesson 25: In the kitchen

Mutfakta

Learn the words

1. **refrigerator**
   Buzdolabı
2. **coffee maker**
   Kahve makinesi
3. **microwave oven**
   Mikrodalga fırın
4. **stove**
   Ocak
5. **blender**
   Karıştırıcı
6. **cupboard**
   Dolap
7. **rice cooker**
   Pilav pişirme makinesi
8. **dish rack**
   Bulaşıklık
9. **pan**
   Tava
10. **toaster**
    Tost makinesi

Learn a verb

clean – cleaning – cleaned – cleaned temizlemek

Sometimes, Mom would spend over ten minutes <u>cleaning</u> one pan.

Learn an idiom

Too many cooks in the kitchen

Meaning: When too many people try to take control.

"There were *too many cooks in the kitchen* and she had made her decision!"

Grammar tenses	Past	Present	Future
Simple	✓		
Continuous	✓		
Perfect	✓		
Perfect Continuous	✓		

Reading

Boom! The rice cooker!

Mom just got back from the department store. She was very excited because she decided to buy some items for the kitchen. Too many things had been being used for years, and it was time that they finally be replaced.

For example, she bought the **toaster** when she first moved into the house, and that was fifteen years ago! It was a good toaster, but it was looking old and used. It was amazing that it was still working.

Some of the **pans** in the kitchen definitely needed replacing. They had been used over and over and they were getting difficult to clean. Sometimes, Mom would spend over ten minutes cleaning one **pan**. It was just getting too tiring for her!

It was last Friday when Mom finally had had enough. She was cooking rice, when suddenly the **rice cooker** made a buzzing sound and exploded! The sound was so loud that she almost burned herself on the **stove**. It was very dangerous, and Mom was worried that the same thing could happen to the **microwave oven**.

That's when she decided it was not worth the risk. She looked around the kitchen to see what else she didn't want. She then went through the **cupboards** to find any items that she could also get rid of.

Her son, Peter, and Dad tried to tell her that she was overreacting, but she told them to stop talking. There were *too many cooks in the kitchen* and she had made her decision!

Peter quickly grabbed his beloved **blender**. There was no way that was going to be thrown out!

Learn the English

Find nine different adjectives from the Reading

1. _____ 4. _____ 7. _____

2. _____ 5. _____ 8. _____

3. _____ 6. _____ 9. _____

Complete the sentence using 3 or 4 words

It was amazing that the toaster _____

Some of the pans were getting _____

Mom almost burned herself _____

Peter quickly grabbed _____

Answer the questions

1. When did Mom buy the old toaster?

_____

2. How long would it take for Mom to clean one of the old pans?

_____

3. What happened to the rice cooker?

_____

4. Which kitchen item did Peter not let Mom replace?

_____

Test

Write the answer next to the letter "A"

True, False or Not given?

A: ___ **1.** The pans needed replacing because they were difficult to clean.

a. True   b. False   c. Not given

A: ___ **2.** Mom bought the toaster fifteen years after she moved into the house.

a. True   b. False   c. Not given

A: ___ **3.** It was really busy at the department store when Mom went there.

a. True   b. False   c. Not given

A: ___ **4.** Mom was worried that the microwave oven might explode.

a. True   b. False   c. Not given

Multiple choice questions

A: ___ **5.** She ___ around the kitchen to see what else she ___ want.

a. looked, didn't   b. looking, not   c. looks, don't

A: ___ **6.** Mom would spend over ten minutes ___ one pan.

a. cleaned   b. cleans   c. cleaning

A: ___ **7.** Was it last Friday that something happened to the rice cooker?

a. Yes, it did.   b. Yes, it was.   c. No, it didn't.

A: ___ **8.** What was looking old and used?

a. The toaster.   b. The stove.   c. The blender.

Answers on page 539

Lesson 26: In the toolbox

Alet çantası

Learn the words

1. **hammer**
   Çekiç
2. **electric drill**
   Elektrikli matkap
3. **screwdriver**
   Tornavida
4. **paintbrush**
   Boya fırçası
5. **shovel**
   Kürek
6. **tape measure**
   Mezür
7. **axe**
   Balta
8. **pliers**
   Pense
9. **ladder**
   Merdiven
10. **wrench**
    İngiliz anahtarı

Learn a verb

use – using – used – used

He tried to <u>use</u> a screwdriver at first, but it didn't work.

Learn an idiom

Tools of the trade

Meaning: Things that are needed for a specific job.

"She needed a proper place to put all of her *tools of the trade*."

Grammar tenses	Past	Present	Future
Simple	✓	✓	
Continuous	✓		
Perfect	✓		
Perfect Continuous			

Reading

The right tools!

The cupboard in the kitchen wasn't working properly. Last Friday when Mom was cooking, the rice cooker blew up and damaged it. Because Dad has so many tools, she asked him to fix the cupboard as soon as possible. It's fortunate that Dad is such a handy guy. Not only did he fix the chair yesterday, but he also repaired the door.

Dad took this opportunity to teach Peter about all the things in the toolbox. Dad climbed the **ladder** and asked Peter to hand him various tools. He tried to use a **screwdriver** at first, but it didn't work. Peter passed him the **electric drill**, and that worked well. However, while using the **electric drill**, Dad had scratched the door of the cupboard.

Fortunately, Dad was also a skilled painter. He got the **paintbrush** and white paint from Peter, and soon the cupboard was looking great. The kitchen looked like new, except for all the tools lying around.

Mom came in and was surprised to see such a mess! There was a **hammer** and **wrench** near the refrigerator, and some **pliers** near the sink. The only tools that weren't in the kitchen was the **shovel** that Mom was using in the backyard and an **axe**!

Despite the mess, Mom wasn't upset. This is because she had just bought many new things for the kitchen from the department store. She now had a new rice cooker and toaster, and was happy the cupboard was fixed so she could put them away. She needed a proper place to put all of her *tools of the trade*.

Peter and Dad quickly cleaned up, and Mom used all of her new kitchen things to make them some lunch.

Learn the English

Complete the questions to the answers

When _____?

The rice cooker blew up last week.

Who _____?

Dad is good at fixing things.

What _____?

Dad taught Peter about the tools in the toolbox.

Why _____?

Mom was happy because the cupboard was fixed.

Answer the questions

1. What things did Dad fix in the kitchen?

_____

2. How did Peter help his father?

_____

3. What had Mom bought from the department store?

_____

4. Who cleaned up all the mess in the kitchen?

_____

Test

Write the answer next to the letter "A"

True, False or Not given?

A: ___ **1.** Dad had bought his ladder at the department store.

a. True   b. False   c. Not given

A: ___ **2.** The door was fixed by Dad yesterday.

a. True   b. False   c. Not given

A: ___ **3.** While fixing the cupboard, Peter asked Dad to hand him various tools.

a. True   b. False   c. Not given

A: ___ **4.** Mom was angry that there were so many tools lying around.

a. True   b. False   c. Not given

Multiple choice questions

A: ___ **5.** While ___ the electric drill, Dad had ___ the cupboard door.

a. used, scratching   b. using, scratched   c. uses, scratch

A: ___ **6.** Mom came into the kitchen and was ___ to see such a mess.

a. surprise   b. surprising   c. surprised

A: ___ **7.** Had Mom bought tools when she was at the department store?

a. No, she hadn't.   b. No, she didn't.   c. Yes, she had.

A: ___ **8.** What is Dad also skilled at doing?

a. Climbing.   b. Painting.   c. Scratching.

Answers on page 539

Lesson 27: Transportation

Ulaşım

Learn the words

1. **catch a bus**
   Otobüsü yakalamak
2. **take a taxi**
   Taksiye binmek
3. **take a ferry**
   Vapura binmek
4. **ride a motorcycle**
   Motorsiklet binmek
5. **take the subway**
   Metroya binmek
6. **take a train**
   Trene binmek
7. **drive a car**
   Araba sürmek
8. **ride a scooter**
   Mobilet sürmek
9. **ride a bicycle**
   Bisiklet sürmek
10. **take an airplane**
    Uçağa binmek

Learn a verb

take – taking – took – taken almak

If she catches a bus, it will <u>take</u> over twelve hours.

Learn an idiom

Lose one's train of thought

Meaning: To forget what you were thinking about.

"She's concerned that if she *loses her train of thought,* she could end up on the wrong side of the road."

Grammar tenses	Past	Present	Future
Simple	✓	✓	✓
Continuous		✓	✓
Perfect		✓	
Perfect Continuous			

Reading

A trip down under!

Emily is planning her trip to Australia. She plans to travel alone, and is trying to work out the best way of traveling to the different destinations. She's never been to Australia before, so it is quite a challenge to get everything organized.

She booked her flight yesterday. She'll be **taking an airplane** in the evening and arriving at the Sydney airport in the morning. From the airport, she will **take a taxi** to her hotel, which should only take fifteen minutes.

The hotel is in a central location, and Emily read that Sydney is a great city to walk around in. She doesn't plan to **drive a car** because she's nervous about driving on the left side of the road. In the USA, cars drive on the right. She's concerned that if she *loses her train of thought,* she could end up on the wrong side of the road!

After Sydney, she'll be heading to Melbourne. She is undecided about which transportation she should choose. She's not sure whether she should go there by bus or train. Melbourne is very far, and she could **take an airplane**, but there are many sights to see on the way. If she **catches a bus**, it will take over twelve hours. However, it would only be eleven hours if she **took a train**.

The place she is most looking forward to going is called Phillip Island. On this island, penguins frequently visit. You can sit on the sand as they walk by. She will **take a ferry** there to enjoy the ocean views.

Even though planning this trip has been challenging, it truly will be the adventure of a lifetime!

Learn the English

Past, Present or Future?

Emily is planning her trip to Australia. _____

She booked her flight yesterday. _____

After Sydney, she'll be heading to Melbourne. _____

On this island, penguins frequently visit. _____

She will take a ferry there to enjoy the ocean views. _____

Answer the questions

1. When did Emily book her flight to Australia?

   _____

2. Which airport will the airplane be arriving at?

   _____

3. Why doesn't Emily want to drive in Australia?

   _____

4. How long does it take to go from Sydney to Melbourne by train?

   _____

Test

Write the answer next to the letter "A"

True, False or Not given?

A: ___ 1. It will take eleven hours if Emily catches a bus to Melbourne.

a. True　　　　　　　　b. False　　　　　　　　c. Not given

A: ___ 2. This is the first time that Emily has traveled alone before.

a. True　　　　　　　　b. False　　　　　　　　c. Not given

A: ___ 3. Emily is nervous about driving a car in Australia.

a. True　　　　　　　　b. False　　　　　　　　c. Not given

A: ___ 4. She's really excited about visiting the place with penguins.

a. True　　　　　　　　b. False　　　　　　　　c. Not given

Multiple choice questions

A: ___ 5. Mary will ___ a ferry to enjoy the ocean views.

a. take　　　　　　　　b. taking　　　　　　　　c. taken

A: ___ 6. She is undecided ___ which transportation she should take to Melbourne.

a. in　　　　　　　　　b. about　　　　　　　　c. at

A: ___ 7. Is Mary's hotel in the middle of Sydney?

a. Yes, it does.　　　　b. No, it isn't.　　　　　c. Yes, it is.

A: ___ 8. What can she do on Phillip Island?

a. Sit on the sand.　　　b. Take a train.　　　　c. Take a taxi.

Answers on page 539

Lesson 28: Clothes

Giysiler

Learn the words

1. **T-shirt** — Tişört
2. **blouse** — Bluz
3. **scarf** — Atkı
4. **coat** — Palto
5. **dress** — Elbise
6. **hat** — Şapka
7. **sweater** — Süveter
8. **jacket** — Ceket
9. **skirt** — Etek
10. **necktie** — Kravat

Learn a verb

wear – wearing – wore – worn giymek

Because she had never gone hiking before, Susan didn't know what to <u>wear</u>.

Learn an idiom

Wear somebody out

Meaning: To make someone tired.

"Finally, her mom *wore her out*, and she agreed to try hiking."

Grammar tenses	Past	Present	Future
Simple	✓	✓	✓
Continuous		✓	
Perfect		✓	
Perfect Continuous	✓	✓	

Reading

The right clothes!

For a while now, Susan's mom has been trying to get her to be more active. While Susan enjoys reading books and does well in school, she has never enjoyed exercise very much. After many weeks of asking her to try things like swimming or basketball, Susan always refused. Finally, her mom *wore her out*, and she agreed to try hiking.

Her friend, Jessica, loves all kinds of exercise, so the two of them planned to go hiking together. Because she had never gone hiking before, Susan didn't know what to wear. She usually likes wearing a **dress** or a **skirt**, but those aren't good clothes for walking in the mountains. Jessica suggested that she should wear a pair of pants and a **sweater**. The weather was pretty cold, so Susan brought a **coat** and a **scarf** as well.

Jessica knows it's important to wear many layers when hiking. This is because the weather can change very quickly where she lives. Although she's only wearing a **T-shirt** and a **blouse**, she will also take a **jacket**, too. She borrowed the **jacket** from her sister whose hobby is going camping, so it's really warm.

The two girls have a classmate whose brother got lost in the forest while hiking, so Jessica wants to be really prepared. She has brought two water bottles and some fruit for a snack. She also has her cell phone for emergency calls.

The scenery at the top of the mountain is really beautiful, so the friends are hoping the weather won't be too cloudy by the time they get there. With any luck, it's going to be perfect weather!

Learn the English

Put the sentences in order

Susan brought a coat because the weather was cold. ___

Susan and her friend planned to go hiking together. ___

They brought food, drinks and a cell phone for emergencies. ___

Susan's mom has been trying to get her to be more active. _1_

Their classmate's brother got lost in the forest once. ___

Susan didn't know what to wear. ___

The scenery at the top of the mountain will be beautiful. ___

Susan refused to try swimming and basketball. ___

Answer the questions

1. Who will Susan be going hiking with?

_____

2. Why didn't Susan know what to wear?

_____

3. Who did Jessica borrow a jacket from?

_____

4. What happened to their classmate's brother?

_____

Test

Write the answer next to the letter "A"

True, False or Not given?

A: ___ 1. Susan refused to play basketball because she got injured.

a. True   b. False   c. Not given

A: ___ 2. Susan went hiking when she was a little girl.

a. True   b. False   c. Not given

A: ___ 3. Their classmate's brother who got lost had to go to the hospital.

a. True   b. False   c. Not given

A: ___ 4. Jessica's sister has a warm jacket for when she goes camping.

a. True   b. False   c. Not given

Multiple choice questions

A: ___ 5. Jessica ___ it's important to ___ many layers when hiking.

a. known, wearing   b. know, worn   c. knows, wear

A: ___ 6. Susan's mom has been ___ to get her to do more exercise.

a. trying   b. tried   c. try

A: ___ 7. Can the weather change very quickly where Jessica lives?

a. Yes, it does.   b. Yes, it can.   c. Yes, it changes.

A: ___ 8. What are the two friends planning on doing together?

a. Going camping.   b. Taking scenery pictures.   c. Going hiking.

Answers on page 539

Lesson 29: More clothes

Daha fazla giysi

Learn the words

1. **pants**
   Pantolon
2. **shorts**
   Şort
3. **shoes**
   Ayakkabı
4. **dresses**
   Elbise
5. **shirts**
   Gömlek
6. **jeans**
   Kot
7. **socks**
   Çorap
8. **gloves**
   Eldiven
9. **pajamas**
   Pijama
10. **boots**
    Bot

Learn a verb

lend – lending – lent – lent ödünç vermek

His father <u>lent</u> him some clothes to wear.

Learn an idiom

Fits like a glove

Meaning: Something is the right size.

"The shorts were too big, but the shirt *fit like a glove*."

Grammar tenses	Past	Present	Future
Simple	✓	✓	
Continuous			
Perfect	✓	✓	
Perfect Continuous		✓	

Reading

Shopping for clothes!

Some people really dislike going shopping for clothes. It can be very uncomfortable for them, especially if they don't know what's currently in fashion. There are so many different kinds of clothing stores that it can be overwhelming.

For example, **jeans** used to be easy to buy because there weren't many styles to choose from. Nowadays, jeans come in all shapes and sizes. There are different colors, various designs and many brands. For women, it gets a lot more complicated when they have to buy **dresses**. There are hundreds of different designs to consider. It is no wonder that some people simply give up when they shop for clothes.

This is how Jason felt when he had to go shopping for new clothes. He hated the thought of spending the day at a department store walking from one store to another, trying on different clothes. As a result, he has worn the same **pants** for the past three years. He has been wearing his **shirts** for five years.

Today, his mother had had enough. She could no longer handle seeing her son wear the same clothes continuously. That evening, Jason opened his wardrobe to take out his **pajamas**. To his surprise, almost all his clothes were gone! Inside was an envelope with a note that said, "Here is $300. Use this money to buy new clothes."

The next day, Jason didn't have any clothes to go outside! His father <u>lent</u> him some clothes to wear. The **shorts** were too big, but the **shirt** *fit like a glove*.

He put his **shoes** on and headed to the department store.

Learn the English

Put a check next to the correct answer

1. Some people don't like going shopping because

- there are too many different choices. ____

- the clothes these days are too expensive. ____

2. Jason has worn the same pants for three years because

- he hates going shopping. ____

- they're his favorite. ____

3. Jason's mother put $300 in his wardrobe so that

- he can buy video games at the department store. ____

- he can buy new clothes at the department store. ____

Answer the questions

1. How have jeans changed over the years?

_____

2. What had Jason's mother had enough of?

_____

3. What was Jason surprised about when he opened his wardrobe?

_____

4. Which clothing did Jason's father lend him?

_____

Test

Write the answer next to the letter "A"

True, False or Not given?

A: ___ **1.** Jason loved the idea of shopping at the department store.

a. True b. False c. Not given

A: ___ **2.** Jason's favorite pair of pants are very colorful.

a. True b. False c. Not given

A: ___ **3.** His mother wasn't very happy with the clothes Jason was wearing.

a. True b. False c. Not given

A: ___ **4.** The department store is very close to Jason's house.

a. True b. False c. Not given

Multiple choice questions

A: ___ **5.** Before, there ___ many styles of jeans to choose from.

a. wasn't b. weren't c. haven't been

A: ___ **6.** Tired of his clothes, Jason's mother had ___ enough.

a. had b. been c. handle

A: ___ **7.** Did Jason's father lend him some clothes to wear?

a. Yes, he did. b. Yes, he had. c. Yes, he lent.

A: ___ **8.** In the evening, what was inside of Jason's wardrobe?

a. New clothes. b. An envelope. c. Some shorts.

Answers on page 539

Lesson 30: In the living room

Oturma odasında

Learn the words

1. **bookcase**
   Kitaplık
2. **television**
   Televizyon
3. **clock**
   Saat
4. **coffee table**
   Sehpa
5. **armchair**
   Koltuk
6. **painting**
   Tablo
7. **TV stand**
   Televizyon büfesi
8. **rug**
   Kilim
9. **sofa**
   Kanepe
10. **vase**
    Vazo

Learn a verb

move – moving – moved – moved hareket etmek

She told him about how she had to unexpectedly <u>move</u> to a new apartment.

Learn an idiom

A race against the clock

Meaning: To not have too much time left to complete a task.

"Because of the short time, it was *a race against the clock* to finish."

Grammar tenses	Past	Present	Future
Simple	✓	✓	
Continuous			
Perfect	✓	✓	
Perfect Continuous			

Reading

Moving day!

Ever since he started his new job, Eric has been very busy. In fact, he seldom has time anymore to stay in contact with all of his good friends. When his old classmate, Betty, called him a few days ago, he was happy to chat with her again. He hadn't spoken with her for over three years.

Betty told him about how she had to unexpectedly move to a new apartment. This was because a storm had broken some windows at her old place. As a result, some rain had gotten in and damaged her things. She had to throw out her favorite **armchair** and a **bookcase**. A **rug** and her **TV stand** also got really wet.

Although Eric wanted to help, he only had an hour while on a break at work. Because of the short time, it was *a race against the clock* to finish. Eric always spends his free time at the gym, so he's very strong. For this reason, Betty wanted help moving the heavy furniture. The two of them moved the **sofa** first because it's the biggest. Eric then brought in a big **vase** and a large **coffee table** by himself.

To thank Eric for his help, Betty gave him a beautiful **painting** that he liked. When he got home after work that evening, he had to decide where to put it. At first, he put it on the wall in his bedroom across from his bed. However, he realized that it would be better if visitors could see it, so he moved it and hung it in the living room. Next to the **television**, he removed the **clock** and replaced it with the **painting**.

Now, any time he has friends come over, they all comment on how great the art looks on his wall.

Learn the English

Find nine different verbs from the Reading

1. _____   4. _____   7. _____

2. _____   5. _____   8. _____

3. _____   6. _____   9. _____

Fill in the blanks

Betty told him about how she had to _____ move to a new _____. This was because a storm had _____ some _____ at her old place. As a _____, some rain had gotten in and damaged her things. She had to throw out her _____ armchair and a _____.

Answer the questions

1. How long hadn't Eric spoken to Betty for?

_____

2. Why did Betty have to move to a new apartment?

_____

3. What did Betty need Eric's help with?

_____

4. What was Betty's gift to Jason for helping her?

_____

Test

Write the answer next to the letter "A"

True, False or Not given?

A: ___ **1.** Eric helped Betty move while on a break from work.

a. True   b. False   c. Not given

A: ___ **2.** After a storm, Betty had to throw out her coffee table.

a. True   b. False   c. Not given

A: ___ **3.** In the end, Eric moved the painting from the bedroom to the living room.

a. True   b. False   c. Not given

A: ___ **4.** The vase that Eric carried for Betty was very expensive.

a. True   b. False   c. Not given

Multiple choice questions

A: ___ **5.** Betty hadn't ___ with Eric for over three years.

a. speaking   b. speak   c. spoken

A: ___ **6.** Eric is quite strong because he ___ his free time at the gym.

a. spending   b. spends   c. spend

A: ___ **7.** Was a storm the reason that Betty had to move?

a. Yes, it had.   b. Yes, it was.   c. Yes, she moved.

A: ___ **8.** What did Eric remove so that he could hang the painting?

a. The television.   b. The art.   c. The clock.

Answers on page 539

Lesson 31: In the bathroom

Banyoda

Learn the words

1. **mirror**
   Ayna
2. **bath towel**
   Banyo havlusu
3. **shower**
   Duş
4. **toilet paper**
   Tuvalet kağıdı
5. **bath mat**
   Banyo paspası
6. **shelf**
   Raf
7. **sink**
   Lavabo
8. **toilet**
   Klozet
9. **bathtub**
   Küvet
10. **soap**
    Sabun

Learn a verb

wash – washing – washed – washed yıkamak

Instead, they have been <u>washing</u> themselves in the bathtub.

Learn an idiom

Throw in the towel

Meaning: To give up or quit.

"Emily had never built a shelf before, and she almost *threw in the towel*."

Grammar tenses	Past	Present	Future
Simple	✓	✓	
Continuous	✓	✓	
Perfect	✓		
Perfect Continuous	✓		

Reading

A new bathroom!

Emily had decided to change her bathroom. She hadn't been happy with it for a long time. The house was over twenty years old, and the bathroom had not been updated since it was built. Recently, the family had avoided taking **showers**. This was because sometimes the water would stop for a few seconds and make a strange sound. Instead, they had been washing themselves in the **bathtub**. The problem with this was it would take a long time to run a bath, and when there are four people living in the same house, it is really inconvenient.

The first thing Emily decided to do was to fix the plumbing in the bathroom to make sure the shower was working properly. While the plumber was at the house, she asked him to put a new **sink** in as well. There was nothing wrong with it, but it looked old and ugly. Once the beautiful new **sink** was installed, it made everything else in the bathroom look even older!

Emily decided to take out the **bathtub** and put a new one in. She also decided to build a **shelf**. She didn't have any tools to build it, so she borrowed some from her uncle. Emily had never built a **shelf** before, and she almost *threw in the towel*. However, she didn't give up, and in the end, she made a big improvement to the bathroom. She put the **shelf** on the back wall across from the **mirror**.

Below the **shelf** was an area where you could place **bath towels**. The last thing she replaced was the **toilet**. Emily looked at the bathroom and was very pleased with herself.

It looked like a new bathroom!

Learn the English

Unscramble the words

ospa _____   swehro _____

imrrro _____   atbhtbu _____

otietl _____   nski _____

Write six things you have in your bathroom

1. _____   3. _____   5. _____

2. _____   4. _____   6. _____

Answer the questions

1. How old was Emily's house?

_____

2. What was the problem with the whole family using the bathtub?

_____

3. Why did Emily decide to put a new sink in the bathroom?

_____

4. Where did Emily put the shelf that she had built?

_____

Test

Write the answer next to the letter "A"

True, False or Not given?

A: ___ **1.** The bathroom had not been updated for over thirty years.

a. True   b. False   c. Not given

A: ___ **2.** Changing the sink made everything else in the bathroom look older.

a. True   b. False   c. Not given

A: ___ **3.** The sink in the bathroom needed replacing because it was broken.

a. True   b. False   c. Not given

A: ___ **4.** Emily asked her uncle to build a shelf for her bathroom.

a. True   b. False   c. Not given

Multiple choice questions

A: ___ **5.** The family had ___ taking showers because of water problems.

a. recently   b. stopping   c. avoided

A: ___ **6.** Emily decided to take out the bathtub and put a new one ___.

a. on   b. at   c. in

A: ___ **7.** Had Emily been unhappy with her bathroom for a long time?

a. No, she hadn't been.   b. Yes, she had been.   c. Yes, she did.

A: ___ **8.** What could be placed below the shelf?

a. The mirror.   b. A toilet.   c. Bath towels.

Answers on page 539

Lesson 32: In the bedroom

Yatak odasında

Learn the words

1. **bed**
   Yatak
2. **pillow**
   Yastık
3. **mattress**
   Döşek
4. **blanket**
   Battaniye
5. **drawers**
   Çekmece
6. **lamp**
   Lamba
7. **alarm clock**
   Çalar saat
8. **wardrobe**
   Gardırop
9. **bed sheets**
   Yatak çarşafı
10. **nightstand**
    Komodin

Learn a verb

change – changing – changed – changed değiştirmek

However, he's thinking about <u>changing</u> his mattress and pillow.

Learn an idiom

Get up on the wrong side of the bed

Meaning: To describe somebody who is in a bad mood.

"Jack hadn't done anything wrong, so he guessed the guy had *gotten up on the wrong side of the bed*."

Grammar tenses	Past	Present	Future
Simple	✓	✓	
Continuous		✓	
Perfect	✓		
Perfect Continuous			

Reading

A love of shopping!

In Amy's opinion, shopping is a great way to spend time. She loves being at the mall, especially when she's with friends. Actually, it doesn't matter to her where she goes to, as long as she can shop. She can <u>change</u> locations and the people she's with, but the important thing for her is the experience of getting new things.

For example, her friend, Jack, just moved into a new house and needs many things in the bedroom. He does have some important items such as a **wardrobe** and a **nightstand**. However, he's thinking about <u>changing</u> his **mattress** and **pillow**. To the left of his **bed**, there aren't any **drawers**. This makes the room look a bit empty.

Of course, Amy saw this as an opportunity to get some new things for her bedroom, too. Because of the cooler December weather, she wants to get new **bed sheets** and a **blanket**. She and Jack made a plan and headed to the mall.

In the first shop, while looking at a **lamp**, the salesclerk wasn't very friendly. Jack hadn't done anything wrong, so he guessed the guy had *gotten up on the wrong side of the bed*. To the right of that store was another one, so they went there instead. They found a nice **lamp** and bought it as a gift for their friend, Kevin.

After hours of walking around the different shops, Jack still hadn't found anything that he liked. Amy, on the other hand, had bought a lot more than she had originally planned. Along with her **bed sheets** and **blanket**, she got an **alarm clock**, too. She also bought many things for her bathroom. Jack was really amazed at Amy's love of shopping!

Learn the English

Find the two mistakes and write the sentence correctly

Jack moved into a new apartment and needs things in the bathroom.

_____

The two friends made a date and headed to the restaurant.

_____

In the second shop, the salesclerk was very friendly.

_____

After hour of walking, Jack hadn't found everything that he liked.

_____

Answer the questions

1. What is one thing Amy likes about shopping?

_____

2. Which room does Jack need new things for?

_____

3. Who did they buy a lamp for?

_____

4. What items did Amy buy for her bedroom?

_____

Test

Write the answer next to the letter "A"

True, False or Not given?

A: ___ 1. Amy's bought a new bath towel for her bathroom.

a. True   b. False   c. Not given

A: ___ 2. Jack's nightstand was given to him by his friend, Kevin.

a. True   b. False   c. Not given

A: ___ 3. The two friends were shopping at the mall for an hour.

a. True   b. False   c. Not given

A: ___ 4. Amy ended up buying many more things than Jack did.

a. True   b. False   c. Not given

Multiple choice questions

A: ___ 5. It ___ matter where Amy ___ shopping.

a. doesn't, goes   b. don't, going   c. doesn't, go

A: ___ 6. To the left of Jack's bed, there ___ any drawers.

a. emptied   b. doesn't   c. aren't

A: ___ 7. After all their time in the mall, had Jack found anything he liked?

a. No, he hadn't.   b. No, he didn't.   c. Yes, he found.

A: ___ 8. Why does Amy want to get new bed sheets?

a. The cooler weather.   b. Hers are the wrong size.   c. For a gift.

Answers on page 539

Lesson 33: Around the house

Evin etrafında

Learn the words

1. **work in the garage**
   Garajda çalışmak
2. **fix the mailbox**
   Posta kutusunu tamir etmek
3. **fix the gate**
   Kapıyı tamir etmek
4. **work in the garden**
   Bahçede çalışmak
5. **clean the pool**
   Havuzu temizlemek
6. **work in the yard**
   Avluda çalışmak
7. **fix the fence**
   Çitleri tamir etmek
8. **clean the balcony**
   Balkonu temizlemek
9. **clean the outdoor furniture**
   Dış mekan mobilyalarını temizlemek
10. **clean the barbecue**
    Izgarayı temizlemek

Learn a verb

fix – fixing – fixed – fixed tamir etmek

Ted won't be able to come because he's busy <u>fixing</u> the gate.

Learn an idiom

On the house

Meaning: To get something for free.

"However, Max's father said he'll deal with it himself, despite the mail carrier saying it would be *on the house.*"

Grammar tenses	Past	Present	Future
Simple	✓	✓	
Continuous	✓		
Perfect	✓	✓	
Perfect Continuous		✓	

Reading

Everybody's busy!

Max and Julie are bored. It's the weekend and the sun's out. Recently, it's been raining a lot and the two of them have been stuck inside. Max suggests that they should go to the park and play soccer. Julie thinks they should invite some people to come, and then they can have a soccer match.

Their uncle won't be able to come because he's busy **fixing the gate**. He accidently drove into it with his car when he was parking. Luckily, it was just the gate that he hit, otherwise he would have to **fix the fence** as well.

Julie decided to call Bob, her classmate from school. He was **cleaning the barbecue** when she called. He told her that he was not allowed out after spilling paint in the back yard. He was painting his skateboard ramp and didn't notice all the blue spots he had splashed on the tables and barbecue. He still has to **clean the outdoor furniture**!

Emily can't play because she hurt her foot while **working in the garage**. She was building a shelf for her bathroom and she dropped a hammer on her toe. It's not serious, but she can't kick a ball.

Finally, Max asks his father to join them. His father says he can, but first he has to do a few things around the house. He's almost done **fixing the mailbox** after the mail carrier knocked it with his bag. He said he would organize someone to come and fix it. However, Max's father said he'll deal with it himself, despite the mail carrier saying it would be *on the house.*

Julie and Max sit in the front yard and wait for their dad.

Learn the English

Unscramble the sentences

1. sun's / and / out / the / the / It's / weekend

_____

2. called / she / barbecue / the / cleaning / when / was / He

_____

3. the / clean / furniture / to / still / He / outdoor / has

_____

4. done / mailbox / He's / fixing / the / almost

_____

Answer the questions

1. Where do Max and Julie want to play soccer?

_____

2. Why is their uncle's fence broken?

_____

3. What color was Bob painting the skateboard ramp?

_____

4. How did Emily hurt her toe?

_____

Test

Write the answer next to the letter "A"

True, False or Not given?

A: ____ **1.** Their uncle has driven into his gate several times before.

a. Trueb. Falsec. Not given

A: ____ **2.** Max has to clean the outdoor furniture because he splashed paint on it.

a. Trueb. Falsec. Not given

A: ____ **3.** Emily dropped a hammer on her toe while she was in the garage.

a. Trueb. Falsec. Not given

A: ____ **4.** The mail carrier said that Max's father has to pay for the broken mailbox.

a. Trueb. Falsec. Not given

Multiple choice questions

A: ____ **5.** Because they've been inside for days, Max and Julie are ____.

a. boringb. boredc. been bored

A: ____ **6.** Emily's toe ____ so she can't ____ a ball.

a. hurts, kickb. hurting, playc. gotten hurt, kicking

A: ____ **7.** Did their uncle have to fix the fence?

a. Yes, he fixed it.b. No, he hadn't.c. No, he didn't.

A: ____ **8.** What was their friend painting in the back yard?

a. The barbecue.b. His skateboard ramp.c. The tables.

Answers on page 539

Lesson 34: Hobbies

Hobiler

Learn the words

1. **do gardening**
   Bahçecilik yapmak
2. **go hiking**
   Dağ yürüyüşüne çıkmak
3. **take photographs**
   Fotoğraf çekmek
4. **play video games**
   Video oyunları oynamak
5. **listen to music**
   Müzik dinlemek
6. **go camping**
   Kampa gitmek
7. **play chess**
   Satranç oynamak
8. **watch movies**
   Film izlemek
9. **go fishing**
   Balık tutmak
10. **sing karaoke**
    Karaoke yapmak

Learn a verb

enjoy – enjoying – enjoyed – enjoyed zevk almak

Kate has always <u>enjoyed</u> teaching her friends about her interests.

Learn an idiom

Face the music

Meaning: To face the consequences of one's actions.

"Peter knows he has to *face the music* and do things differently."

Grammar tenses	Past	Present	Future
Simple	✓	✓	✓
Continuous		✓	
Perfect	✓	✓	
Perfect Continuous			

Reading

Many hobbies!

Rather than sitting around and wasting time, Matthew likes to be active. This is why he has many hobbies. Not only does he **listen to music** and **go hiking**, he also enjoys **watching movies** at the cinema. In fact, he just watched a movie with his good friend, Kate.

One of the reasons the two get along so well is because Kate also has many interesting hobbies. While Matthew doesn't **take photographs** or **sing karaoke** like Kate does, he enjoys learning about new things from her. They both like to be outside, so when Kate **does the gardening**, Matthew helps her. Kate has always enjoyed teaching her friends about her interests.

While walking home, Kate saw her other friend, Peter, who looked worried. He always spends a lot of time **playing video games**, so his grades at school aren't very good. Peter knows he has to *face the music* and do things differently. Kate had read an article about how doing exercise is a good way to help memory. She suggested that an outdoor hobby might be helpful for him to make some positive changes. Peter liked the idea because he knows being active could help his grades.

Going camping is something Peter's older brother enjoys. He plans to try that next Saturday. They will also **go fishing** on their trip. Peter also decided to **play video games** less. Along with that, Peter meets with his friends who do different things. Once a week, he meets with Matthew to **go hiking** in the mountains nearby. To challenge his mind, he also asked Kate to start teaching him how to **play chess**.

Now, Peter is much happier and isn't feeling worried anymore!

Learn the English

Write the names: Matthew, Kate, Peter or Peter's brother?

_____ enjoys teaching others about her interesting hobbies.

_____ asked Kate to teach him how to play chess.

_____ enjoys going camping.

_____ doesn't like to sing karaoke.

_____ spends a lot of time playing video games.

_____ likes to be active and has many hobbies.

_____ had read an article about the benefits of exercise.

Answer the questions

1. Why do Matthew and Kate get along so well?

_____

2. Who likes to take photographs?

_____

3. Where was Kate going when she saw Peter?

_____

4. What does Peter's older brother like doing?

_____

Test

Write the answer next to the letter "A"

True, False or Not given?

A: ___ **1.** Matthew likes to sing karaoke with his friend, Kate.

a. True b. False c. Not given

A: ___ **2.** Both Matthew and Kate do the gardening together.

a. True b. False c. Not given

A: ___ **3.** Peter's older brother asked Kate to teach him how to play chess.

a. True b. False c. Not given

A: ___ **4.** Peter's worst grades at school are in his music class.

a. True b. False c. Not given

Multiple choice questions

A: ___ **5.** Matthew ___ movies at the cinema.

a. enjoy to watch b. enjoying watch c. enjoys watching

A: ___ **6.** Kate ___ that an outdoor hobby might ___ helpful.

a. suggesting, being b. suggests, been c. suggested, be

A: ___ **7.** Does Peter always spend a lot of time playing video games?

a. Yes, he does. b. Yes, he spends time. c. Yes, he always.

A: ___ **8.** What will Peter and his brother do on their trip?

a. Go fishing. b. Play video games less. c. Listen to music.

Answers on page 539

Lesson 35: Countries

Ülkeler

Learn the words

1. **Japan**
   Japonya
2. **Canada**
   Kanada
3. **Brazil**
   Brezilya
4. **Australia**
   Avustralya
5. **South Africa**
   Güney Afrika
6. **China**
   Çin
7. **Mexico**
   Meksika
8. **Argentina**
   Arjantin
9. **New Zealand**
   Yeni Zelanda
10. **Kenya**
    Kenya

Learn a verb

write – writing – wrote – written yazmak

He even <u>wrote</u> a travel book about his unforgettable experience.

Learn an idiom

Second to none

Meaning: To describe something that is the best.

"He said watching the migration is *second to none*."

Grammar tenses	Past	Present	Future
Simple	✓	✓	
Continuous		✓	
Perfect	✓	✓	
Perfect Continuous		✓	

Reading

Snowboarding again!

Helen's family loves to travel. Right now, they are in an airplane flying to **New Zealand**. The family chose to go there instead of the more popular tourist destination, **Australia**. This is because they want to go snowboarding on this trip. **New Zealand** has a lot more snow than **Australia**. Last year, Helen went snowboarding for the first time in **Canada** with her friend, Susan, and she absolutely loved it. She has been thinking about the snow every day since coming home!

Helen's mother had actually wanted to travel to **Kenya** to watch the migration of animals across the Masai Mara wildlife park. It has been a dream of hers to see this great wonder of the world. Her friend, John, traveled from **South Africa** to **Kenya** to watch all the wild animals moving together across the land. He said watching the migration is *second to none.* He even wrote a travel book about his unforgettable experience.

However, Helen didn't want to go to Africa. She's been begging her parents to take her to another country that has snow all year. At first, they considered going to **Japan**, but Helen's father often travels to **China** on business, and didn't want to go to another Asian country this year.

Helen's father agreed to go to **New Zealand**. However, he has been working a lot this year, and he would have preferred to sit on a beach in **Mexico** for two weeks and drink coconut water all day.

"Put your seats in an upright position."

Helen looked out the window and saw some sheep.

Learn the English

Write the opposite with the word "not"

Helen's family loves to travel.
Helen's family doesn't love to travel.

She has been thinking about the snow.
_____

He said watching the migration is second to none.
_____

Helen's father often travels to China.
_____

Helen's father agreed to go to New Zealand.
_____

Answer the questions

1. What does Helen want to do in New Zealand?
_____

2. Why did Helen's mother want to travel to Kenya?
_____

3. Who wrote a book about his experience in Africa?
_____

4. How does Helen's father want to spend his vacation?
_____

Test

Write the answer next to the letter "A"

True, False or Not given?

A: ___ **1.** Helen's father didn't want to travel to another Asian country this year.

a. True b. False c. Not given

A: ___ **2.** Helen went snowboarding for the first time in New Zealand last year.

a. True b. False c. Not given

A: ___ **3.** When John was in South Africa, he spent a lot of money.

a. True b. False c. Not given

A: ___ **4.** Seeing snow was an amazing part of Helen's trip to Canada.

a. True b. False c. Not given

Multiple choice questions

A: ___ **5.** John ___ a book about his travel experience in Africa.

a. wrote b. written c. writing

A: ___ **6.** Helen has ___ her parents to take her to a country with snow.

a. being begging b. been begging c. begging

A: ___ **7.** Does Australia get a lot more snow than New Zealand?

a. Yes, it does. b. No, it doesn't. c. Yes, it gets.

A: ___ **8.** What would Helen's father like to do on a beach all day?

a. Go swimming. b. Look at sheep. c. Drink coconut water.

Answers on page 539

Lesson 36: Landscapes

Manzaralar

Learn the words

1. **river**
   Nehir
2. **beach (es)**
   Kumsal
3. **mountain**
   Dağ
4. **volcano (es)**
   Yanardağ
5. **forest**
   Orman
6. **lake**
   Göl
7. **waterfall**
   Şelale
8. **island**
   Ada
9. **ocean**
   Okyanus
10. **jungle**
    Orman

Learn a verb

prepare – preparing – prepared – prepared hazırlamak

Tom had <u>prepared</u> a presentation about forests and how to clean them up.

Learn an idiom

A drop in the ocean

Meaning: To only make a tiny impact.

"Although they know it's just *a drop in the ocean*, it felt like a good start."

Grammar tenses	Past	Present	Future
Simple	✓	✓	
Continuous			
Perfect	✓	✓	
Perfect Continuous			

Reading

Clean landscapes!

While growing up, Tom and his family loved the great outdoors. They visited many wonderful locations and Tom loved learning about how things work in nature. It is no wonder that his favorite subject is science.

In class, he learned about **volcanoes** and how they form **mountain** peaks. Tom's dream is to one day go hiking in the **jungles** of South America and see the incredible **waterfalls** there.

After learning about so many incredible places, Tom understands the importance of protecting the environment. Last week in his science class, the topic was pollution. It was really shocking to hear about how polluted the **oceans** and **lakes** have become. Tom had prepared a presentation about **forests** and how to clean them up. Many classmates wanted to help, so they formed a group to try to change things. Although they know it's just *a drop in the ocean*, it felt like a good start.

He was so focused on his presentation that Tom forgot about his other homework. The teacher was quite angry about this. While his classmates had prepared videos and speeches about **islands** and **rivers** for geography class, Tom hadn't done anything.

After school, he went and spoke to his teacher, explaining why he hadn't done his homework. He also suggested that he could make a video about pollution and give a quiz to the class. The teacher saw how concerned Tom was about the earth, so she was happy to let him do this project to catch up. As a geography teacher, she wants to encourage students to take care of the landscapes for the future.

Learn the English

Find nine different adjectives from the Reading

1. _____   4. _____   7. _____

2. _____   5. _____   8. _____

3. _____   6. _____   9. _____

Complete the sentence using 3 or 4 words

Tom loved learning about how _____

He understands the importance of _____

Tom forgot about _____

The teacher was _____

Answer the questions

1. What is Tom's dream to do one day?

_____

2. Which subject did he make a project about pollution for first?

_____

3. Why was Tom's teacher angry with him?

_____

4. How will Tom catch up in his geography class?

_____

Test

Write the answer next to the letter "A"

True, False or Not given?

A: ___ **1.** In Tom's science class last week, the topic was volcanoes.

a. True   b. False   c. Not given

A: ___ **2.** Tom spoke to his geography teacher in her office.

a. True   b. False   c. Not given

A: ___ **3.** It was shocking to hear about the pollution in the water.

a. True   b. False   c. Not given

A: ___ **4.** While growing up, Tom often went camping with his family.

a. True   b. False   c. Not given

Multiple choice questions

A: ___ **5.** When he was younger, Tom started ___ about nature.

a. preparing   b. learning   c. working

A: ___ **6.** Unlike his classmates, Tom ___ anything for his presentation.

a. hadn't done   b. didn't done   c. wasn't done

A: ___ **7.** Did Tom and his classmates form an environmental group?

a. Yes, they formed.   b. Yes, they had.   c. Yes, they did.

A: ___ **8.** What did Tom suggest giving to the class to catch up?

a. A video.   b. A quiz.   c. A speech.

Answers on page 539

Lesson 37: Everyday life

Günlük yaşam

Learn the words

1. **woken up**
   Uyandım
2. **brushed my teeth**
   Dişimi fırçaladım
3. **done homework**
   Ödevimi yaptım
4. **cooked dinner**
   Yemek yaptım
5. **taken out the trash**
   Çöpü attım
6. **eaten breakfast**
   Kahvaltı ettim
7. **gone to school**
   Okula gittim
8. **taken a shower**
   Duş aldım
9. **gone to sleep**
   Uyudum
10. **gone shopping**
    Alışverişe gittim

Learn a verb

wake – waking – woke – woken uyanmak

Firstly, Ted has decided to <u>wake</u> up earlier.

Learn an idiom

Hit the nail on the head

Meaning: To say something that is correct.

"Ted thinks Kevin has *hit the nail on head*."

Grammar tenses	Past	Present	Future
Simple		✓	✓
Continuous		✓	
Perfect	✓	✓	✓
Perfect Continuous			

Reading

Let's get organized!

Ted is trying to improve his time management. He often turns up late to appointments. His friends are starting to get annoyed with him. His friend, Kevin, is always on time and told him that he's always late because he doesn't write down his daily schedule. Ted thinks Kevin has *hit the nail on head*. Therefore, Ted is working on a daily schedule now to make his everyday life more organized.

Firstly, Ted has decided to wake up earlier. Before, he had **woken up** at six o'clock in the morning, but recently he has gotten lazy and now gets up at eight o'clock. He will have to have **gone to sleep** by ten o'clock in the evening if he wants to be up two hours earlier. Ted sets his alarm clock immediately to make sure he doesn't sleep late.

To go to bed by ten, Ted needs to make sure he has **done homework** by nine o'clock. This is because he still has to take a shower before bedtime. Last night, he had **taken a shower** at ten o'clock and it took about thirty minutes. However, he had also **brushed his teeth** and this took ten minutes.

Ted is pleased with how he has organized his schedule in the evening. However, he still has to find some time to do the chores. Now that he is waking up at six, it should be easier to get more things done. If he can make sure that he has **taken out the trash** before breakfast, then he will have more time to relax in the morning and also prepare for the day. Once he has **eaten breakfast**, he will head off to school.

On the weekends, Ted decides that he can sleep in late. It's okay to be a little lazy sometimes!

Learn the English

Complete the questions to the answers

Who _____?

Kevin is always on time.

How _____?

He will set his alarm clock two hours earlier.

When _____?

He will have done his homework by nine o'clock.

Which _____?

His chore in the morning is taking out the trash.

Answer the questions

1. Why is Ted working on a daily schedule?

_____

2. What time had Ted woken up at before?

_____

3. How long does it take for Ted to take a shower?

_____

4. When will Ted sleep in late?

_____

Test

Write the answer next to the letter "A"

True, False or Not given?

A: ___ **1.** Just recently, Ted bought himself a new alarm clock.

a. True   b. False   c. Not given

A: ___ **2.** Waking up at six gives Ted enough time to take out the trash.

a. True   b. False   c. Not given

A: ___ **3.** Kevin is annoyed with himself for always being late.

a. True   b. False   c. Not given

A: ___ **4.** Ted decided to write down his new schedule in a notebook.

a. True   b. False   c. Not given

Multiple choice questions

A: ___ **5.** Before, he had ___ early in the morning.

a. woken up   b. waking up   c. woke on

A: ___ **6.** After he ___ breakfast, he will head off to school.

a. is eaten   b. eating   c. has eaten

A: ___ **7.** Were Ted's friends unhappy with his poor time habits?

a. Yes, they unhappy.   b. Yes, they were.   c. Yes, they did.

A: ___ **8.** What does *hit the nail on the head* refer to in the article?

a. Ted has no schedule.   b. His friends are annoyed.   c. Ted is organized.

Answers on page 539

Lesson 38: Languages

Diller

Learn the words

1. **English**
   İngilizce
2. **German**
   Almanca
3. **Portuguese**
   Portekizce
4. **Japanese**
   Japonca
5. **Vietnamese**
   Vietnamca
6. **Spanish**
   İspanyolca
7. **French**
   Fransızca
8. **Chinese**
   Çince
9. **Hindi**
   Hintçe
10. **Arabic**
    Arapça

Learn a verb

speak – speaking – spoke – spoken konuşmak

Jessica was sitting next to one of the meeting rooms, and she heard a lot of people <u>speaking</u> inside.

Learn an idiom

Speak the same language

Meaning: To share the same understanding and be in agreement.

"The two of them were really *speaking the same language*."

Grammar tenses	Past	Present	Future
Simple	✓	✓	
Continuous	✓		
Perfect	✓		
Perfect Continuous		✓	

Reading

<u>So many languages!</u>

Early in the morning, Jessica went to the library to find some books about art. When she first arrived, there were very few people. She asked the librarian to recommend some things, and it turns out the librarian loves art, too. They discussed some famous artists like Van Gogh and Picasso for almost an hour. The two of them were really *speaking the same language*.

As it got to around noon, more and more people started showing up. Jessica was sitting next to one of the meeting rooms, and she heard a lot of people speaking inside. However, they weren't speaking **English**, they were using **German**. She had only studied **Arabic** and **Spanish** before, so she didn't understand them when they spoke. Jessica looked through the window and saw Helen's brother inside. He looked like he was really having fun.

Next to the door, Jessica noticed a poster on the wall for the library's language club. It invited people to go to their website to choose a language to learn. This reminded Jessica about her aunt and uncle, who have been studying both **Japanese** and **Vietnamese**. They had traveled to Asia many times and loved conversing with the locals. Perhaps it was time for Jessica to study something like **Portuguese** or **French** because she has always wanted to go to France and Portugal.

It was lunchtime, so Jessica decided to head home. As she was going out the door, she overheard some people having a conversation in **Chinese**. Upon hearing them, she decided to definitely start learning a new language!

Learn the English

Put the sentences in order

Jessica discussed famous artists with the librarian. ___

Jessica noticed a poster on the wall for the language club. ___

Jessica went to the library to find some books about art. _1_

Some people were having a conversation in Chinese. ___

She'd like to learn Portuguese and French. ___

Jessica heard some people speaking German. ___

Jessica decided to leave the library at lunchtime. ___

The poster reminded Jessica about her aunt and uncle. ___

Answer the questions

1. Where did Jessica go to find books about art?

_____

2. What did the poster at the library invite people to do?

_____

3. Which languages had Jessica studied before?

_____

4. Why is Jessica thinking about studying Portuguese and French?

_____

Test

Write the answer next to the letter "A"

True, False or Not given?

A: ___ **1.** The library got a lot busier around lunch time.

a. True b. False c. Not given

A: ___ **2.** The librarian loves languages and can speak German.

a. True b. False c. Not given

A: ___ **3.** Helen's brother was there with two of his friends.

a. True b. False c. Not given

A: ___ **4.** Jessica's aunt and uncle have been to Asia once before.

a. True b. False c. Not given

Multiple choice questions

A: ___ **5.** Jessica and the librarian ___ some famous artists.

a. discussing b. discusses c. discussed

A: ___ **6.** They were ___ German, so she didn't understand them when they ___.

a. using, spoken b. speaking, spoke c. use, speak

A: ___ **7.** Did Jessica look through the window of the meeting room?

a. Yes, she did. b. No, she didn't. c. Yes, she had.

A: ___ **8.** Around lunchtime, where did Jessica decide to go?

a. Chinese class. b. France. c. Home.

Answers on page 539

Lesson 39: Pets

Evcil hayvanlar

Learn the words

1. **dog**
   Köpek
2. **fish**
   Balık
3. **bird**
   Kuş
4. **rabbit**
   Tavşan
5. **guinea pig**
   Kobay faresi
6. **cat**
   Kedi
7. **turtle**
   Kaplumbağa
8. **mouse**
   Fare
9. **hamster**
   Hamster
10. **snake**
    Yılan

Learn a verb

feed – feeding – fed – fed beslemek

Mice, on the other hand, can be <u>fed</u> almost anything.

Learn an idiom

The teacher's pet

Meaning: A student whom the teacher favors.

"Her science teacher is very proud of her decision and Emily has become a *teacher's pet* herself!"

Grammar tenses	Past	Present	Future
Simple	✓	✓	✓
Continuous		✓	✓
Perfect		✓	
Perfect Continuous			

Reading

Emily's new pet!

Emily is thinking about getting a pet. She has never had a pet before, so she's not sure which animal she should get. She lives in a small apartment and doesn't have a back yard. Therefore, her place wouldn't be very suitable for a **dog**. This is disappointing because she loves **dogs**. Emily will probably get a **mouse**, but she's still not sure.

She spoke to her classmate, Jason, about it. He has a pet **hamster**. He thinks a **hamster** is more expensive than a **mouse**. While both animals are omnivores, a **hamster** likes to eat a lot of leafy vegetables. Mice, on the other hand, can be fed almost anything, which makes them a little cheaper than **hamsters**.

Jason suggested to Emily that she should consider a **cat**. However, Emily has recently decided to become vegetarian. This is because her science teacher explained to her what the main causes of the climate crisis are. One of the reasons is not only humans, but also pets are eating too much beef. Her science teacher is very proud of her decision and Emily has become a *teacher's pet* herself!

Emily doesn't want to get a pet that eats too much meat. **Cats** love eating meat, so she won't be getting one. It's another reason why she doesn't want a **dog**. Jason suggested that she should consider a **rabbit**. Like **guinea pigs**, they are herbivores, so there is no meat in their diet. However, **rabbits** also have nice personalities and become very friendly with their owners, similar to a **dog**.

Emily was excited to hear that. She has made her decision. She's going to get a pet **rabbit**!

Learn the English

Put a check next to the correct answer

1. Jason thinks mice are cheaper than hamsters because

- they can eat almost anything. ____

- they are smaller than hamsters. ____

2. Emily doesn't want a meat-eating animal because

- her science teacher eats too much beef. ____

- her teacher taught her about the causes of the climate crisis. ____

3. Emily has decided to get a pet rabbit since

- they are herbivores and are friendly animals. ____

- they are similar to guinea pigs. ____

Answer the questions

1. Which pet is Emily's small apartment not suitable for?

_____

2. What does a hamster like to eat?

_____

3. Why doesn't Emily want to get a cat?

_____

4. Which animal will Emily be getting?

_____

Test

Write the answer next to the letter "A"

True, False or Not given?

A: ___ **1.** According to Jason, a hamster is cheaper than a mouse.

a. True b. False c. Not given

A: ___ **2.** Emily's place isn't big enough to get a dog.

a. True b. False c. Not given

A: ___ **3.** Over the years, Jason has had many pet hamsters.

a. True b. False c. Not given

A: ___ **4.** Emily's science teacher's explanation changed her mind about cats.

a. True b. False c. Not given

Multiple choice questions

A: ___ **5.** Rabbits ___ nice personalities and are very friendly.

a. have had b. have c. has

A: ___ **6.** Emily ___ never ___ a pet before.

a. is, having b. had, has c. has, had

A: ___ **7.** Has Emily made her decision about getting a new pet?

a. Yes, she made. b. No, she hasn't. c. Yes, she has.

A: ___ **8.** Which animal is a herbivore?

a. A dog. b. A rabbit. c. A guinea pig.

Answers on page 539

Lesson 40: Fast food

Hazır yemek

Learn the words

1. **doughnut**
   Tatlı çörek
2. **cheeseburger**
   Çizburger
3. **chicken nuggets**
   Tavuk nugget
4. **pancake**
   Krep
5. **taco**
   Tako
6. **french fries**
   Patates kızartması
7. **onion rings**
   Soğan halkası
8. **hot dog**
   Sosisli sandviç
9. **fried chicken**
   Kızarmış tavuk
10. **burrito**
    Burrito

Learn a verb

try – trying – tried – tried denemek

Matthew <u>tried</u> the burrito because he had heard it was the best.

Learn an idiom

You are what you eat

Meaning: The food that you eat affects your health.

"Always being so tired made him realize that *you are what you eat*."

Grammar tenses	Past	Present	Future
Simple	✓	✓	
Continuous	✓		
Perfect	✓		
Perfect Continuous		✓	

Reading

Good and bad habits!

Everyone knows that it's difficult to start and keep good habits. Lately, Ted has been getting advice from his friend, Kevin, about how to set up his timetable and be healthier. However, on weekends, Ted allows himself to be a bit lazy and eat some unhealthy food, too.

Before Kevin started coaching him, Ted loved to eat **doughnuts** and **pancakes**. He would order some **fried chicken** and **onion rings**, and then for dessert have something sweet. Of course, all that junk food made Ted feel unenergetic. In gym class last week, he was constantly out of breath. Always being so tired made him realize that *you are what you eat*. Around that time is when he asked Kevin for help. Along with organizing Ted's timetable, Kevin told him to stop eating things like **cheeseburgers** and **french fries** all the time.

On Saturday, Ted went to meet his friend, Matthew. Rather than being late to meet him, Ted had to skip breakfast so he could arrive on time. Everyone is sick of him always being late, so Ted was trying to change that. Because it was the weekend, Ted wanted to go to a fast food restaurant, which Kevin had recommended.

Matthew tried the **burrito** because he had heard it was the best. Ted, on the other hand, was really hungry, so he tried the **tacos** and a **hot dog** with **chicken nuggets** on the side. Of course, Ted's meal was the most expensive, and it wasn't very healthy, either. After they left the restaurant, Ted began to feel guilty about eating so much. He also wasn't happy about how unhealthy his food was.

Ted realized he still has to work on improving his good habits.

| Learn the English |

Find nine different verbs from the Reading

1. _____   4. _____   7. _____

2. _____   5. _____   8. _____

3. _____   6. _____   9. _____

Fill in the blanks

Before _____ started coaching him, Ted loved to eat doughnuts and _____. He would order some fried chicken and onion _____, and then for _____ have something _____. Of course, all that _____ food made Ted _____ unenergetic.

Answer the questions

1. What made Ted realize you are what you eat?

_____

2. Which foods did Kevin tell Ted to stop eating?

_____

3. Where did the boys go to eat on the weekend?

_____

4. Why was Ted feeling guilty after leaving the restaurant?

_____

Test

Write the answer next to the letter "A"

True, False or Not given?

A: ___ 1. In gym class last week, Ted felt tired while playing basketball.

a. True   b. False   c. Not given

A: ___ 2. Ted allows himself to eat unhealthy food and be lazy on Fridays.

a. True   b. False   c. Not given

A: ___ 3. The fast food place they went to was close to Ted's house.

a. True   b. False   c. Not given

A: ___ 4. At the restaurant, Ted ordered a lot more food than his friend.

a. True   b. False   c. Not given

Multiple choice questions

A: ___ 5. In order to be on time, Ted ___ breakfast.

a. skipped   b. ate   c. bought

A: ___ 6. Ted's meal ___ the most expensive, and it ___ very healthy.

a. was, wasn't   b. had, didn't   c. is, hadn't

A: ___ 7. Had Kevin given Ted advice about what foods to not eat?

a. Yes, he gave.   b. Yes, he had.   c. Yes, he advised.

A: ___ 8. What did Ted think about improving on?

a. His guilty feeling.   b. The cost of food.   c. His good habits.

Answers on page 539

Answers

Lesson 1 test	1. b 2. a 3. b 4. c 5. b 6. c 7. c 8. a
Lesson 2 test	1. a 2. c 3. b 4. b 5. c 6. b 7. a 8. c
Lesson 3 test	1. c 2. b 3. b 4. c 5. b 6. a 7. c 8. b
Lesson 4 test	1. b 2. c 3. c 4. a 5. a 6. c 7. c 8. b
Lesson 5 test	1. b 2. b 3. a 4. c 5. b 6. c 7. a 8. a
Lesson 6 test	1. c 2. a 3. c 4. b 5. b 6. b 7. c 8. a
Lesson 7 test	1. c 2. a 3. b 4. b 5. a 6. a 7. b 8. c
Lesson 8 test	1. a 2. a 3. c 4. c 5. c 6. a 7. b 8. b
Lesson 9 test	1. c 2. c 3. a 4. b 5. b 6. c 7. a 8. b
Lesson 10 test	1. b 2. a 3. c 4. a 5. b 6. c 7. a 8. c
Lesson 11 test	1. a 2. b 3. a 4. c 5. b 6. b 7. c 8. a
Lesson 12 test	1. c 2. a 3. b 4. b 5. c 6. b 7. a 8. c
Lesson 13 test	1. b 2. b 3. a 4. a 5. c 6. a 7. b 8. b
Lesson 14 test	1. a 2. b 3. c 4. a 5. a 6. a 7. c 8. b
Lesson 15 test	1. c 2. b 3. a 4. b 5. c 6. c 7. a 8. a
Lesson 16 test	1. b 2. c 3. a 4. c 5. b 6. a 7. c 8. c
Lesson 17 test	1. a 2. a 3. b 4. c 5. c 6. b 7. b 8. a
Lesson 18 test	1. b 2. b 3. c 4. a 5. a 6. b 7. a 8. b
Lesson 19 test	1. c 2. a 3. c 4. b 5. b 6. c 7. a 8. c
Lesson 20 test	1. b 2. c 3. b 4. a 5. b 6. b 7. c 8. a

Lesson 21 test	1. a 2. c 3. a 4. c 5. c 6. a 7. b 8. b
Lesson 22 test	1. c 2. b 3. b 4. a 5. b 6. c 7. b 8. a
Lesson 23 test	1. b 2. c 3. b 4. a 5. a 6. c 7. a 8. b
Lesson 24 test	1. a 2. b 3. c 4. b 5. c 6. b 7. c 8. c
Lesson 25 test	1. a 2. b 3. c 4. a 5. a 6. c 7. b 8. a
Lesson 26 test	1. c 2. a 3. b 4. b 5. b 6. c 7. a 8. b
Lesson 27 test	1. b 2. c 3. a 4. a 5. a 6. b 7. c 8. a
Lesson 28 test	1. c 2. b 3. c 4. a 5. c 6. a 7. b 8. c
Lesson 29 test	1. b 2. c 3. a 4. c 5. b 6. a 7. a 8. b
Lesson 30 test	1. a 2. b 3. a 4. c 5. c 6. b 7. b 8. c
Lesson 31 test	1. b 2. a 3. b 4. b 5. c 6. c 7. b 8. c
Lesson 32 test	1. c 2. c 3. b 4. a 5. a 6. c 7. a 8. a
Lesson 33 test	1. c 2. b 3. a 4. b 5. b 6. a 7. c 8. b
Lesson 34 test	1. b 2. a 3. b 4. c 5. c 6. c 7. a 8. a
Lesson 35 test	1. a 2. b 3. c 4. a 5. a 6. b 7. b 8. c
Lesson 36 test	1. b 2. c 3. a 4. c 5. b 6. a 7. c 8. b
Lesson 37 test	1. c 2. a 3. b 4. c 5. a 6. c 7. b 8. a
Lesson 38 test	1. a 2. c 3. c 4. b 5. c 6. b 7. a 8. c
Lesson 39 test	1. b 2. a 3. c 4. a 5. b 6. c 7. c 8. b
Lesson 40 test	1. c 2. b 3. c 4. a 5. a 6. a 7. b 8. c

CPSIA information can be obtained
at www.ICGtesting.com
Printed in the USA
BVHW021700170323
660679BV00011B/297